THE NMA HANDBOOK
FOR MANAGERS

THE NMA HANDBOOK FOR MANAGERS

By the National Management Association

Edited by Patricia H. Virga, Ph.D.

PRENTICE HALL
Englewood Cliffs, New Jersey 07632

Prentice-Hall International, Inc., *London*
Prentice-Hall of Australia, Pty. Ltd., *Sydney*
Prentice-Hall Canada, Inc., *Toronto*
Prentice-Hall of India Private Ltd., *New Delhi*
Prentice-Hall of Japan, Inc., *Tokyo*
Editora Prentice-Hall do Brasil Ltda., *Rio de Janeiro*
Prentice-Hall Hispanoamericana, S.A., *Mexico*

© 1987 *by*

PRENTICE-HALL, INC.
Englewood Cliffs, N.J.

10 9 8 7 6 5 4 3 2 1

Library of Congress Cataloging-in-Publication Data

The NMA handbook for managers.

Includes index.
1. Management—Handbooks, manuals, etc.   I. Virga,
Patricia H.   II. National Management Association (U.S.)
HD31.N56 1987   658   87-14511

ISBN 0-13-622903-4

PRINTED IN THE UNITED STATES OF AMERICA

Contents

CHAPTER 3   **HOW TO USE COMMUNICATION AS**
                  YOUR FOUNDATION FOR SUCCESS   **69**

CHAPTER 4   **HOW TO DEAL EFFECTIVELY**
                  WITH OTHERS IN THE WORKPLACE   **113**

CHAPTER 5   **WHY PERFORMANCE IS**
                  THE MANAGER'S BOTTOM LINE   **147**

CHAPTER 6   **WHY A NEW EMPLOYEE IS ALWAYS
                 A MANAGEMENT CHALLENGE   187**

**CHAPTER 7   HOW THE MANAGER'S FUNCTION AS A
                   COUNSELOR AFFECTS PERFORMANCE   227**

CHAPTER 10   LAW FOR THE MANAGER   337

What This Book Will Do for You

Management effectiveness requires multiple skills and abilities. The *NMA Handbook for Managers* is specifically designed to provide you with all the strategies, tools, and techniques you need to increase your management skills and, as a result, become an even more effective manager than you already are.

Here are some specific ways in which the *NMA Handbook for Managers* can help you—ready for your implementation in the workplace. This handbook will show you:

- The practical techniques you need to handle the four prime management responsibilities.
- How to balance the managerial and technical work you face each day.
- How to use problem-solving techniques to help you reach good decisions analytically.
- How to use the "Feedforward Concept."
- Proven successful organizational strategies and techniques.
- How to develop and use the six critical qualities you must have for successful, effective communication.
- How to control the communication transaction.
- What meetings can accomplish for you—if you use the right strategies.
- How to deal with conflict in the workplace.
- How to build trust.
- The ten key qualities of a winning manager and how to develop them.
- How a control system can help you monitor performance.
- Proven techniques for dealing with waste and absenteeism.
- How effective management can really pay off for you.
- How to select, screen, and interview—a step-by-step plan.
- The four key elements of growth and change—and how to use them to impact your management.
- Tested counseling strategies and techniques that make your job easier.

- Where and how to acquire power.
- How to develop and implement your personal leadership style.
- How to create an innovative climate—and work within it.
- How to organize your departments efficiently.
- How to get the most from your company's MIS.
- Techniques for keeping track of the money—through cost accounting and smart budgeting.
- How the international dimension affects you as a manager.
- Why and how managers must be able to administer the law.
- How to protect yourself from improper agreements.
- Guidelines for understanding and dealing with labor law and other laws governing employment.

Through these time-tested, innovative, and practical strategies, you can achieve increased managerial effectiveness. By any measure, that leads to professional success.

Introduction

In today's industry, it's no longer enough for a manager to simply go to work, do the job, and make sure everyone else does his or her job. Your role is much more complex than ever before, and to succeed you must be effective as a manager.

This book is about effectiveness. And it's about success. *The NMA Handbook for Managers* provides you with the many concepts and techniques that can make you an effective manager. It shows you how to apply proven methods in daily situations. Every page is filled with information, strategies, and examples that will help you master your constantly evolving management role. In so doing, it presents you with the challenge of achieving personal satisfaction, goals, and pride. That's success!

Chapter 1 takes you from the comfort of your present management role to what you are about to become—a more efffective manager. And it leaves you right at the doorstep of the future by preparing you for the challenges ahead. You'll see how to evaluate yourself and the others around you, as well as your work environment. You'll also find the key elements that spell success or failure in management.

In Chapter 2 you'll find the four major management functions fully described. Through discussion, examples, and actual case studies, you'll clearly see what you must do and how to do it in order to function most effectively in management.

This country can proudly boast of a multitude of resources and the greatest of these is its people. Ironically, it's also the most difficult resource to manage. Each person is unique and complex, with needs, feelings, and desires. Fitting each individual into a structured business environment successfully is the special challenge that faces today's managers. The key is communication.

Much of this book is concerned with communication and the ability to build effective interpersonal relations. In Chapter 3 you'll explore human communication—reading, speaking, and writing. You'll be provided with the proven techniques for dealing with others in the workplace. Chapter 4 emphasizes achieving honest and authentic levels of communication. Interpersonal skills such as giving recognition, mutual problem solving, and active listening will provide you with the tools you need in order to achieve and maintain healthy relationships with your workers.

These interpersonal skills gained as a result of implementing Chapter 4 are applied again in Chapters 6 and 7. You'll greet the challenge of a new employee by being ready with proven interviewing techniques, orientation programs, and training sessions. You'll come to understand your new employee and how you can best help this person become a productive asset to your organization. With that comes a sense of satisfaction perhaps unrivaled by any other part of your management job.

In Chapter 7 you take on yet another role related to interpersonal relations—that of counselor. No longer can a manager survive without being able and ready to counsel employees. What you need to know about this subject—from concept to process—is found in this chapter. Most important, you'll come away knowing what you *can* do and what you can't.

Of course, your first concern as a manager is to get the job done. This means performance—your bottom line. Getting the most from your employees is the subject of Chapter 5—and very much at the heart of this book. You'll see how to use a system that focuses on building employee performance through planning, monitoring, and controlling the work situation. It's practical, it's proven, and *it works*.

Every manager is a leader. In Chapter 8 you'll see how to grasp the opportunity for personal growth as you manage better. You'll see what it takes to be a leader, how to make your personal style work for you, and how to create a climate for innovation. This chapter focuses on *you* and helps you develop qualities that will make you an even more effective leader.

Chapters 9 and 10 provide you with the information you need in order to be an informed manager. Two important, necessary areas are addressed here: business concepts and law. You'll find discussions of economics, business organization, management information systems, finance and budgeting, quality assurance, and productivity—and how you can use this information to "power" your management strategies and techniques. In the last chapter you are provided with an overview of the legal system, with emphasis on those laws and regulations that affect your organization. Use it as a helpful reference.

So there you have it! Here are not only the challenges but the winning strategies and techniques you need to meet them. The rest is up to you. You can thrive as a manager by being ready and willing to apply the techniques and tools provided in this book. The payoff? Effectiveness and success!

—The National Management Association

Acknowledgments

The National Management Association acknowledges the support and assistance of H.A. Waggener; James M. Daily, Ph.D.; William McGrath, J.D.; and the staff of The National Management Association.

Special thanks go to Dr. Thomas J. Von der Embse, Ph.D., A.P.D., who designed and wrote the *NMA First-Line Supervisor* training program. Dr. Von der Embse is Professor of Management at Wright State University and is an accredited Personnel Diplomate in managerial training and development. He holds Senior Professional stature in the American Society for Training and Development (ASTD).

Pat Virga thanks Barbara Scheibel for typing all those hundreds of manuscript pages with accuracy, proficiency, and professionalism.

CHAPTER 1

How to Handle Multifaceted Management Responsibilities

An effective supervisor is one who can step on people's toes without removing the shine.

—BITS AND PIECES

WELCOME to the world of management! What's it all about? Why should you get involved? What's in it for you? There is not just one answer to these questions—they can be a bit complex. Yet, there's no mystique about management, just tried-and-true methods, concepts, and skills. All you really need is an interest and willingness to try.

This chapter serves as an introduction to first-line management and sets the stage for the chapters that follow. The concern is to facilitate your awareness of the first-line manager's role, its requirements, challenges, and setting. Next, you'll gain a working knowledge of key management concepts and approaches. Upon this foundation, then, you'll develop key skills, including leadership, communication, motivation, and management.

CHALLENGE = EC³

As a manager, you might have your own reasons for choosing management work, but from your organization's perspective, reasons for "why management" are very clear: Organizations must have managers in order to function. Whether it be a single formal manager, an informal group leader, or a shared group management, the role exists in every type of organization.

Management is concerned with monitoring, facilitating, and directing the accomplishment of organizational objectives. Throughout this book, only those who manage at the level where work is actually carried out and who are called manager, foreman, team leader, operating manager, or a similar title are considered managers.

What's in it for you? There are many benefits from being a manager. Some are obvious, such as increased organizational status, higher salary (usually), better working conditions, and increased responsibility and authority. Some are not so obvious—for example, the personal satisfaction of achieving your organization's goals. To put it simply, if you want to develop and influence others, management offers much more reward than operative work.

Ultimately, management offers important work that contributes to the employer, the company, the customer, and the community. Said another way, EC^3—Employees, Company, Customer, and Community—make up the cornerstone of what managers want: *challenge*. Here's the formula:

Challenge = EC^3

Employees need to know what is expected of them and how their work relates to the whole process. As manager, you are a key person in satisfying these basic needs. In a real sense, to employees and their families, you *are* the company.

By your efforts toward productivity and efficiency, you help make your company competitive. By meeting critical schedules and quality standards, you help to satisfy customers' needs and keep your company's good reputation. By being responsible to yourself and your workers, you become an example to the community and the people around you.

FIVE POINTS OF VIEW ON MANAGEMENT

A useful way to understand the manager's role is to look at what middle and top management expect of you. In today's organizations, you'll find basically five different views, and one will generally predominate depending on the company. Let's look briefly at each:[1]

1. *The Person in the Middle.* You're the pressure point when the goals of management and workers are in conflict. Your behavior usually involves compromise—finding some way out that will satisfy both sides.

2. *The Key Person.* You're the conduit through which everything flows—all the policies and directives of management and feedback about and from workers. You'll find this role prevalent in peaceful working environments where the manager is considered a strong position.

3. *One of the Workers.* This view occurs when the manager's job is not clearly defined. EXAMPLE: Positions with titles such as *Lead Man, Crew Chief, Chief Technologist, Head Accountant* are often basically technical jobs with some small amount of management responsibilities.

4. *Human Relations Specialist.* You are seen as the key person for handling human problems in getting out the work. This is especially prevalent in organizations where technical specialists are in charge of different aspects of the work but are not directly responsible for the performance of the department. EXAMPLE: Engineers and draftsmen may instruct assemblers directly while the manager concentrates on human problems, working conditions, morale, and so on.

5. *The Keystone—Supporting Link for the Organizational Arch.* This represents the ideal notion that the manager connects and supports the two sides of the organizational arch—management and workers. The keystone is not just a conduit but a building block in its own right. It absorbs pressure from both sides and exerts pressure of its own. (See Figure 1.1.)

HOW TO BUILD YOUR EFFECTIVENESS

A *process* is defined as a series of factors (or steps) linked together in a system. The management process (Figure 1.2) shows what an effective manager does, the skills involved, the setting, and

---

[1] Adapted from Keith Davis, *Human Behavior at Work* (New York: McGraw-Hill, 1977).

FIVE VIEWS OF THE MANAGER''S ROLE

View #1

The Man in the Middle

View #2

The Key Man

View #3

One of the Workers

View #4

The Human Relations Specialist

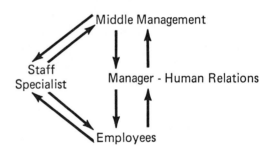

View #5

The Keystones

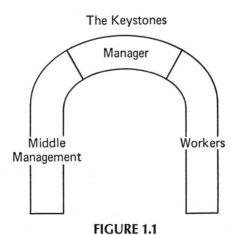

FIGURE 1.1

the required working knowledge. The process continually feeds back into what the manager does—building, maintaining, and monitoring both individual and group performance. You will have an opportunity to return to this process throughout this book, and throughout your career.

The Ten Cornerstones of an Effective Manager

In the final analysis, your success depends mainly on skillful handling of problems and opportunities in order to achieve your organization's objectives.

The effective manager:

- Pulls for neither work nor management nor self-interest exclusively but rather for the interests of the organization.
- Possesses human skills—understanding, supportiveness, ability to communicate clearly, ability to work with others.
- Possesses conceptual skills—understanding the big picture, ability to organize, ability to make predictions and solve problems.
- Has influence—gets ideas and recommendations accepted by superiors; is supported and respected by upper management.
- Favors neither the task nor the worker exclusively but is concerned with both to the appropriate degree.
- Uses scientific approaches when needed but also trusts an intuitive sense.
- Looks for ways to build developmentally rather than find expedient "Band-Aids."
- Perceives himself or herself as a manager rather than a worker and identifies self as a team member.
- Identifies with the company objectives, though not necessarily with other managers' values.
- Maintains a stable sense of value about self and society.

WHAT'S SPECIAL ABOUT BEING A MANAGER?

Three characteristics make the manager's role a unique and special one. First, you are directly responsible for the product or service of the organization. You are the closest to actual operations, and you actually fulfill the mission of the organization. Second, you are involved in more operational and technical work than those at other management levels. Finally, you stand in the "middle," be-

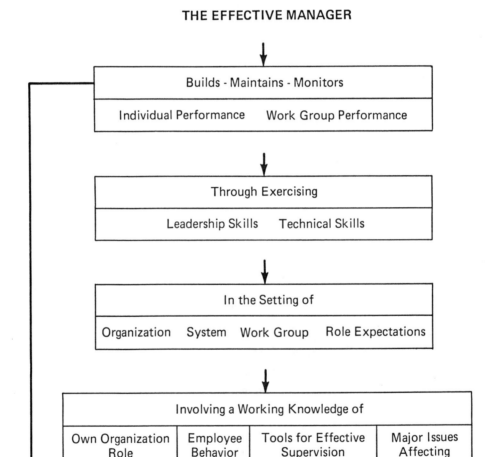

FIGURE 1.2

tween management and workers. You are the only manager to supervise nonmanagerial people. Your workers are likely less concerned about the company and more about their day-to-day problems.

With this in mind, you face a unique challenge because:

1. *You represent management.* You are entrusted with the responsibility to accomplish objectives within the policy framework of the department and the organization.

2. *You represent the workers.* You are obligated to get the legitimate needs and desires of your workers recognized by higher management and reflected in policies and working conditions.

To help you succeed, here's what you need to do:

1. *Build relationships with other managers at approximately the same level.* As part of a larger team, your ability to work together is critical to a smoothly running division or department.

2. *Build relationships with employees who work for other managers.* When you have frequent contact with employees from other sections, it's quite easy to unintentionally undercut other managers. This can start a complicated series of events that can upset the other manager and other workers.

3. *Build relationships with staff personnel.* You represent your department to staff people and influence their attitude toward assisting and cooperating with your department.

WHAT TO DO: Your effectiveness as a manager will depend largely upon your skill in conducting the just mentioned relationships. You personally should:

1. Be objective and constructive in your contacts.

2. Respect the motives and abilities of others with whom you come in contact.

3. Be clear in your thinking regarding your proper role in the organization and your overall obligations, particularly to your own manager.

4. Be particularly cautious in dealing with employees in other sections who report to other managers.

5. Conduct your activities with an eye to your impact on the organization as a whole.

PRACTICAL TECHNIQUES FOR HANDLING THE FOUR MANAGERIAL RESPONSIBILITIES

Whenever two or more people engage in a work activity together, there exists a need for coordination and direction. The more people become involved, the greater the need for "formal" management. As you move up the organizational ladder, your ability to manage becomes more important. By the same token, your technical knowledge usually becomes less important. KEEP THIS IN MIND: As a manager, you need to maintain a balance between managerial and technical competence.

You need to recognize that managing is a skill quite different from many other kinds of work. Like other professions, managing consists of a set of skills and abilities that are developed by gaining an understanding of the underlying principles and then by applying them to practical situations. Managers find that the development process goes throughout their entire careers.

The manager performs four main managerial responsibilities: planning, organizing, directing, and controlling. *Planning* means anticipating events that will affect the department and converting general plans and objectives into daily activities. *Organizing* means obtaining and arranging the necessary resources for performing the work. *Directing* means making appropriate work assignments through delegation and instruction. *Controlling* means making certain that performance meets the necessary standards and monitoring the flow and output of work.

In a practical sense, your major planning responsibilities are of a short-term nature. They involve mainly the preparations of a budget and the scheduling of work assignments. Both can affect personnel in a significant way. Virtually every department has unique problems or needs that will play upon your planning decisions, particularly with regard to work assignments. Here are guidelines that will help you improve your effectiveness in this area:

1. Make assignments on an equitable basis.
2. Give explicit instructions on what is expected in the assignment.
3. Try to match as closely as possible the assignment to the employee's qualifications.
4. Adjust the workload according to what the employee can handle.

5. Think ahead.

6. Be receptive to change.

Your organizational work involves two areas: personnel and facilities. Of the two, the most difficult is organizing and coordinating the efforts of people. Here are four suggestions to help you develop organizing abilities:

1. Make certain the facilities, equipment, and supplies are set up and ready for use.

2. Build teamwork.

3. Improve methods and procedures.

4. Coordinate the activities of the work group.

The job of directing involves instructing and coaching your workers as they discharge their responsibilities.

EXAMPLE: You hire a draftsman. He just completed school. Before he begins, he needs to know how things are done by your organization, his own working role, and how it relates with others. Then, you can explain work assignments, arrange shift and days off, and the other details.

It's important to get off on the right foot. So, take time right at the beginning to brief your employees. To direct your employees effectively, you are required to:

1. Devote time and attention to their orientation.

2. Form individual relationships that lead to positive and open interactions.

3. Give assistance and guidance through counseling and coaching.

4. Build confidence by providing clear and accurate expectations of your workers' activities.

5. Keep open channels of communication with other departments.

Controlling implies evaluation, enforcing standards and regulations, taking disciplinary action, grappling with reports and budgets, and handling complaints. Most managers consider this part of the job least desirable of all. But without it, there's little chance for success.

From time to time, every manager will find it necessary to take disciplinary action. This is not always pleasant or easy to do without wrecking otherwise productive relationships. To make this part of your job as easy as possible, keep these points in mind:

1. Controlling is an ongoing activity. Prevention is much less painful than disciplinary action after the fact.

2. Continual feedback is necessary for assessing progress, direction, and consequences of performance. Feedback requires follow-up.

3. Building positive mental discipline means more than just taking disciplinary action. It means developing positive attitudes and work habits.

SUGGESTION: Try the "hot stove" approach. That is, take disciplinary action immediately after the infraction and keep it objective and resolute.

4. You remain accountable for overall operation of the department, including budget and communication. A positive attitude will make you more effective.

HOW TO BALANCE YOUR MANAGERIAL AND TECHNICAL WORK

Nearly every manager performs work related to his or her department's area of specialization. This is called "technical" work because it involves skills necessary for building the product or service of that profession.

EXAMPLE: A foreman on a construction project might pitch in and help the bricklayers.

You probably enjoy doing technical work because it takes you back into an old, familiar place. But sooner or later, you must make a choice as to which you want most—the managerial or the technical. THINK FOR YOURSELF: There's no general advice to give here. Rather, you need to look at the components and responsibilities of your position and the situation itself.

The "50 Percent Rule" states that any position that is called managerial should involve at least 50 percent managerial work. If that level falls short, it is not really a managerial position.

NOTE: Unions, by and large, have a clearer designation of a manager than nonunionized organizations. The legal definition under the Taft–Hartley Act basically parallels their descriptions.

HOW TO DEVELOP THE SKILLS YOU NEED

Compared with middle and top management, first-line managers require about the same amount of human skill, less conceptual skill, and more technical skill. You can see this in Figure 1.3. This book is concerned largely with human and conceptual skills, since these are the areas that are generally most unfamiliar.

DISTRIBUTION OF SKILLS AT VARIOUS MANAGEMENT LEVELS

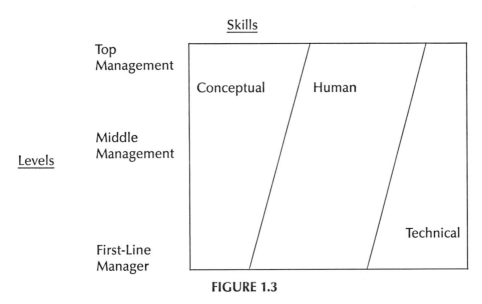

FIGURE 1.3

It's possible to identify those areas where your managerial skills are most important. The ten highest ranked priorities, roughly in order of importance, are as follows:

1. Scheduling and day-to-day planning (Facilitating)
2. Assigning and delegating work (Directing)

3. Quality and cost control (Monitoring)
4. Communicating policy and procedure (Directing)
5. Motivating and directing people (Directing)
6. Discipline (Monitoring)
7. Training workers (Facilitating)
8. Evaluating performance (Monitoring)
9. Maintaining equipment and supplies (Facilitating)
10. Safety (Facilitating)

HOW TO USE SOPs AND SOTs (SIGNIFICANT OTHERS) IN THE WORKPLACE

SOPs and SOTs—Significant Other People and Significant Other Things—comprise your work environment. By identifying them, you'll have a clear idea of what aspects *really* make a difference to you.

SOPs include all persons who affect your work in some way. Figure 1.4 shows what a mental picture might include. The inner circle is you, the manager. The middle circle includes employees, your boss, expert staff, and so on who directly affect your work situation. The outer circle is made up of people who are not as immediately in focus but who may become important at various times.

The significance of the areas can be expected to change from time to time, even daily. And so, too, will your mental picture change in focus. REMEMBER THIS: Each person in your mental picture has a legitimate role as seen in that person's frame of reference. Cultivate the benefits of working with *all* the people in your mental picture.

Significant nonhuman elements (SOTs) also affect your environment. These tend to be more abstract and sometimes more technical than the human dimensions. Here are the major nonhuman elements:

1. *The Management System.* The basis or philosophy of management driving your organization.
2. *The Work System.* The way the work is accomplished, including division of labor, degree of teamwork, and so on.
3. *The Reward and Evaluation System.* How people are compensated and how they are evaluated.

4. *Objectives and Policies.* The organization's mission, goals and values, and its operating guidelines.

5. *Information and Computer System.* The channels, users, and formats of information flow.

6. *The Prevailing Attitudes and Values.* The organization's genuine orientation to how people and customers are valued.

7. *The Industry.* All organizations that produce the same goods or services.

8. *Competitive Environment.* The degree and types of competition.

A MENTAL PICTURE OF THE "PEOPLE" ENVIRONMENT

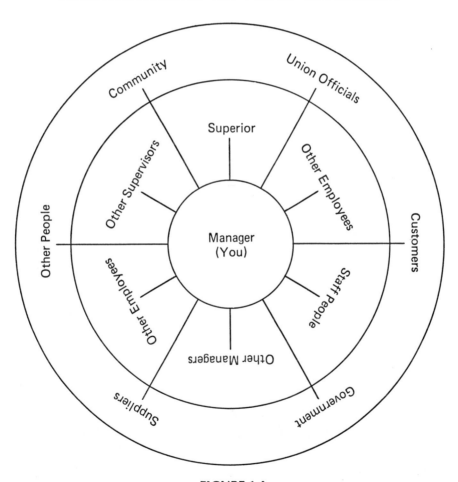

FIGURE 1.4

HOW TO MAP THE TERRITORY AND LEARN THE ROPES

It's essential that you learn and understand your company's organizational structure and how you fit into it. WHAT TO DO: Begin by obtaining a table of organization. See where you fit in. Then determine to whom you are accountable; that is, to whom you report. Most of the time, you are accountable to only one superior.

> EXAMPLE: Figure 1.5 shows a typical organization chart. Suppose you are Unit A foreman. Note that you are four levels removed from the chief executive and that you report to the production vice-president. Consider this situation: Sometimes Quality Control wants to direct your unit concerning a special project. You are required to report to Quality Control temporarily for its special project. What do you do?
> ANSWER: As long as the project is coordinated at your superior's level or above, you can reconcile your accountability to your superior by knowing where the directive came from and how it fits into the overall plan.

The organizational chart and your job description provide information about your position, but these are like road maps that show the main highways and not the side road. To understand your job more completely, it helps to develop your own personal chart.

Charting your work activities involves keeping a record of everything you do at work over a defined period of time. Figure 1.6 shows a form you can use to keep such a record. REMEMBER: It's important to record the amount of time spent in each activity.

WHAT TO DO: A personal strategy for mastering your work situation involves using your time most effectively. It involves developing skills, some of which may not be easy to learn. Here are six practices that will help in developing and evaluating your own work activities:

1. *Use your time wisely.* To do this, know where it is actually going. Then answer this question, "Am I spending the biggest portion of my time on the most important activities?" Specifically identify the full range of job activities and then establish the priorities as you see fit. (See Chapter 8 for further details.)

2. *Focus on results.* In order for you to work toward results, your employees must be concentrating on the right tasks. And that's your major responsibility—to help them channel their efforts in the right direction. To become results oriented, ask yourself this, "What

skills will I (and my employees) need to get better results, using my (our) time and energy more efficiently?"

3. *Concentrate on strengths.* Overlooking strengths while focusing on weaknesses often imposes a barrier to accomplishing your needs. It's a good idea periodically to review your records and your subordinates' records to get a fresh perspective on background

**AN ORGANIZATION CHART
WITH FOCUS ON THE PRODUCTION DIVISION**

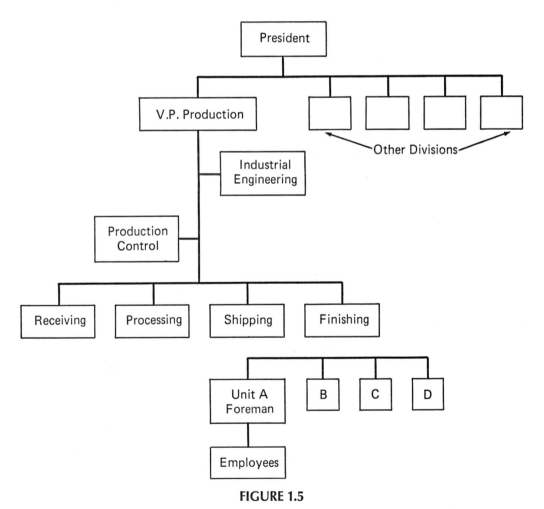

FIGURE 1.5

WORK ACTIVITIES AND TIME LOG

First Half-Day	T	Second Half-Day	T	Planning	Planned
Activity		Activity		Your Objectives for the Day	T

Monday

Tuesday

Wednesday

FIGURE 1.6

WORK ACTIVITIES AND TIME LOG

	First Half-Day		Second Half-Day		Planning	
	Activity	T	Activity	T	Your Objectives for the Day	Planned T
Thursday						
Friday						
Saturday						
Sunday						

FIGURE 1.6 (continued)

and accomplishments. Once you identify an individual's strengths, these should become the center of attention as long as they are important to the job.

4. *Recognize and do what is important.* Emphasize the important tasks and relationships. When this is understood and clearly executed by your employees, your department's contribution will be perceived positively.

5. *Keep in touch with your needs.* If you belittle the existence of your own needs, problems will result.

6. *Maintain a balanced perspective.* Balance is the process of establishing and maintaining equilibrium in order to have the appropriate perspective. The five areas where balance is especially important are (1) behavior, (2) attitudes, (3) leadership style, (4) evaluations, and (5) problem analysis. These will be further explored throughout this book.

The main problem in implementing a strategy for mastering your work environment lies in your own resolve to carry it out. SUGGESTION: Discuss matters with your immediate superior, especially in the earlier phase when you're learning the ropes. Test out your strategy by going over them with him or her. Remember, your chief may have useful ideas about your approach.

THE HUMAN FACTOR: WHAT MAKES PEOPLE TICK?

Probably one of the biggest obstacles in getting out the work of your department is the so-called "human" factor. Technical skill is really only the first step. Keep in mind these three formulae:

Performance = Motivation × Skills

Skill = Ability × Training

Motivation = Situation × Attitudes

Motivation can be achieved by properly getting at the way people behave. Much of the theory and skills in accomplishing this are discussed in other chapters, but here is a brief overview.

Recent research in behavior science has uncovered five basic *needs* common to all people:

1. *Physiological.* This means getting the basic necessities of life and any other things that make life more enjoyable. This is why people work—to make money in order to fulfill basic needs.

2. *Security.* This concern shifts to the future. Job security is central because it provides both economic and psychological security.

3. *Social.* Most people want to be accepted by others as a member of a group, both on and off the job. As a manager, you have an important task in building social satisfactions at work. From the moment you introduce a new employee to others in the unit, personal relationships begin to form. REMEMBER THIS: If social needs are stifled, you can expect that social behavior will appear in some other form, perhaps in labor disputes or turnover.

4. *Ego.* Quite distinct from social needs, ego needs are oriented toward the individual. Ego satisfactions bring identity and esteem to the person. WARNING: There's a tendency among long-time friends and co-workers to take good work for granted. If you hold this attitude, you may unintentionally be frustrating your workers' ego needs. When good performance goes unrecognized and unappreciated, you run the risk of losing your employees or creating hostile attitudes.

> EXAMPLE: Professional employees such as air traffic controllers tend to vigorously defend their position if their professional integrity is questioned. When they strike, they'll usually insist that their action is in the interest of better passenger safety, and so on. Their ego needs will become their priority.

5. *Self-fulfillment.* People oriented toward self-fulfillment are concerned about whether their work is developing their capabilities to the highest extent. They usually want assignments that challenge their abilities.

If all people have the same basic needs, why do they act so differently? The answer is twofold: (1) people have different ways of satisfying their needs and (2) the needs themselves change constantly. THE KEY: How well you know your people and understand these differences.

One of the biggest mistakes you can make is to assume that because the work is complex and important, people who perform it are concerned with the highest need levels, or vice versa. Actually, a person's need level is not determined by the work but by the individual's orientation toward the work. The type of work is only a general indicator of need levels, useful when you view it as one of many factors in understanding needs.

Values are expressions of what people hold as important and, as such, are closely related to the ego and self-fulfillment needs. A person's values determine to a large extent his or her conduct in day-to-day situations.

There are many instances where an individual's values come into conflict with those of the group.

> A CASE-IN-POINT: Joe, an experienced worker in Shipping and Receiving is considered very efficient and responsible. He works with two young men who are casual about their responsibilities. When a shipment comes in, the young men are often not around, and Joe finds himself handling the shipment alone. Joe has talked with both men about it, but they tell him to "cool it" and "stop working your tail off." Joes tries to solve this dilemma by asking for a transfer. He says he's bored and wants something different. But clearly, Joe's values of "a fair day's work" are in conflict with those of his peers, and Joe is trying to escape from the situation.

As manager, you will need to get behind the real reason for workers' conflicts. Very often, incompatible values lie at the root. Your appropriate response will be to protect the worker's self-image, regardless of how the conflict gets resolved.

People's values determine their attitudes toward issues in society and work. You might find yourself perplexed about why your employees do not share your own sense of responsibility about work. The answer often lies in the different expectations of managers and employees, particularly with regard to family, hobbies, or community activities. Behavioral scientist Robert Dubin has shown that the individual's work values depend largely on his or her "central life interest," or, in other words, orientation toward work or nonwork activities.

As a manager, you have only indirect control over the values people hold. But you can influence them by your own example.

FIVE CRITICAL STEPS TO PROBLEM SOLVING

The key to effective problem solving lies in developing a perspective that lets you see the problem from all angles and in relation to the objectives that govern a situation. By experiencing different situations, being close to the objectives, identifying the barriers included in achieving the objectives and the factors that caused the barriers to develop, you can be assured that you'll not just be doing things right but doing the right things.

Most important problems are human in nature and require experience, judgment, and intuition. Normally, we respond naturally in some fashion and simply get the matter resolved. However, when the problem becomes complex while still not an emergency, a more deliberate approach will help. The management problem-solving process follows a logical framework similar to that used in other professions. It should become second nature to you. Here are the five steps involved in the problem-solving process:

Step One: Size Up the Situation. Determine what happened, under what circumstances it happened, and what approach caused it to happen. Then define the problem itself. This means separating the individual's concerns from the organization's objectives.

> SUGGESTION: Determining causes are vital for preventing the problem from recurring. If you pursue causes rather than symptoms, you're headed in the right direction.

Step Two: Get Relevant Information. You probably need more information to support and confirm your diagnosis. This means gathering facts by consulting with others, reviewing personal records, and sometimes by doing a time-consuming investigation. With more information, the solutions—or at least the alternatives—become apparent.

Step Three: Evaluate Alternatives. Your experience combined with an ability to anticipate the probable outcome are crucial factors in determining the wisdom and appropriateness of selecting a particular course of action. Two skills are required here: (1) predictive ability and (2) good judgment. Both are developed by experience and education.

Step Four: Test Possible Solutions. Try out the alternative on a tentative basis while preparing yourself to change course if necessary. REMEMBER: Be flexible, and don't be afraid to change your mind.

Step Five: Select the Best Solution. There's a point at which decisive action is necessary. Make a firm commitment and implement the solution. NOTE: A thorough solution includes measures to prevent its recurrence and is part of the follow-up procedures that complete the process.

A CASE-IN-POINT: A crane operator moves dangerously close to an overhead high-voltage line. You immediately intervene and take charge. After the emergency has been handled, you then begin to look at what happened. What is the problem? The operator thinks the problem is his safety. Another might think it's the operator's carelessness. Organizationally, the problem is how to meet and maintain its safety standards. As the manager, it's best to define the problem from the organizational point of view. Upon looking further into this case, you find that the operator was not properly trained to handle his instructions. So, your alternative presents itself: Train him. But do you have time? Is he trainable? Will the budget permit it? After thinking it over, you decide to go ahead. However, you discover that this employee is deficient in the fundamentals of his specialty. What then? After trying other possibilities, you decide that this ineptitude is rooted in a serious background educational deficiency that cannot be corrected at organizational time and expense. Your final decision is to recommend dismissal and replace the employee. At that point, you stay with this decision. Also, you recommend screening new applicants for appropriate background and experience.

HOW TO MAKE THE RIGHT DECISIONS

Since the last phase of the problem-solving process involves making the decision, the only real distinction between the two is in the implementation and follow-up.

Effective decision making requires that follow-up be thorough and that you anticipate the consequences. A formula expresses this idea well:

EDM = Q + A

or

Effective Decision Making = Quality + Acceptance

when

Quality = The merits of the decision

and

Acceptance = The willingness of others to go along with the decision

Interpreting and applying policy is a special case of decision making. Policies are similar to prepared cake mixes. The ingredients are furnished along with the instructions, but the cook (manager) must still mix (synthesize) and bake (apply) them.

While not as challenging as arriving at solutions creatively, this area is extremely important simply because managers spend so much time and energy doing it. If the policies were readily and clearly understood by employees, your role could be the "big chief" described earlier in this chapter. Since the opposite tends to be the case, you play a vital and challenging role in interpreting policy.

> RULE OF THUMB: Unless a union contract requires it, uniformity of policy applications is not as important as consistency of judgment. The difference? Uniformity follows the policy to the letter, while consistency of judgment applies the policy situationally, following the implicit rather than the letter. It breeds trust from your employees.

WHY SUCCESS BEGINS WITH YOU

The old axiom "Know thyself" takes on added significance when it comes to achieving your ideal personal style. In a very real sense, you alone are responsible for yourself and your well-being.

WHAT TO DO: Determine what you consider most important to you. Figure 1.7 is a questionnaire that will help you rate your most commonly held values. To determine your score in each area, follow the instructions. If you score less than four, the values in that area are insignificant. A higher score indicates where your central life interest lies.

Once you have determined your score, you might then decide if the value orientation reflected in the scores is really what you want. You can then decide what to do about the differences: whether to work around conflict areas, attempt to change them, or accept them as part of the challenge of management.

HOW TO DEAL WITH CHANGE

Change is inevitable and often beneficial. Nevertheless, it can also cause havoc in your life. To best deal with change, it needs to be evaluated on its own merits and undertaken with an awareness of its consequences.

LIFE AND WORK VALUES QUESTIONNAIRE

Directions: Indicate the importance of the following values to you by circling the appropriate number.

PART 1: LIFE VALUES

	Maximum Importance	Highly Important	Moderately Important	Fairly Important	Of Little Importance	Of Minimal Importance	No Importance
Family Relationship (desire for harmony between you and your family)	7	6	5	4	3	2	1
Wealth (many possessions and plenty of money for the things you want)	7	6	5	4	3	2	1
Wisdom (mature understanding, insight, good sense, and judgment)	7	6	5	4	3	2	1
Religion (religious belief, being in relationship with God)	7	6	5	4	3	2	1
Love (warmth, caring, unselfish devotion that freely accepts another in loyalty and seeks his/her good)	7	6	5	4	3	2	1
Aesthetic (appreciation and enjoyment of beauty for beauty's sake in the arts and in nature)	7	6	5	4	3	2	1
Altruism (regard for or devotion to the interest of others, service to others)	7	6	5	4	3	2	1
Physical Appearance (concern for one's attractiveness, being neat, clean, well groomed)	7	6	5	4	3	2	1

FIGURE 1.7

	Maximum Importance	Highly Important	Moderately Important	Fairly Important	Of Little Importance	Of Minimal Importance	No Importance
Morality (believing and keeping ethical standards, personal honor, integrity)	7	6	5	4	3	2	1
Emotional Health (peace of mind, inner security, ability to recognize and handle inner conflicts)	7	6	5	4	3	2	1
Health or Physical Well-Being (condition of being sound in body)	7	6	5	4	3	2	1
Honest (frank and genuinely yourself with everyone)	7	6	5	4	3	2	1
Justice (treating others fairly or impartially, conforming to truth, fact, or reason)	7	6	5	4	3	2	1
Knowledge (seeking truth, information, or principles)	7	6	5	4	3	2	1

Total Score: _____ ÷ 14 = Your Score: _____

FIGURE 1.7 (continued)

LIFE AND WORK VALUES QUESTIONNAIRE

Directions: Indicate the importance of the following values to you by circling the appropriate number.

PART 2: WORK VALUES

	Maximum Importance	Highly Important	Moderately Important	Fairly Important	Of Little Importance	Of Minimal Importance	No Importance
Loyalty (maintaining allegiance to a person, group, or institution)	7	6	5	4	3	2	1
Skill (able to use one's knowledge effectively, being good at something important to you or to others)	7	6	5	4	3	2	1
Power (possession of control, authority, or influence over others)	7	6	5	4	3	2	1
Recognition (being important, well liked, accepted)	7	6	5	4	3	2	1
Leadership (desire to be a leader rather than a follower within an organization)	7	6	5	4	3	2	1
Autonomy (ability to be a self-determining individual, personal freedom, making own choices)	7	6	5	4	3	2	1
Challenge (demanding, different and difficult tasks, dislike for routine)	7	6	5	4	3	2	1
Creativeness (creation of new ideas and designs, being innovative)	7	6	5	4	3	2	1

FIGURE 1.7 (continued)

	Maximum Importance	Highly Important	Moderately Important	Fairly Important	Of Little Importance	Of Minimal Importance	No Importance
Affiliation (sense of belonging within an organization)	7	6	5	4	3	2	1
Achievement (accomplishment, results brought about by resolve, persistence, or endeavor)	7	6	5	4	3	2	1
Physical Safety (safety within your job, freedom from worry about harm or injury)	7	6	5	4	3	2	1
Self-esteem (favorable regard for one's accomplishments and activities)	7	6	5	4	3	2	1
Financial Security (providing for financial needs of the family without worry)	7	6	5	4	3	2	1
Income (amount and level of salary or wages from work)	7	6	5	4	3	2	1

Total Score: _____ ÷ 14 = Your Score: _____

FIGURE 1.7 (continued)

Directions: Record your score in the table below:

Spiritual		*Psychological*	
Morality	____	Emotional health	____
Religion	____	Power	____
Honesty	____	Recognition	____
Justice	____	Self-esteem	____
Aesthetics	____	Achievement	____
Altruism	____	Leadership	____
		Challenge	____
		Autonomy	____
Total:	____ ÷ 6 =	Total:	____ ÷ 8 =
Your Score:	____	Your Score:	____

Economic		*Intellectual*	
Loyalty	____	Knowledge	____
Affiliation	____	Skill	____
Love	____	Creativeness	____
Family relationships	____	Wisdom	____
Total:	____ ÷ 4 =	Total:	____ ÷ 4 =
Your Score:	____	Your Score:	____

Physical	
Appearance	____
Health	____
Safety	____
Total:	____ ÷ 3 =
Your Score:	____

FIGURE 1.7 (continued)

As a manager, you are involved in change from two perspectives: (1) creating and implementing change in others and (2) bringing about change in yourself. When analyzing these two areas, it's important to use the same approach.

A useful method of analyzing changes comes from a process called force-field analysis, developed by behavioral scientist Kurt Lewin (see Figure 1.8). Force-field analysis is designed to analyze the positive and negative forces in a situation, identifying these forces and their effects on a change situation. Reactive (depressing) forces—such as employee attitudes, resources, red tape, and so on—collide with proactive (elevating) forces—such as need, survival, competition, and so on.

By identifying the forces in a situation, you can develop a change strategy. By doing so, you're in the driver's seat, where you can influence results. Here are some guidelines to help you along:

1. Identify the objectives you seek and the change you want to make.

2. Develop a list of benefits and possible negative consequences.

3. Do a force-field analysis.

4. Develop a plan of action for dealing with the reactive factors and strengthening the proactive forces.

5. Keep your options open.

6. Use causative thinking. Plan and act *as if* the change will be successfully accomplished.

FORCE-FIELD ANALYSIS

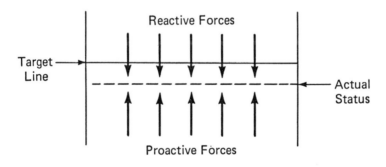

FIGURE 1.8

HOW BALANCE CAN BECOME YOUR KEY TO INNER SATISFACTION

Achieving balance means establishing an equilibrium that is needed to handle various demands in a situation. Here are five areas in which you can achieve balance:

1. *Behavior.* When relationships get out of balance, people get irritated, statements are misinterpreted, communication becomes erratic, and the parties involved feel uncomfortable with one another. Cooperation and productivity deteriorate, and so the organization suffers along with the people involved. Balancing relationships is not a simple matter that can be reduced to a list of do's and don'ts. It involves knowing people and their needs, responding appropriately to others, and being objective in dealing with them.

2. *Attitudes.* The "odd-even negative number" phenomenon makes three points: (1) whenever there is an even number of negative attitudes, the relationship is in balance, (2) introducing an odd number of negative attitudes will throw a relationship out of balance, and (3) when this occurs, forces are triggered that will restore balance.

> EXAMPLE: Suppose you have a subordinate whose work you like. The subordinate likes the seniority system, but you don't. Here, you have two pluses and a minus. The relationship is out of balance. To restore balance, you can (1) change your view on seniority to match your subordinate's, (2) influence your subordinate to change his or her mind, (3) drop that particular topic from the relationship, or (4) change your mind about the employee's performance, making it negative. This would restore the balance but ruin the working relationship. YOUR BEST BET: Create all positives whenever possible.

3. *Leadership style.* Balance in leadership style implies adapting to the needs of the situation or, in some cases, adapting the situation to your style. IMPORTANT: There should be a correlation between what employees expect and how you actually approach a situation.

4. *Evaluation.* Here, evaluations by the manager should match the evaluation of the employees. When evaluations are out of balance, tension will result until manager and employee iron out their differences. WHAT TO DO: Emphasize performance—what the person did—and avoid implications about the employee's personal worth.

5. *Problem solving.* This involves weighing the factors and alternatives in a problem situation in order to arrive at the best overall solution. Balance relates to the quality of the solution itself, which reflects how well the analysis was done.

In the final analysis, managing stress (discussed in Chapter 8), adapting to necessary change, and maintaining balance are pre-requisites to managing others. They'll see the effects, and so will you.

HOW TO TELL IF YOU'RE BECOMING AN OBSOLETE MANAGER

While it's true that people never become obsolete, their think-ing and behavior sometimes do. How do you know when you are in danger of becoming obsolete? Answer the following questions. Your responses will give you a good idea of where you stand.

How well do these describe you: (a) very well, (b) fairly well, (c) not well, or (d) not at all?

_____ 1. I find myself very sensitive to criticism.

_____ 2. The more I do, the less progress I seem to be mak-ing.

_____ 3. It upsets me when I am approached about changing anything.

_____ 4. Lately, more and more things seem to irritate me. My habits (drinking, smoking) are getting more in-tense.

_____ 5. I get enthusiastic about new opportunities, but the excitement cools down before long.

_____ 6. Lately, I have been jumping from topic to topic; sometimes tossing around several ideas at a time.

_____ 7. Just thinking about teamwork is tiring. I find it more a bother than a benefit.

_____ 8. I get the feeling there are a lot of things passing me by that I should know, but I'll leave that to the young, inexperienced kids at this point.

_____ 9. I find there is very little new about managing that I have to learn at this time since we manage by tried and true methods.

_____10. I feel I've proven myself in any job; now it's the organization's turn to carry me for awhile.

Score yourself on these ten items by giving 0 points to those that describe you *very well* (a's), and 3 to those *not at all* (d's). If you scored 24–30, you are ahead of the race with obsolescence; 16–23, you're keeping up; 8–15, falling behind; and 0–7, time to regroup because you're now obsolete.

Recognize that it's never a hopeless case. Sure, if you are on the brink and the only way out seems to be upgrading all your technical knowledge, then it will be extremely hard to catch up. On the other hand, if catching up means to you a revitalized enthusiasm for learning new ideas and you have a strategic program for managerial self-improvement, you will be surprised at how fast you can catch up and stay ahead of the race.

Here are nine suggestions for renewing your competency and avoiding obsolescence (they are also useful for handling stress):

1. *Do a self-assessment.* This way you can determine where you are behind and where you need to catch up. As you do this, be sure to emphasize your strengths and avoid any preoccupation with weaknesses.

2. *Visualize what you want to be as a competent person.* What competency level do you want in your technical specialty? Your managerial job? Understand that technical and managerial leadership seldom go together. But if you truly want to do both, then visualize the behavior and the skills that are needed.

3. *Prepare yourself for maximum adaptability.* If you're not sure at this time whether your career is in management or in another area, you can do yourself a favor and prevent obsolescence by seeking developmental experiences that prepare you for a variety of possibilities.

4. *Take charge of your life and your work.* Master the things that are really essential and do not worry about those that are not.

5. *Identify very clearly what it takes to stay abreast of your field.* Once you know what is really important, you'll catch up faster than you think. Do not get bewildered when you find a whole new terminology that you never heard of. A lot of it is jargon—cosmetic language that even your specialists do not know. Look for *real* breakthroughs, *truly new* ideas and concepts. You can usually find them by reading the best periodicals and journals in the field, or in popular magazines as well.

6. *If you are headed for a management career, prepare yourself for a continuous educational process.* It will likely be both informal and formal. If learning is low on your priority list, you should turn to a career other than management.

7. *Maintain a position to fall back on.* What will you do if management is not for you? Have you burned your bridges behind you? Think about alternate plans if you decide to change career direction.

8. *Take charge of your own development.* People who do this are the most satisfied and healthiest individuals in the world of work.

9. *Center your development on your basic values.* Most other things will change, and unless you have a framework for coping with the change, you'll become like the rudderless boat tossing with every wave of change.

MANAGEMENT IN THE YEAR 2000

Here are some thoughts about management in the next decade and beyond:

1. The current professional-development emphasis will continue and grow. Managers and employees will place high value on taking charge of their own lives.

2. At the same time, employees will become more cooperative, and management-employee relationships will be more a partnership because there will be a better understanding of common needs. Personal development will focus not just on narrow specialties but on ways to be a more effective employee overall.

3. Managers are likely to specialize more. The baby-boom people entering managerial positions during the 1980s are producing very crowded conditions in management ranks. There will always be few positions at the top of the organization, so in the competition for management positions, people will want to make themselves as visible and in demand as possible. Therefore, they will seek areas of specialized knowledge, expertise, and achievement that will make them stand out and be recognized.

Many positions in management will require special skills such as conflict resolution, counseling, training, planning, and numerous topics addressed in this book. By becoming an expert in these areas, your chances for promotability and survival are increased. Do not forget your present job and its needs. Your future is, and always will be, determined by your *current* performance and effectiveness.

4. Planning and evaluation will be more long-term. Along with a greater emphasis on self-development, progress and growth will be observed more over the long haul. Thus, creative and planning skills will be more important, as well as building teamwork.

5. There will be less emphasis on managerial movement and mobility. People are becoming and will continue to be more community conscious. As they plant these roots more firmly, they are less likely to move unless the incentives are very great.

6. Your future in management could well depend on Japanese management techniques. But they are only the beginning. You will need to be abreast of developments in other countries and how they affect your operation.

You can meet these and other challenges by assessing and building your strengths. The future is not "out there" somewhere; you'll find it within yourself. You and your organization will create your future by proceeding right now to accomplish your most important goals.

CHAPTER 2

How to Become Even More of a Manager

Anticipation of problems is half the battle. And the only way to anticipate is to think.

—BITS AND PIECES

AS time goes on, you'll find yourself becoming more and more a manager; that is, the one who makes things happen. As the role of the manager changes, so too will the nature of your work. You'll find yourself increasingly involved in the four management functions: planning, organizing, directing, and controlling. So, it's important that you understand the functions and apply them in your daily routine. Concepts such as the systems approach and feedforward control can help provide you with the necessary tools to handle your new managerial responsibilities. These topics and more are presented in this chapter. They are your guide to becoming more and more a manager.

HOW MANAGERS MAKE THINGS HAPPEN: THE FOUR VITAL INGREDIENTS

Managers make things happen first by planning, then by organizing, next by directing, and finally by controlling. Your day-to-day responsibilities as they relate to the four management functions are summarized in this checklist:

CHECKLIST OF MANAGEMENT FUNCTIONS

Planning:

- Plans the work of the department; develops personnel schedules; interprets higher level plans as they apply to the department.

- Develops the budget for the department; makes necessary adjustments as directed and requested by the appropriate administrator.

- Anticipates future needs with regard to personnel, facilities and funds; informs superiors and takes appropriate follow-up measures.

- Makes decisions that commit the manager and the department to a particular course of action.

- Carries out the overall plans of the organization as they pertain to the department.

- Consults with others on future needs and how those needs will be met.

Organizing:

- Staffs the department or unit; takes a significant role in hiring personnel.

- Builds the work unit into an effective team by coordinating individual efforts.

- Secures and allocates resources needed for the job; makes certain supplies and facilities are available and adequate.

- Creates a climate that encourages individual performance.

- Makes certain that positions and roles are clearly defined and understood.

Directing:

- Orients employees concerning performance requirements, work assignments, and roles.

- Issues instructions concerning work assignments.

- Interprets policies and directives to employees.

- Assists and counsels employees about their work-related problems.

- Maintains communication channels and provides significant information.

Controlling:

- Evaluates employee performance.

- Establishes and enforces departmental work standards.

- Checks and monitors the work of subordinates.

- Takes appropriate disciplinary action when necessary.

- Gives meaningful feedback to employees concerning progress of their work.

- Maintains an equitable disciplinary system.

- Reports to higher management on departmental performance.

- Keeps costs within budget.

- Enforces safety and security regulations.

- Supplies other departments with information necessary for coordination.

- Listens to suggestions and criticisms.

- Maintains open channels for handling grievances.

- Keeps accurate records.

Now, let's take a closer look:

1. *Planning* is concerned with two questions: (1) What objectives should the organization pursue in order to accomplish its mission? and (2) What strategies will assure that these objectives are reached?

2. *Organizing* defines responsibilities and structures official relationships among people in the organization. Its purpose is to assure that all system components, including managers and employees, have a useful role in achieving objectives.

3. *Directing* is making sure tasks are done well and completed on time. As a manager, you must create a working climate that

motivates employees to do their best, then see that the job gets done.

4. *Controlling* includes the feedback, decision, and corrective action elements of organizational systems. This means you are controlling when you detect deviations from the plan and correct them quickly and effectively before the mission is in jeopardy.

The four management functions are sequential; that is, they must be done in order. Figure 2.1 shows the process as it begins and moves, one at a time, through the four functions and returns to the beginning again.

SEQUENTIAL MANAGEMENT FUNCTIONS

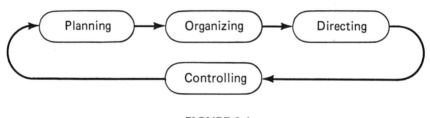

FIGURE 2.1

THE FIVE STEPS TO PLANNING WELL

Planning is the process of deciding where the organization is to go and how it should get there. It focuses on the primary mission of the organization and then selects objectives, strategies, and policies that enable individuals to work together to accomplish the mission. It maps the course from where you are to where you want to be.

Planning is first in the sequence of management functions. Alone, it's insufficient. But without it, actions may be random and ineffective.

Managers at every level of the organization are involved in planning. Top-level managers are responsible for strategic or long-range planning to assure future success. Middle-level managers develop operational plans that set specific objectives and schedules to implement the strategic plans. Lower-level managers implement day-to-day plans that make things happen according to short-range and long-range plans.

Step One: Analyze Your Situation

Situation analysis—defining your current status—may be divided into two parts: external and internal.

External analysis involves a close look at environmental systems to identify opportunities and constraints. Perhaps there is an opportunity in the marketplace or a technological improvement that can be applied to your product or service. Certainly, there are laws, regulations, and economic circumstances that require you to conform. By planning, you can succeed in spite of them.

Of course, you are interested in *current* opportunities and constraints, but you must look ahead and try to identify those that will affect you in the future. Therefore, *forecasting* plays a key role in planning.

If you could forecast with accuracy, planning would be easy. However, uncertainty is one of the facts of life. WHAT TO DO: You must use every available information source and technique to forecast future conditions and assess their impact.

Forecasting applies mostly to probable events in the environment, but it also allows you to anticipate changes within your organization. You can predict the impact on your system from changes in laws, competition, technology, population shifts, and market conditions. The problem is to forecast these conditions in time to modify your plans to accommodate them.

Basically, there are two types of forecasting: objective and subjective. *Objective forecasting* is done by analyzing what has happened in the past and projecting the findings into the future. The basic assumption is that historical trends will continue into the future. Several statistical techniques such as regression and correlation analysis may be applied to project future trends by analyzing historical data.

Since the organization and its environmental systems are interdependent and overlapping, events in the environment have a profound impact on the organization. You cannot make effective plans without considering such factors. One way is through *economic forecasting*.

Economic forecasting has flourished widely since World War II. Today, there are forecasts of national income, productivity, gross national product (GNP), unemployment, wholesale and retail prices, capital investments, and many other factors. They are published by groups of specialists who collect and analyze data with sophisticated econometric models. Respected national and regional forecasts are produced regularly by the President's Council of Economic Advisors, the Conference Board Forum, the Wharton School at the University of Pennsylvania, and many large banks and university groups. SUGGESTION: Take advantage of economic forecasts such as these and assess the impact of predicted trends on your organization.

Subjective forecasting is based on judgment and intuition. One type of subjective forecasting is known as the Delphi Technique, named after the Oracle of Delphi in ancient Greece. Here's how it works: Suppose you would like a forecast of when solar energy will be a competitive alternative for heating buildings. You would survey several experts in the field and record their opinions. The results are made available to the experts, who then may wish to revise their predictions. This may be repeated. When their opinions begin to form a pattern, you can use it as a forecast.

Most organizations use a forecasting technique called Jury of Executive Opinion. Here, top managers pool their knowledge and hunches to forecast an estimate of future events. This is often the way sales forecasts are developed.

PUTTING IT TOGETHER: In practice, managers employ both objective and subjective forecasting. It's dangerous to accept an objective forecast without considering probable changes in conditions. Therefore always use your best judgment in addition to objective forecasts.

Internal analysis shows the current status of internal affairs. It tells you how well you are accomplishing your mission and points out your strengths and weaknesses.

Every organization is strong in some areas but weak in others. Many fast-growing companies have strong managers, increasing sales, and good products or services but lack working capital and adequate facilities. The idea is to recognize realities so you can capitalize on your strengths and remedy your weaknesses.

A good approach to internal analysis is to examine each functional area with a critical eye, making note of strong and weak points.

> EXAMPLE: You may look at your financial management and find a strong capital structure and good cash flow but cash is not being put to work. Perhaps it could be used to replace that obsolescent machine you identified as a weakness in the production area. Or, you could buy money market certificates and draw

interest on them. All major functional areas (finance, marketing, production, personnel, and the rest) should be analyzed in this manner.

The external and internal analysis yields a profile of the environment and the organization. WHAT TO DO: Match strengths and opportunities. Then set objectives for improving weaknesses. Finally, devise strategies for succeeding in spite of constraints.

Step Two: Define Your Goals

Objectives are goals to be pursued, targets to be reached. They serve two purposes: to provide the guidelines for progress and the benchmarks for measuring progress.

> EXAMPLE: The situation analysis may reveal an opportunity to sell your product in a new marketing area. You can set an objective to begin selling the product in that marketing area within the next six months. If you make this happen, you will have attained this objective.

Objectives are of two types: (1) general objectives that provide broad guidelines and direction to help you make plans for accomplishing your mission and (2) performance objectives that are specific and measurable. They state what is expected and when.

> EXAMPLE: A general objective might be to improve profitability. A related performance objective would state: "To increase net profit after taxes by 10 percent during the next fiscal year." CAUTION: When setting performance objectives, carefully study the difficulties that might be encountered in reaching them. Make objectives challenging yet attainable.

GENERAL OBJECTIVES FOR A
MANUFACTURING ORGANIZATION

- To grow and survive as a corporation.

- To produce high-quality products.

- To increase sales.

- To respond quickly to customer needs.

- To be a socially responsible corporate citizen of the local community.

- To develop loyal and satisfied employees.

- To operate within budgetary limits.

Setting objectives is not an easy task. Often, they conflict, and compromises must be arranged.

> EXAMPLE: An organization sets its first objective to cut production and administrative costs by 5 percent. However, a second objective is to increase sales by 20 percent. Trying to do both would prove quite a challenge.

The process of setting objectives may follow something like this: Since general objectives are derived from the mission or basic purpose of the organization, top-level managers may write them down and distribute them to their subordinates. Each work unit is asked, "What will you do to help accomplish these objectives?" Then, in consultation with subordinates, each manager develops performance objectives. These are then discussed with superiors and modified to ensure that they are challenging, attainable, and compatible with other objectives and company policies. Thus, performance objectives are negotiated at every level of the organization. This approach serves several purposes. It starts with the basic purposes of the organization; gets everyone involved in the planning process; motivates people to attain objectives; resolves conflicts among objectives; and results in measurable objectives against which progress can be compared.

Every manager should know how to write good performance objectives. Start with the word "to" followed by a verb and in clear and concise language, state what will be accomplished and when it will be accomplished. EXAMPLE: "To increase productivity from ten units per labor-hour to twelve by January fifteenth next year."

CHECKLIST FOR EVALUATING PERFORMANCE OBJECTIVES

- Does it support the organization's mission?

- Will it help attain one or more general objectives?

- Does it conform to the organization's policies?

- Is it measurable? (Are quantities and times specified?)

- Is it simple and easily understood?

- Can one person be made responsible for it?

- Is it challenging but attainable?

Step Three: Select a Strategy

Objectives define *what* must be accomplished. Strategies outline *how* to go about it. Possible courses of action are considered and the best chosen. This means that (1) you should take time to think of as many possible strategies as you can and (2) you should gather sufficient information and do the necessary analysis to make certain you select the best one.

> A CASE-IN-POINT: Suppose you wish to go to Chicago on the twenty-seventh of next month. This is the objective. How will you get there? There are many routes and modes of transportation. Some, such as flying by way of Miami, are obviously inappropriate if you wish to minimize time and cost. But there are reasonable alternatives, such as driving, flying direct, or going by bus. Based on the amount of time and money available, the urgency of the trip, and your own preference, you select the mode of transportation and route best for you.

Selecting strategies is the most interesting part of planning because it involves creativity and personal preference as well as objective analysis. After all, you cannot choose the best way to attain objectives unless you think of it and can demonstrate that it is truly better than other ways.

Step Four: Set Policy Guidelines

Policies are general statements that guide the decisions and actions of managers and employees. They are broad enough to allow subordinates to make decisions within the stated guidelines.

> EXAMPLE: Your policy may be to select qualified inside candidates for promotion rather than recruit from outside. With such a policy, you would look outside the organization only if you had no qualified employees as candidates.

Policies must be clear and carefully communicated to subordinates. In most cases, it's wise to get subordinates to participate in making a policy. Why? Because they will then be more likely to understand it and accept its guidance.

Step Five: Develop Action Plans and Programs

Ordinarily, the action plan involves the various functional areas of the organization. You may develop a program for marketing, one for production, one for finance, one for personnel, and others as necessary. All these programs start from the same corporate objectives, strategies, and policies. This promotes coordination and synergy even though many groups are involved.

Programs include the tasks that must be done, the schedules that must be met, and the milestones that must be reached in order to implement the strategy. In addition, specific responsibilities are assigned to individuals. Facilities and equipment needs are defined. Personnel requirements are developed. All this is priced and budgets are prepared. When these detailed action programs are completed, approved by top management, and funded, the plan is complete.

There are three major types of plans:

1. *Strategic plans* usually map the organization's multiyear direction. They include broad general objectives and strategies designed to guide the organization toward long-term goals. Strategic plans must be updated periodically (usually once a year) so they will stay in tune with the dynamic environment and the changing needs of the organization.

2. *Operational plans* (normally, one year or less) include specific performance objectives and programs for short-run activities. There are definite tasks, schedules, and budgets. Progress is carefully plotted to make sure objectives are met on time.

3. *Project plans* are prepared for a specific purpose. When that purpose has been achieved, the plan is completed.

> EXAMPLE: You need a project plan to build a house, design a new product, or conduct a market survey. All these plans include detailed schedules, procedures, task assignments, and budgets.

HOW TO ALLOW FOR THE UNEXPECTED THROUGH CONTINGENCY PLANNING

What if the forecast is wrong? After all, no one can predict the future precisely. Unforeseen events can disrupt best-laid plans.

A CASE-IN-POINT: Forecasting models at General Motors showed a market trend toward smaller automobiles in the 1975–1980 time period. Planners set objectives to produce small cars and to down-size larger cars on an orderly schedule over the five-year period. Engineers designed the subcompact Chevette and reengineered the larger cars. Things were going well. Record sales were chalked up until 1979. Then consumers—pressed by energy problems, rising inflation, and threats of recession—abandoned their love affair with larger cars and bought subcompacts in record numbers. Chevette factories could not keep up with the new demand. Small foreign cars made deep inroads into American markets. General Motors had not planned on such a rapid switch in demand, so large cars had to be sold with little or no profit while factories worked at top capacity to turn out Chevettes and Citations, which had been sold to the marketplace ahead of schedule.

What happened? The forecasts were basically correct, but they were off in the timing and intensity of the change. Managers cannot count on forecasts to be accurate and precise all the time. There are too many uncertainties in future events. WHAT TO DO: The prudent manager will accept forecasts for what they are—the best reasonable estimates of the future. Then he or she prepares the contingency plan—just in case!

You can prepare for most major forecast deviations by asking these questions:

1. What could happen that would substantially change the forecast?

2. What is the probability that such contingencies will occur?

3. How would they affect my plans?

4. What can I do to meet these contingencies?

5. What safeguards (or insurance) can I build into my plans to minimize any adverse impact on my organization?

6. Are the safeguards worth their cost?

Contingency planning offers feasible alternatives in emergency situations. Of course, you cannot allow for everything that could happen, but planning for contingencies will remove the surprise element from many deviations from forecast and allow you to react in a rational way.

HOW GOOD ORGANIZATION CAN BE THE KEY
TO CORRECT ACTION

The functional activity of acquiring resources, including people, and arranging them so the tasks outlined in the programs can be accomplished successfully is called organizing. Through organizing, you can coordinate the efforts of many people working simultaneously toward systems objectives.

The purpose of organizing is to arrange jobs and work relationships in such a way that everyone works effectively in a united effort. Organizing does something positive for everyone associated with an organization. For managers, it defines roles, areas of responsibility, channels of communication, and official relationships among individuals and groups. For nonmanagers, it describes job requirements and relationships with managers and other employees. For outsiders, such as salespeople and customers, organizing clarifies points of contact.

THE COMPANY PICNIC

The importance of organizing is illustrated in this story about a company picnic. Committees were appointed to plan the food and games. The food committee circulated a letter instructing employees to bring a meat dish, a salad, a vegetable, or a dessert. At the appointed time, everyone gathered in the park and placed their covered dishes on the picnic tables, only to discover that nearly everyone had brought desserts. There were twenty desserts, four vegetables, four salads, and two fried chickens for thirty families. The food committee failed to organize the picnic. Efforts were not coordinated, and confusion reigned. Both committee members and picnickers were disappointed and unhappy (except, perhaps, for some of the children who were happy with nothing but desserts).

The organizing function seeks to answer many questions, among them:

1. How should the organization be structured?
2. What will be the horizontal and vertical lines of communication?
3. Should the organization be centralized or decentralized?
4. How shall line and staff relationships be set up?
5. What skills are needed?

6. Who should be hired?

7. What training is necessary?

8. How can the organization satisfy the personal and social needs of its people?

9. How can potential conflicts be eliminated?

10. Will the informal organization support or disrupt the formal organization?

11. Can responsibility be delineated?

12. Where should authority be centered?

IMPORTANT: You must perform the organizing function in such a way that these questions are resolved and the organization becomes an efficient and effective system. In short, you must organize for *action.*

HOW TO USE THE SYSTEMS APPROACH TO GET THINGS DONE

Think of a system as an entity whose purpose is to do a job for which it is designed.

EXAMPLE: The electric company is a system designed to generate and distribute electricity to its customers. It uses manpower, fuel, and so on to generate power. The accounting department records financial data (bookkeeping), identifies costs, and prepares financial reports. A maintenance crew keeps equipment running and productive. A foreman and workers, with their equipment, make the product or render services. All these are subsystems within the system and have specific missions. Through interaction and cooperation of the components, they accomplish their missions and, finally, the overall mission of the organization.

As a manager, the systems approach can help you to see the organization as an entity with a mission and at the same time deal with the components (subsystems) as individual and necessary elements. The systems concept can help you:

1. Focus on the basic mission of the organization.

2. Provide an overall perspective on individual activities within the organization.

3. Emphasize the interdisciplinary nature of the organization.

4. Convey the dynamic character of the organization.

5. Relate all the parts to the whole organization.

6. Relate the organization to its environmental suprasystem.

7. Promote coordination and communication.

Organizational systems are perpetually changing. There is no such thing as a static condition or equilibrium when it comes to complex systems. As a manager, you need to constantly monitor the organization and anticipate what will happen. A good manager recognizes the fact that changes will occur with or without direction. Its your job to see that resources (human and otherwise) are used to produce goods and services within the limits of internal and external constraints in such a way that the value of the output is worth more than the value of the input plus the cost of conversion. When this is done, the organization becomes a *synergistic* system, or, in other words, a profitable one.

PROVEN WAYS THE MANAGER CAN BE AN ORGANIZER

You may not see yourself as an organizer because a lot of what you do is already organized by the time it reaches you. This may be true for the overall project, but there is much that you must do to make certain that people and other resources come together at the right time and in the right place. You are organizing when you:

1. Staff the department: hire, screen, transfer, fire, or work with the personnel department.

2. Coordinate the work of the unit with other units, with specialists, and with other managers so as to produce desired results.

3. Obtain the necessary resources to do the job and allocate those resources appropriately.

4. Make sure that people and jobs are matched reasonably well.

5. See that jobs are adequately defined and that people understand what they are expected to do.

WORKING WITH INFORMAL ORGANIZATIONS

The informal organization develops naturally whenever people work together for an extended period of time. It operates primarily to meet those needs of its members that are not and cannot be noted within the formal structure. The informal organization, like the formal, is structured and consists of a network of relationships among people, as shown, for example, in Figure 2.2. The dotted lines depict informal relationships among people that develop across department lines.

Informal organizations satisfy needs—probably social needs— by maintaining informal relationships. Within your department, the same kind of organization will occur, but it will be more cohesive than the network across departments. HERE'S SOME ADVICE: You cannot control its development, and you cannot extinguish it. So work with it, through it, and, in some cases, around it.

The informal organization has many of the features of the formal organization: its own leadership, status system, rewards and punishments, standards, and the world's most effective communication system—the grapevine. TAKE NOTE: An effective informal system will not only increase employee satisfaction but it can also enhance productivity. If you invite the group to help solve departmental performance problems and set standards, you will usually get improved cooperation along with group norms compatible with formal standards. (NOTE: See Chapter 4 for a further discussion of group dynamics.)

HOW TO USE DIRECTION TO GET RESULTS THROUGH PEOPLE

Directing is a familiar activity for managers. It's where the action is and what you do most of the time. Directing includes communicating, leading, motivating, resolving conflicts, evaluating performance, and sometimes taking disciplinary action. While planning and organizing prepare the system to accomplish its mission, directing activates it and makes things happen.

Directing is performed by managers at all levels. As a manager, you are part of the group you supervise, even though your relationship with your subordinates sets you apart from them. You are responsible for their work as well as your own, and you must make

INFORMAL ORGANIZATION OVERLAYING THE FORMAL

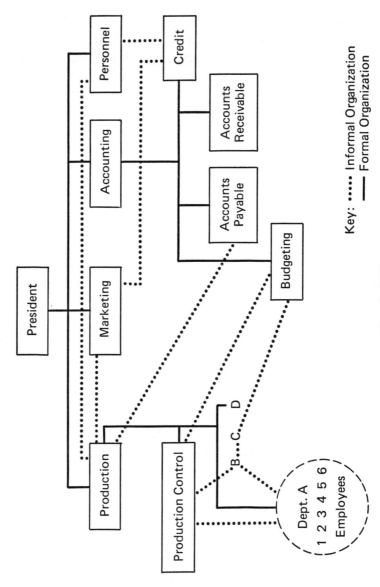

Key: ••••• Informal Organization
     ——— Formal Organization

FIGURE 2.2

sure their efforts as well as yours are directed toward organizational objectives. You make assignments, monitor progress, coordinate actions, and correct errors. Most importantly, you see that everyone works toward the common goal. This means that you lead and influence them in performing their work.

Your leadership style will be governed by your attitudes and assumptions about people. "Theory X" holds that people are basically self-centered and must be told what to do. "Theory Y" holds that people are socially oriented and will voluntarily do what is best for the organization. According to Douglas McGregor, the autocratic leader makes "Theory X" assumptions about people, while the participative leader makes "Theory Y" assumptions.[1] (More on this in Chapter 8.)

An objective of most organizations is to keep employees productive and satisfied. Managers have a great deal to do with achieving this objective. Your personal style should fit the situation in such a way that your subordinates will be motivated to be productive. This will result in higher morale, higher achievement, lower employee turnover, lower absenteeism, and fewer accidents.

As a manager, your function of directing is not unlike a navigator of a ship. A navigator charts the direction and guides it accordingly. You, like a navigator, steer rather than drive. You should have a firm hand on the wheel and the throttle but focus on the end results rather than the thrill of controlling the "ship's" course.

Managers tend to see directing as the major part of their job, and if this is done well, their work is also done. Not so! Directing is important but certainly no more so than planning, organizing, and controlling. While directing may be more visible and more enjoyable, without the other functions, you are little more than a straw boss.

Here are the most important principles involved in directing:

1. *Unity of direction.* A single plan and common set of objectives must govern operations that involve various people and resources. People must know what the objectives are, and these objectives must be common to all units.

2. *Decentralized decision making.* This principle pushes the decision authority down to the lowest levels having the requisite

---

[1] Douglas McGregor, *The Human Side of Enterprise* (New York: McGraw-Hill, 1960).

information and skill. It generally produces more effective decisions. When decisions are made at the level where they are to be implemented, there is usually greater commitment by those involved.

3. *Factoral selection.* The decision maker needs control over the selection and allocation of the factors needed to accomplish the task. EXAMPLE: You need to have a voice in staffing your unit. When someone else hires, you lose control over the consequences.

4. *The law of this situation.* Decisions should be made according to what the situation demands. If followed, the law of this situation leads to the best possible decision. It suggests that you review your better judgment in light of other realities and base your ultimate decision on all factors.

HOW TO ISSUE INSTRUCTIONS AND ASSIGN WORK TO GET THE RIGHT RESULTS

Much of your success in getting the results you want will depend on how well you issue instructions and assign work. You'll find that the employees who are most receptive to instructions are those who accept your influence in other ways. There may be no one best way to give instructions, but here are some helpful guidelines:

1. Have a clear understanding concerning what is to be done.
2. Acknowledge what you do not know.
3. Be aware of the employee's frame of reference.

A CASE-IN-POINT: Consider which way you prefer to receive instructions: "Bob, here's what you need to know about the Ajax account. I've written it out in detail so there shouldn't be any questions." or "Bob, here's a brief on the Ajax account. Look it over and let me know what other information you'll need to develop your approach." Just as you would prefer the second approach, so would your employees.

IMPORTANT: The need, or rationale, should always be stated. Also, the assignment should describe the overall situation along with whatever details are needed.

Parts of the directing function include giving information and interpreting policies. Without these types of communication, it would be impossible for you to effectively direct the work of others.

Employees need information, not only about their work, but also about the organization, its people, and its products.

As a manager, you play a vital role in giving and receiving certain kinds of information. This implies being informed yourself about what is happening. WHAT TO DO: Take an active role in getting what you perceive to be important information. Deal with controversial matters as matter-of-factly as possible, with emphasis on what will be done about it. Above all, communicate in a straightforward way when you have information employees need or when they have questions that you can answer.

The most useful guide for interpreting policy and procedure is to understand what the policy means, the reasons for it, and what results it is expected to achieve. This will give you a grasp of the spirit of the policy which can then be communicated to employees.

THE MANAGER AS A COACH

Despite the wide recognition and acceptance of the need for coaching, research has shown that relatively few managers perform well in this capacity. Generally, this is due to a lack of commitment and a systematic method for guiding the personal improvement of employees. To help you become a better coach, follow these five steps:

1. Prepare by assessing your employee's performance.
2. Set the stage first by opening avenues for communication. HINT: Don't expect great progress in the beginning. Things take time to develop. Try this lead, "Let's talk about how your work is progessing."
3. Discuss constructively what can be improved. IMPORTANT: The suggestions must be specific. Try to give examples of what you mean. It's a good idea to let your employee look for ways to improve.
4. Implement improvements. HINT: Draw upon your own personal experiences as they relate to the situation at hand. This can help your employee.
5. Follow up.

Good communication is vital to the coaching process. Listening along with nondirective counseling techniques (where the counselee directs his or her own development) will help ensure your success. Involve your employee in finding solutions.

HOW TO DELEGATE

Delegation means assigning responsibility and authority to accomplish a task. It's essentially an act of trust and confidence, coming as a result of proper coaching. The main purpose of delegation is to get better performance in the areas that really count—profits, quality, service, and personal commitment.

The benefits of delegation can be summarized in terms of their effects on both you and the employee. Delegation:

1. *Increases personal development.* Every organization needs skilled and talented people.

2. *Permits the delegator to accomplish his or her own work.* Although delegation takes time, eventually employees will be able to handle a greater workload. This frees you for the important managerial responsibilities.

3. *Develops cooperation and trust among subordinates.* When you recognize your employees' ability to take on responsibility, they are more likely to be cooperative.

4. *Fosters commitment to the organization and its objectives.* When people are given responsibility and commensurate authority, they feel they have a greater stake in the organization and its future.

It's not enough to understand the merits of delegation. Effective delegation lies in implementation, and that depends a great deal on your approach. The overall delegation process consists of five steps:

1. *Preparation.* There is an old axiom that says "To fail to plan is to plan to fail." This is important to remember when delegating. In the preparation stage, you determine exactly where the employee stands in capability and experience. Then, you decide what can be delegated. Obviously, your priorities will make an important difference. CAUTION: Be aware of the limits of delegation as defined by the job description and union restrictions.

2. *Clarification.* Basically, you develop an understanding of what is expected. Be sure there are no misunderstandings that could cause problems. EXAMPLE: If a subordinate is told to go

ahead and overhaul one of his machines, he might not be sure what this means. What are the budget limits? Who can he call for help? Can he go outside the company for service? You need to anticipate and provide concrete answers.

3. *Agreement.* Even if both you and the employee are clear about expectations and authority, you must both agree on the assignment. Say so explicitly, if necessary.

4. *Assignment.* This step goes beyond the position description in that it implements specific authority and responsibility to the employee.

5. *Follow up.* This stage is one of the most difficult because it requires evaluation and, if necessary, corrective action. It also requires that you provide the necessary support in the form of resources and psychological reinforcement.

If you neglect to give support for the authority you delegate to an employee, you're essentially giving him "enough rope to hang himself." No one deliberately wants to see a person "hang" on the corporate ladder, but there is good reason to suspect it often happens.

> A CASE-IN-POINT: An engineering project manager was assigned to conduct a feasibility study for a major product design change. The director of engineering gave the project manager "complete authority" to perform the study and make a recommendation by a certain date. Once given the authority to proceed, the project manager lined up the necessary personnel. However, department managers were not told of the project and were reluctant to give up personnel. By the time the project group jelled, there were only two months left to complete the study, and as a result, the report was incomplete. The director of engineering reprimanded the project manager and turned the project over to a different group.

To help you determine what and when to delegate, and to see the results of what you delegate, consider the concept of the *learning curve.* It's shown as a graphic scale for observing an employee's progress. Figure 2.3 depicts a fairly typical learning trend. In the first month or so, the gradient level is steep, meaning that the employee learned the first three skill levels of the job in that time. Then he or she plateaued—stayed at the same level—for another month and a half and then spurted again to a higher level.

A LEARNING CURVE

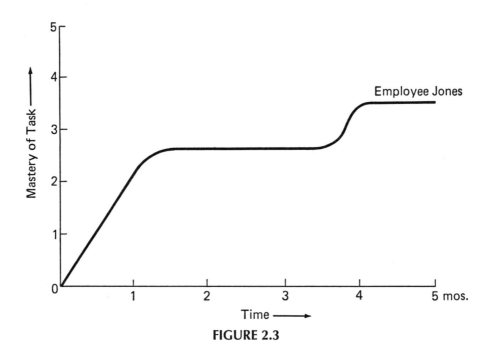

FIGURE 2.3

The learning curve points out a well-established principle: When learning a new task, learning increases first at a rapid rate and then levels off temporarily. As a manager, you may not be able to change the process but you assist the employee in coping with it. YOUR STRATEGY: During the plateau, forego delegating more responsibility, and stress instead the preparation of further delegation once proficiency increases.

WHAT GOOD CONTROL CAN MEAN TO YOU

No organizational system can be expected to attain its objectives without control. Even if managers prepare a superior plan and establish an efficient organization, they cannot assure success unless they take measures to ensure that the organization will operate according to that plan.

In every instance, a control system includes these four elements:

1. *A good plan.* There is no such thing as organizational control without a plan. Even when plans are unwritten, an objective or expectation must exist in your mind. Otherwise the organization has no direction and cannot fulfill its mission.

2. *Feedback.* This includes everything you read, see, or hear about your organization and the environment in which it operates. Often, feedback can warn you of potential problems before they become significant.

3. *Analysis.* This phase serves two purposes: to see if a problem exists and, if it does, to select the best possible corrective action. RULE OF THUMB: A problem exists if there is a significant deviation from the plan or if such a deviation is likely to happen. In either case, you must take corrective action.

4. *Corrective action.* Even if you have timely feedback and exercise good judgment in choosing the best remedy, you are not likely to keep your organization on course if you fail to take corrective action.

Effective action must be *timely, economical, appropriate, clear,* and *acceptable.* These characteristics should be used as guidelines for establishing and evaluating control systems. Of course, control is tied irrevocably to the plan since the plan establishes the benchmarks for evaluating feedback. The plan should specify measures of effectiveness; that is, criteria that inform the manager about the status of important operations and when action is necessary.

> EXAMPLE: Personnel turnover is a good measure of effectiveness because it alerts the manager to possible problems. An increasing personnel turnover rate means that more employees are leaving the organization and may point to conditions causing dissatisfaction and low morale. Knowing this, you can take steps to identify the problem and, if necessary, take corrective action.

USING THE POWERFUL MANAGEMENT TOOL: THE "FEEDFORWARD CONCEPT"

As noted, the term "feedback" is used to describe the status reports that a manager receives from his organizational system. Almost automatically, however, a good manager will interpret feedback in terms of its implications for the future of the organization.

Control action is directed toward changing something so it will act differently in the future. This forward-looking attitude and future-oriented action is called *feedforward control.*[2] It is dedicated to the concept that we must anticipate deviations from the plan far enough in advance to take corrective action.

> EXAMPLE: A demand forecast may indicate that sales will fall 20 percent below target next quarter. By increasing promotion, lowering prices, and opening a warehouse store, you may be able to meet the target.

Management science techniques are very helpful in feedforward control. PERT (Program Evaluation and Review Technique) is a planning and control network technique that maps critical activities. Here's how it works: Critical activities are identified on a project schedule. The project manager then monitors these activities and keeps them moving on time. If trouble with a noncritical activity arises, PERT can predict when it will become critical enough to delay the project. Thus, the manager can take corrective action before the project runs behind schedule. In addition, PERT can compute the probability of completing the project on schedule and can point out the activities that must be expedited to finish ahead of schedule. See Figure 2.4. An extension of PERT, called PERT-COST, can estimate how much it will cost to expedite activities.

Perhaps the most powerful management tool for feedforward control is *simulation.* It is based on a model of the salient features of the organizational system. When programmed for the computer and exercised with the proper data, a simulation model becomes a dynamic replica of the system and behaves in much the same way as the real system.

DECISION MAKING: THE HEART OF YOUR JOB

Managers make decisions when confronted with a choice between two or more alternatives. If there are no alternatives, there's no need for a decision. However, this situation rarely happens. Usually, there are two or more alternatives; the problem is to decide which one is the best.

---

[2] Harold Koontz and R.W. Bradspies, "Managing Through Feedforward Control," *Business Horizons*, Vol. 15, No. 3 (June 1972).

PERT DIAGRAM (HYPOTHETICAL)

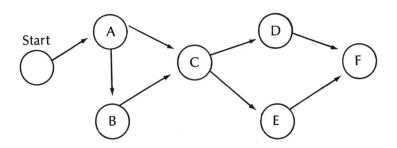

Events: A, B, C, D, E, F, where F is completion of the project.
FIGURE 2.4

The process of decision making involves the following sequence of activities:

1. Recognizing that a decision is required.
2. Identifying alternatives.
3. Evaluating alternatives by comparing advantages and disadvantages.
4. Exercising judgment and choosing the best alternative.
5. Implementing the choice.

Finally, *monitoring* the system after implementation assures that the problem has really been solved and the new system is performing as expected. If the system deviates from expectations, you now have another problem to solve. And this is why managers are needed.

Figure 2.5 can serve as a useful decision framework. It shows that there are four decision-making approaches, each representing a choice for the manager-leader, depending on the kind of situation he or she faces:

1. *The routine-thinking approach.* When the situation is governed entirely by policies, rules, and traditions, the decision is already made, so your main task is to apply the policy or rule.

FOUR APPROACHES TO DECISION MAKING

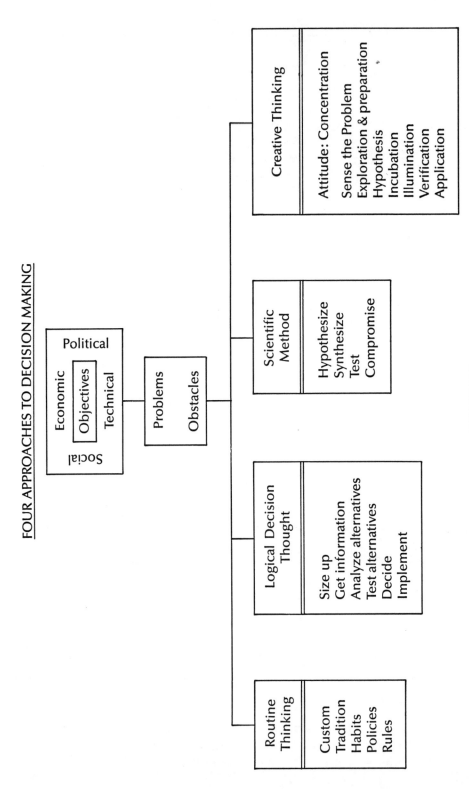

FIGURE 2.5

2. *The logical, or rational, decision-making approach.* The keynote of the rational approach is its logic. It makes sense to most decision makers, and by using it you can ensure that nothing important has been omitted. It is useful in any situation requiring judgment.

3. *The scientific method.* Very similar to the rational approach, the main difference in the scientific method is that it investigates the problem and tests it out more formally than the rational approach. The scientific approach is most useful in solving problems involving technology, product, or process, where you can experiment and test out a hypothesis.

> EXAMPLE: Suppose you want to find out if a particular machine is operating properly. You might set up a controlled two-hour test and record the machine's performance statistically. Here, the scientific method can tell you whether your predictions or hunches about the machine are valid.

4. *Creative thinking.* This is mainly an intuitive process that discovers things by hunches, ideas, and feelings rather than by logical analysis.

HOW TO MAKE THE CORRECT BIG DECISIONS USING ANALYTICAL TOOLS

Making decisions is the most pervasive activity of your job. A few are so important that you need to gather much data and compare alternatives in depth before deciding. These important decisions fall into several categories:

1. A decision that will have a great impact on the organization and its people. EXAMPLE: "Should we move our plant to another state?"

2. A decision that will have ripple effects and deeply affect subsequent decisions. EXAMPLE: "Shall we establish a policy to fill vacancies with internal candidates or recruit from outside the organization?"

3. A decision that is complex and requires extensive research and analysis. EXAMPLE: "Should we build a new plant or renovate our old one?"

4. A decision in which the risk is great. EXAMPLE: "Should we add solar energy water heaters to our product line?"

5. A decision that involves heavy capital investment. EXAMPLE: "Which large computer system should we buy?"

The analytical techniques can be very helpful in testing alternatives. Simple arrays of alternatives and criteria can help you view all the possibilities at one time.

A CASE-IN-POINT: You have a problem with an obsolete computer system. Its capacity is limited and down-time for maintenance is increasing. You gather information about your needs, establish criteria, and procure information about new computers. There are five alternatives. They are shown in Figure 2.6 using only plus (+) and minus (−) to indicate strong features and weak alternatives. Figure 2.7 shows the same information but uses weighted criteria and a scale (1–10) for rating the alternatives. This method requires more information, but it's worthwhile if the consequence of your decision has a major impact on the system. In both tables, Computer System B is the best choice. The comparative analysis shows simply that System B is equal to or better than the other systems except in initial cost. The weighted analysis scales both the criteria and the scores to show not only that System B is better but how much better it is.

Implementing the chosen alternative is not always simple. Once the decision is made to buy Computer System B, a project plan must be made to:

1. Continue the old system until the new one is ready.

2. Arrange financing.

3. Buy the new system.

4. Schedule installation and training.

5. Adapt operating programs to the new systems.

6. Install and test.

7. Change over to the new system.

8. Shut down and dispose of the old system.

COMPARATIVE ANALYSIS OF ALTERNATIVES

(Computer systems are compared with one another, not with present system)

Criteria					
Tangible benefits	A	B	C	D	E
Low cost of system	+ +	−	− −	+	+
Meets ROI* target of 20% after tax	+	+	−	+	+
Lower order processing cost	+	+	+	−	−
Lower inventories	+	+	+	+	+
Lower maintenance costs	−	+	−	+	+
Lower programming costs	+	+ +	+	−	−
Faster turnaround	+ +	+ +	+	+	+
Better reliability	+	+	+	+	+
Intangible benefits					
Better service to customers	+	+	+	+	+
Quicker reports for managers	+	+ +	−	+ +	+
Better formats and displays	−	+	−	+	−
On-line display	−	+	−	+	−
On-line printing	+	+	−	+	+

*Return on Investment

FIGURE 2.6

Many pitfalls can occur during this process. It is usually traumatic for people to adapt to new systems and procedures. Instructions are misunderstood; initial operations slow; errors abound; costs are high. These and a dozen other difficulties will probably happen. WHAT TO DO: A prudent manager will realize this and include time and money for contingencies in the implementation plan.

To repeat an essential point, managers make decisions not only with current information about a situation, but also with an esti-

WEIGHTED ANALYSIS OF ALTERNATIVES
(Scale = 1 to 10, 10 is best)

Criteria	Criterion Weight	Computer Systems[1]									
		A		B		C		D		E	
		Score	Weighted Score[1]	Score	Weighted Score	Score	Weighted Score	Score	Weighted Score	Score	Weighted Score
Tangible Benefits Cost of System	2	10	20	6	12	3	6	8	16	9	18
Meets a ROI target of 20% aftertaps	3	9	27	7	21	4	12	7	21	8	24
Order processing cost	1	8	8	7	7	7	7	3	3	4	4
Inventory cost	1	7	7	9	9	8	8	7	7	7	7
Maintenance cost	1	4	4	9	9	5	5	7	7	7	7
Programming cost	2	6	12	10	20	8	16	4	8	5	10
Turnaround speed	3	10	30	10	30	8	24	8	24	7	21
Reliability	3	8	24	9	27	8	24	8	24	9	27
Intangible Benefits Better service to customers	3	8	24	8	24	8	24	8	24	8	24
Quick reports to managers	4	9	36	10	40	5	20	8	32	9	36
Better formats and displays	2	5	10	9	18	4	8	8	16	6	12
On-line display	1	na[2]	0	8	8	na	0[3]	7	7	na	0
On-line printing	1	8	8	9	9	na	0	8	8	8	8
Total Weighted Score			210		234		154		197		198

[1] Weighted score is obtained by multiplying criterion weight by score for each computer.
[2] Not available.
[3] Batch processing.

FIGURE 2.7

mate of conditions in the future. Since you cannot predict the future perfectly, some risk is involved. It follows that decisions will be made under one of these three conditions:

1. *Complete certainty.* When you know what the outcome will be when you select an alternative. Since you have complete knowledge about the consequences, you compare the alternatives and choose the one with the highest payoff. EXAMPLE: A financial manager must decide how to invest cash to keep it productive. Alternatives are to (1) put it into an insured savings account, (2) buy government bonds, or (3) buy money market certificates. For all practical purposes, the return from these three investments is certain. So, you choose the one that best fits the need for maximum return with high liquidity. Unfortunately, few decisions are made under conditions of such complete certainty.

2. *Complete uncertainty.* When you have no idea about the consequences of your decision. No information is available to help you choose. Fortunately, you are seldom faced with such conditions. Some information is usually available.

3. *Risk.* Most decisions are made under conditions of risk. EXAMPLE: Thirty thousand dollars is spent on an advertising campaign with the expectation that sales will increase. The probability is high that sales will indeed rise but not guaranteed. WHAT TO DO: When faced with a decision under conditions of risk, try to get sufficient information to determine how probable the outcome will be for each alternative. When information is poor, risk is high. Therefore, the quality of the available information has a direct bearing on how risky decisions will be for managers in the organization.

Risk analysis uses probabilities to determine whether a decision is likely to be a good one.

EXAMPLE: In Figure 2.8, four products could be manufactured by a plant. Product No. 1 offers a high expected profit but also high risk. The expected value, obtained by multiplying the expected profit times the probability that the expectation will be achieved, shows that Product No. 3 has the highest payoff ($200,000) and is the best choice based on the information available. Notice that both the expected profits and the probabilities are estimates; so you must use judgment, too.

Payoff tables also demonstrate the use of probabilities.

EXPECTED VALUE OF ALTERNATIVE PRODUCTS						
Alternative Products	Expected Profit	×	Probability of Product	=	Expected Value of Products
1	$100,000		10%		$10,000
2	70,000		20%		14,000
3	40,000		50%		20,000
4	40,000		20%		8,000
			100%		

FIGURE 2.8

EXAMPLE: The question is whether to expand by building a large plant or a small plant. Figure 2.9 shows the net payoff over the five-year life of the plant, all expected costs and revenues considered. There are probabilities for low, moderate, and high sales based on forecasts of economic conditions.

The expected payoff of the large plant is $52,000—$12,000 greater than the payoff of the small one. There is an 80 percent probability (50 percent plus 30 percent) that profits will be between $40,000 and $120,000 if you build the large plant. Thus, you would probably choose to build the large plant even though there is a 20 percent probability of a $20,000 loss. There is some risk, but the opportunities are great.

This question may also be analyzed by using a *decision tree* (Figure 2.10). This method of analysis reveals another option: Build a small plant now, then decide whether or not to build an addition to the plant at a later date when the sales outlook will be clearer.

On the basis of the decision-tree analysis, the two-stage approach would yield a higher payoff than building a large plant immediately. This approach would enable you to save the cost of the additional capital that would be tied up in a large plant during the first two years when it would not have been operating at capacity.

Most decisions can be made without these sophisticated analytical techniques. However, when they can be economically applied, such methods greatly increase your ability to make sound decisions in complex situations. Your understanding of how they work may not directly affect your day-to-day operation, but it will help you become more and more a manager.

PAYOFF TABLE ($)

Sales Forecast	Estimated Profits		Probabilities	Expected Value	
	Small Plant	Large Plant		Small Plant	Large Plant
A	B	C	D	(B × D)	(C × D)
Low	10,000	(− 20,000)	.20	2,000	(− 4,000)
Medium	40,000	40,000	.50	20,000	20,000
High	60,000	120,000	.30	18,000	36,000
				TOTAL (Payoff) 40,000	52,000

FIGURE 2.9

DECISION TREE ($)

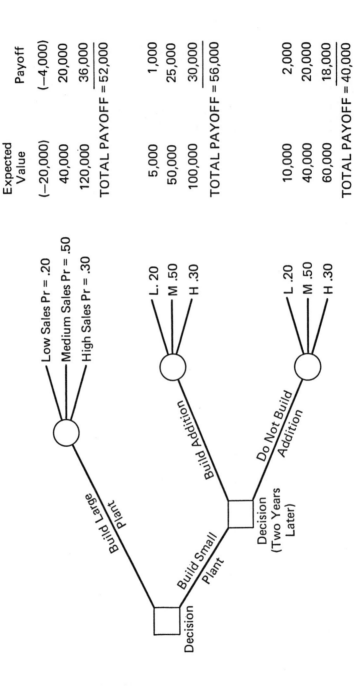

	Expected Value	Payoff
Low Sales Pr = .20	(−20,000)	(−4,000)
Medium Sales Pr = .50	40,000	20,000
High Sales Pr = .30	120,000	36,000
		TOTAL PAYOFF = 52,000
L .20	5,000	1,000
M .50	50,000	25,000
H .30	100,000	30,000
		TOTAL PAYOFF = 56,000
L .20	10,000	2,000
M .50	40,000	20,000
H .30	60,000	18,000
		TOTAL PAYOFF = 40,000

Build Large Plant

Build Addition

Do Not Build Addition

Build Small Plant

Decision

Decision (Two Years Later)

FIGURE 2.10

CHAPTER 3

How to Use Communication as Your Foundation for Success

A manager's number one problem can be summed up in one word: Communication.

—THE EDITORS OF PERSONNEL JOURNAL

MANAGERS at all levels need to be versed in the concepts and techniques of communication that will help them manage with greater impact. And no level of management is more crucial in this respect than first-line managers.

Every day you interact frequently and closely with people in a variety of situations. If you understand the communication process and appreciate the importance of each stage, your chances for success are indeed very good. As you build your communication skills you'll develop an awareness of the dynamics that occur in the communication process and an appreciation of good supervisory communication.

You may perhaps already know some of the fundamentals of communication described in this chapter, but you may not always be aware of them. Some were already mentioned in Chapter 1. And some will be completely new. All together, this chapter forms the basis for the next challenge—building strong interpersonal relationships. And with that comes success.

HOW THE PROCESS WORKS

Communication is the process of transmitting information, meaning, and a frame of reference between people. It's essential that people comprehend the meaning of messages and respond accordingly. Additionally, communication is only complete when each party understands the other's frame of reference (empathy) and can accurately predict how the other will interpret the message. In other words, you're putting yourself in the other person's shoes and seeing the situation from the other's vantage point.

There are at least four purposes for communication in an organizational setting:

1. *Functional.* When the intention is to accomplish something.

2. *Manipulative.* When the motive is to somehow persuade or maneuver someone to the manipulator's own ends.

3. *Educational.* When someone needs to be prepared beyond their immediate needs.

4. *Social.* When maintaining nonwork relationships.

Five major factors come into play in the communication process: (1) the message; (2) the personalities, background, and experience of the sender and the receiver; (3) the medium; (4) the organization; and (5) any other parties affected by the communication. Figure 3.1 depicts the communication event in its simplest form. CAUTION: Matters can get complicated quickly when any of the factors plays upon the event.

Basically, four elements are exchanged in a communication: feelings, thoughts, information, and opinions. These are exchanged in an interaction or *transaction*, the "rules" of which must be agreed upon by the parties involved beford the communication can be complete.

> EXAMPLE: Tom says "Hello" to Fred, who says "Hello" in return. Suppose, though, that Fred adds, "How are you?" but Tom does not reply. Chances are that both will go away uncomfortable because one did not commit to the full extent of the transaction.

According to Dr. Eric Berne, the originator of Transactional Analysis, people have three basic hungers: for stimulation, for structure, and for recognition.[1] These are the universal forces that explain behavior and underlie various motives that people exhibit in their transactions.

BASIC COMMUNICATION MODEL

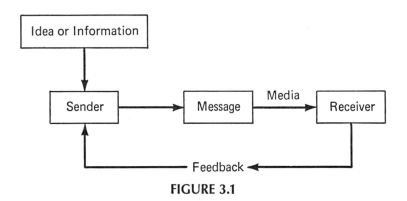

FIGURE 3.1

Recognition hunger seeks what Transactional Analysis terms *strokes;* that is, any form of recognition. Strokes are given and received through transactions; therefore, communication becomes the basic process for satisfying recognition hunger. So powerful is this hunger that people will perform any conceivable act to gain it. IMPORTANT: Whether or not you intend it, your transactions convey strokes—be they positive (reward) or negative (punishment).

> EXAMPLE: Notice the manager who punishes an employee for absenteeism only to find the problem continuing, even increasing. What's happening? The employee is getting negative strokes, which he prefers to none at all. In order to make the manager's program work, positive strokes for compliance must have a greater value to the person than the strokes he gets for the deviant behavior.

There are essentially four types of communication, each of which employs different media: (1) talking, (2) writing, (3) reading, and (4) listening. The first two are involved in sending messages, while the last two involve receiving them. Not coincidentally, then,

---

[1] Eric Berne, *The Structure and Dynamics of Organizations and Groups* (New York: Grove Press 1963).

there are two types of communication roles: the sender and the receiver.

None of the types of communication is inherently superior to the others. You might know, however, that one study showed that managers spend more time listening than any other type of communication.[2]

One other type of communication exists—*nonverbal*, by way of feelings, gestures, and perhaps thought patterns. It's especially important because it conveys feelings, and feelings influence behavior, which in turn affects all organization levels and all types of situations.

It has been said that an optimist looks at half a glass of water and sees it half full, while a pessimist looks at it and sees it half empty. Such differing attitudes constitute what is called a *frame of reference*. The frame of reference results from an individual's past experiences and training and influences how that person interprets messages of everyday living.

> EXAMPLE: Your company announces that employees will have an additional vacation day over a holiday. Some employees feel pleased about it. Some see it as a way to get more work out of them when they return. Others think business is slumping, and this extra day foreshadows a layoff. Still others see it as a way to gain leverage with the union. IMPORTANT: Being aware of your employee's frame of reference will enable you to anticipate their reactions and communicate in a way the employee understands.

Perception is a process whereby you "see" and interpret events. Think of a frame of reference as a window of perception. Like a window, everything is filtered through it. So, if you want to change someone's perception, you need to introduce other information into their frame of reference.

> A CASE-IN-POINT: Suppose your employee says, "You want to eliminate overtime, but we can't complete the schedule without it." You reply, "I realize it seems impossible, but we're getting an additional person to handle the bundling operation. That will free you up entirely for press work." What have you accomplished? By adding information, you have introduced another perspective which, if your employee agrees, will lead to the desired change in behavior.

---

[2] Alfred Cooper, "The Art of Good Listening," *Manage* (February 1959), Vol. II.

Along with the various types of communication, there are several levels at which people communicate:

1. *Technical.* Information is passed among people and/or machines without any attempt to understand the material.

2. *Ritualistic.* Feelings are conveyed simply in the context of social etiquette. EXAMPLE: "Hello," "How are you," and similar "polite" greetings.

3. *Activity oriented.* The emphasis is on accomplishing work. Most of the information exchanged is factual, and opinions are given related to the tasks at hand.

4. *Social involvement.* Communication is generally stroke oriented, and people exchange feelings not only about their work but about personal matters as well.

5. *Authentic communication.* At this level, people experience a true sharing of ideas, views, ideals, and feelings. The parties involved feel spontaneous and see themselves as freely choosing their role in the relationship.

Authentic communications allow for real intimacy in the sense that human beings work together, solve problems, and share their views and aspirations. CRITICAL FACTORS: Trust, honesty, and understanding are essential; and they must begin with you.

RULE OF THUMB: To manage effectively, you must comunicate at least at Level 3 and preferably higher.

At every level, there are potential barriers to good communication, including these four:

1. *Physical.* Limitations posed by geography and/or capability. Physical barriers or disabilities can usually be overcome.

2. *Social.* Status; that is, one's standing in the social environment—often an "invisible door" that undermines the open-door policy.

3. *Psychological.* The fantasies and images people have about a situation—major determinants of whether a person will react appropriately. Psychological barriers are the most difficult to identify and resolve. Why? Because such barriers are mainly internal, consisting of messages people have about how they should think and behave, what they should feel, and how they should perceive the other person. In Transactional Analysis, these messages are

called *injunctions,* meaning they were assimilated from authority figures in previous experiences.

    4. *Organizational.* Barriers that include language, structure, climate, traditions, and the information system at work within the organization. More on this later.

THE PARABLE OF THE SPINDLE

> In a well-known restaurant, many customer orders were not being handled properly. Social scientist William H. White noted that cooks, who had higher status, were taking orders from waiters and waitresses, who were considered lower status. This created an inconsistency in the workers' hierarchy, resulting in poor communication and cooperation. To resolve the conflict, White recommended the use of an impersonal item—a spindle—as a buffer between the waiters and the cooks. With the spindle, the cooks no longer perceived themselves as taking orders from waiters. The result: The customers got their food!

Networks refer to the format used in communicating. For example, the "grapevine" usually has a branching network, which explains its speed and efficiency. A scalar network is top-down and follows the chain of command. More on this later.

The *medium* is the mechanism used to transmit the message. Commonly used organization media include the bulletin board, form letter, personal letter, telex, intercom, phone, video, and face-to-face exchange. PRINCIPLE: The more important the message, the hotter and more dynamic the medium should be. The more dynamic the medium, the greater the demand for attention placed on the observer or listener.

> EXAMPLE: If your department's new quota is set at 120 percent of the previous year, assuming this is important information, it would not be appropriate to announce this via a form letter. Rather, it should be conveyed face to face or by audio-visual means. Overall, the media can be rated according to these dimensions, as in Figure 3.2.

What is the significance in all of this for you? For one, by knowing the strength of media in capturing people's attention, you can better select the appropriate one. Second, people equate the importance of the message with the medium used; thus, your choice is highly critical. By selectively choosing the communication me-

RATING THE TYPICAL ORGANIZATION COMMUNICATION MEDIA

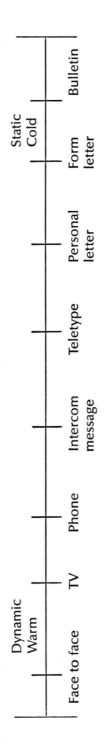

FIGURE 3.2

dium, reserving the warmest for the most important messages, your employees will become more sensitive to and participate more in face-to-face transactions. REMEMBER THIS: The content of the message is the primary element in the communication process. The medium is still only a vehicle for delivering the message.

SIX QUALITIES NECESSARY FOR COMMUNICATING WELL

Authentic communication is not always easy to achieve. The key lies in the attitude you take and the qualities you interject into the lines of communication. The manager who communicates well demonstrates these six qualities:

1. *Authenticity.* Honest, straightforward, open, and sincere.
2. *Empathy.* Able to put oneself in another's shoes and see things from that person's standpoint.
3. *Assertiveness.* Authentically state your feelings and needs; ask for what you want.
4. *Goal orientation.* Steadfast commitment to organization goals, keep goals uppermost in mind.
5. *Judgment.* Make decisions appropriate to the situation; say and do the right things at the right time.
6. *Listening.* Keep tuned into events and feedback, and process what you observe; be willing to hear and understand what others are saying and feeling.

HOW TRANSACTIONAL ANALYSIS PROVIDES A SYSTEM FOR EFFECTIVE COMMUNICATION

Transactional Analysis (TA) is a system developed by the late Eric Berne, a psychiatrist, to help his patients become well. Taking Berne's work, W. Ray Poindexter, M.D., continued to study human behavior in organizations. Much of the following discussion is based on their work.[3]

TA, as Berne intended it, is a system for effective communication and interaction among people. Those who use TA properly will be in charge of themselves and their destinies.

---

[3] See Eric Berne, *The Structure and Dynamics of Organizations and Groups* (New York: Grove Press 1963), and W. Ray Poindexter, *The Poindexter Organization* (Agoura, CA: TRANSAN Publications 1977).

The basis for control (social and self) in transacting with others is the personality structure as influenced by the experiences of life. (See Figure 3.3.) Experiences consist of everything that happens to an individual. They are recorded in three distinct ego states within the personality: Parent, Adult, and Child. An *ego state* is a consistent pattern of feelings and experiences that are expressed and observed in corresponding actions. Each is identifiable by both the type of messages residing in it as well as its impact on others. Each is a separate and distinct source of behavior.

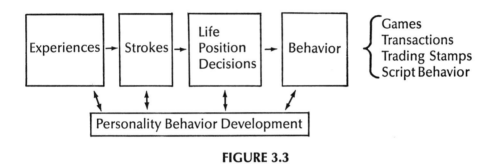

FIGURE 3.3

Experiences are resistered in the brain and stored much like videotape. These tapes, or associations, can be replayed consciously and often unconsciously.

> EXAMPLE: A manager reacts nervously to the company president. Why? The president's gray hair triggers a boyhood memory when he was chased by a gray-haired man with a stick.

In the TA system, very few tapes are unimportant to the development of effective human beings. Tapes exist for a purpose, for problem solving at some later time. They include everything incorporated from parent figures, and from perceptions of events, feelings, and distortions associated with the memories.

Let's consider the three ego states in more detail:

1. *Parent.* When you think, talk, act, or feel as one of your parent figures did when you were little. You're in this state when you protect, nurture, scold, criticize, make moral judgments, and give opinions.

2. *Adult.* When you deal with reality, collect facts, appraise objectively, calculate probabilities, and make decisions thoughtfully. The Adult is open to options and makes objective evaluations concerning how to deal with reality.

3. *Child.* When you feel, talk, think, and act as you did when you were a little girl or boy.

> EXAMPLE: Suppose you are watching a football game and your favorite team is losing. Your Adult perceives that the score is 52-10. Your Child is sad and perceives that your team is getting clobbered. Your Parent concludes that the team is playing lousy ball and that the coach should be fired.

Effective communication is not so much a matter of which ego state you are transacting from but whether you have engaged the constructive, or "OK," side of the ego state. This is depicted in Figure 3.4.

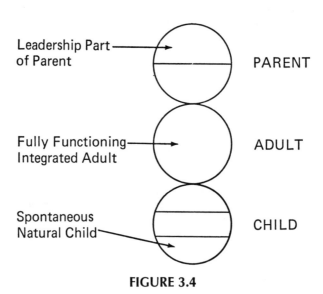

FIGURE 3.4

In the diagram, a vertical line separates positive and negative sides of Parent and Child ego states.

> EXAMPLES: The Not-OK side of the Parent gives negative criticism, "smother" love, rescues people instead of giving them a chance to solve problems for themselves. The OK side of the

Child dreams and hopes, expresses its needs and wants openly, loves, makes friends, and likes to act naturally. The Not-OK Child feels guilty, adapts and obeys mechanically, shows uncontrolled rage, manipulates others by devious means, ducks blame, complains, gripes, and threatens others.

The foundation for OK/Not-OK feelings about yourself and others lies in past experiences. The sum total of positive/negative feelings of yourself and others, derived from these experiences, forms what is called your *life position*. This is the view you hold toward yourself and others.

Life positions are the greatest single influence on human behavior. If you want to predict someone's behavior, knowing the basic life position will help you anticipate how effectively he or she will communicate.

Figure 3.5 shows the "OK Corral" and depicts the four different life positions.

THE OK CORRAL

You're OK

	4	1	
I'm not OK			I'm OK
	3	2	

You're not OK

FIGURE 3.5

1. *Position 1: I'm OK, You're OK.* This means "I'm OK with me, and you're OK with me." In this position, communication is productive.

2. *Position 2: I'm OK, You're not OK.* This is the "Get Rid Of" position in which you see others as threatening and/or inferior, and you want to put them down in some way to make yourself feel superior.

3. *Position 3: I'm not OK, You're not OK.* You are a "dropout" because you have low regard for yourself and others.

4. *Position 4: I'm not OK, You're OK*. This is the dependency relationship, in which you hold others in high esteem and literally draw your energy from that dependency. You feel guilty and often inferior around others.

A *winner* invests his or her energy in positive, get-on-with-it endeavors. *Losers*, on the other hand, are stuck in the past or the future, investing their energy in finding fault, making excuses, worrying about what to do or what people will say, and so on. The loser is quick to declare that something can't be done, even if people are willing to devote their time, energy, and brainpower to the task.

People in the Life Position 1 are winners. Those in Positions 2, 3, and 4 are destined to be losers, or at least nonwinners. You can move into the Life Position 1 by developing positive qualities, including self-expectancy, motivation, and so on. You'll find more on this subject in the next chapter.

HOW TO CONTROL THE COMMUNICATION TRANSACTION

The basic communication transaction is depicted in Figure 3.6. Here you see a model of the communication flow, including the sender and receiver, frame of reference, ego state involvement, and message exchange.

The sender's stimulus triggers the receiver's response, which in turn constitutes the transaction, or exchange. A good transaction is one in which the real issue is dealt with directly and the people involved are in touch with their feelings about what is happening. WHAT TO DO: By expressing your own feelings, you invite others to express theirs. The transactions might not all be complementary, but, nonetheless, the tone is set for productive discussion that focuses on resolving the issue. Then the outcome is predictably successful for all. In other words, everybody wins because you are willing to arrive at a mutually satisfactory solution. HERE'S THE KEY: The value of TA as a system lies in its predictability, and as such is your pathway to success. You will normally get the response you aim for; so you therefore can control your communication by transacting out of your preferred ego state to the intended ego state of the other.

In total, there are nine transactional options available between two people (3 × 3 ego states). The five most common are shown in Figure 3.7. You can increase the combinations by adding OK and

BASIC COMMUNICATION TRANSACTION MESSAGE

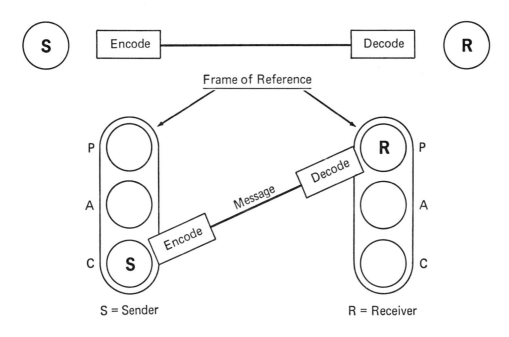

S = Sender   R = Receiver

FIGURE 3.6

Not-OK ego states and then further by advanced structural breakdown of the Parent, Adult, and Child. THE RESULT: You have a *very*
wide range of choices when you transact with others.

An exchange aimed at positive results between ego states is
considered a parallel or complementary transaction and can go on
for an indefinite period of time. However, a transaction is "crossed"
when the receiver responds to the sender from an unexpected ego
state. Then, communication stops, and both parties leave with bad
feelings. The communication process need not end here, however.
WHAT TO DO: Choose to continue the exchange by hooking into the
ego state you actually seek.

EXAMPLE: Ron says to Sally, "What time is it?" Ron asks for a
simple, direct Adult response but instead gets, "Isn't it time you
got yourself a watch?" The communication is crossed because
Ron expected an Adult reply but the Parent spoke instead. Ron
chooses to reply cheerfully, "It sounds like asking for the time is

a heavy thing with you?" Ron is now approaching her Child, and she replies, "I'm sorry, Ron, I was just distracted. It has nothing to do with you." So, her Adult responded to his Adult by way of her Child. Now the transaction is parallel.

THE FIVE MOST COMMON TRANSACTIONS

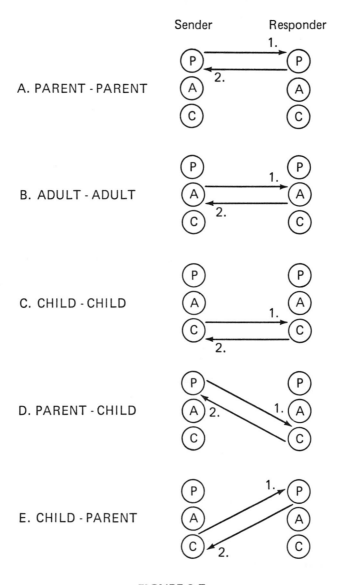

FIGURE 3.7

In order to deal effectively with feelings of others, you must first get in touch with your own. This principle—self-awareness—will apply to other important areas discussed throughout this book. KNOW THYSELF is a prerequisite to knowing others and to communicating effectively with them.

BEHAVIOR PROFILES

Based on observation, research, and data already collected, six basic behavioral profiles can be described:

1. LOW PARENT–HIGH ADULT–HIGH CHILD
   This may be the most productive combination, where the charm of the OK Child adds warmth, intuition, and creativity to the power of the Adult. If Critical Parent behavior is minimal and values are held in the Adult, rationality is emancipated.

2. HIGH PARENT–HIGH ADULT–LOW CHILD
   Able to switch easily between Parent and Adult, this manager is often a high achiever. His rationality is ruled by the demands of his Parent. Education and experience are essential ingredients to his success. Key question: Can he distinguish between his opinion and the facts?

3. LOW-PARENT–HIGH ADULT–LOW CHILD
   Infrequently seen, this individual is object-and fact-oriented. His behavior may be repetitious and boring and his relationships sterile and unfeeling. He has difficulty working with others.

4. HIGH PARENT–LOW ADULT–HIGH CHILD
   Difficult to work with, this person is hard-working, moralistic, judgmental, and authoritarian one moment, and the next moment he wants to be liked, applauded, and taken care of. Working with this person is difficult because of this love-hate behavior.

5. LOW PARENT–LOW ADULT–HIGH CHILD
   A Child-dominant person may be enormously appealing. He prospers in sales and in organizations where personal charm and intuition are useful. Often he is not a good manager since decisions are made in the Child and redistorted by fantasy. For him the key question is: Who are my friends?

6. HIGH PARENT–LOW ADULT–LOW CHILD
   Unfortunately, this profile is frequently seen in industrial or-

> ganizations where "We've always done it this way" thinking prevails. This manager, by treating subordinates as children, fosters dependency. This domineering manager believes that "People don't want responsibility" and that "They only work to earn enough money to buy a new fishing rod." Suitable for the industrial age, this profile is hopelessly outmoded for the day of technology and rapidly evolving problems.

RESOLVING COMMUNICATION PROBLEMS SUCCESSFULLY

Why, then, do communication problems exist? Because the sender's intent conveys the real meaning of the message, whether subtle or overt. If the sender's frame of reference does not complement the receiver's, then the transaction is incomplete, and bad feelings are likely to result. Whenever a person says one thing and actually means something else, you have the ingredients of an ulterior transaction. Such nonverbal ulterior messages are likely to breed resentment and misunderstanding. They are usually part of a larger psychological game that is occurring between the parties involved.

> EXAMPLE: Figure 3.8 shows a relatively simple ulterior transaction involving the game of "Kick Me." The dotted line depicts the ulterior, or below-the-surface, transaction. What's happening is that Smith is asking to be kicked (Life Position 4) and Jones is happy to oblige (Life Position 2). What appears to be a normal business situation is actually a psychological drama.

There are many types and variations of the ulterior transaction. What's important is to recognize and deal with it effectively when it occurs. Here are some useful guidelines:

1. Learn to recognize ulterior motives and covert behavior. Remember that logical thinking is never enough to identify a motive.
2. Learn to get in touch with how you are feeling. Keep yourself operating in the present.
3. Focus on what is going on inside yourself. Notice your physical reactions.
4. Say to yourself, "Right now I feel _____." Be honest with yourself in recognizing your feelings; process it through your Adult and then decide how to deal with it.

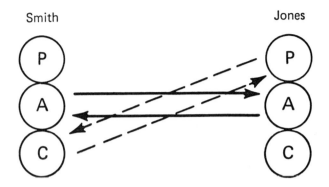

Smith   Jones

Adult-Level Transaction

Smith: Here's the report.
         Sorry it is late.
Jones: It's too late to use
         in my presentation.

Ulterior Parent — Child Transaction

Smith: "Kick me. I'm bad."
Jones: "Okay. Here's your kick."

FIGURE 3.8

Expressing your feelings in a transaction can have a positive effect by inviting the other person to do likewise. This approach not only leads to problem solving but helps relieve stress.

Whenever you diminish any aspect of a situation, and others in it, you are practicing what is called *discounting*. Discounting detracts in some way from the willingness and ability to solve a problem. It usually happens when you ignore any or all of these areas: (1) the stimulus, (2) the problem, or (3) the options. Also, take note not only of *what* is being discounted but the degree to which the stimulus, problems, and options are discounted.

REMEMBER: Discounting of any type detracts from authentic, straightforward communication. It usually creates bad feelings, reduces your effectiveness in some way, and detracts from continued productive communication. Ask yourself, "Which people do you like to deal with?" Most likely, these people do not discount but rather confront problems directly.

WHAT TO DO: Adult functioning is a safeguard against discounting. Try to remain objective and transact through your Adult.

Anytime the Parent or Child ego states overlap, or "slops over," the Adult, biases, prejudices, and distortions are likely to creep in. This situation is called *contamination.* Contaminations are insidious. Why? Usually some grain of truth exists but is used to form generalizations that distort the situation at hand.

> EXAMPLE: "Hiring elderly people is costly." This may be true some of the time, but should this statement govern policy formation? If it does, you have a contamination.

In dealing with contaminations, it is very important to recognize that a fallacy exists in what the person is saying or experiencing. Also, avoid arguing about the validity of the person's actions. WHAT TO DO: Reflect back to the person what he or she is saying.

> EXAMPLE: An employee says, "My boss doesn't like me. He never assigns me challenging work." Your best reply would be, "I hear you saying that you are not getting challenging work because the boss doesn't like you." This points out objectively the fallacy of the other's statement.

PROVEN TECHNIQUES FOR BECOMING A MORE ASSERTIVE MANAGER

Simply stated, assertiveness is the appropriate expression of one's thoughts and feelings. Assertive people:

1. Feel free to say what they feel, think, and want.
2. Can communicate with people at all levels, be they friends, strangers, family, subordinates.
3. Go after what they want—make things happen, rather than waiting for things to happen.
4. Act in ways they respect.

Assertive philosophy says that by standing up for yourself and letting yourself be revealed to other people, you gain self-respect and the respect of others.

Assertiveness seems distasteful to some people because they think that it means being obnoxious and insistent on getting one's own way. Not so! That is aggressiveness, not assertiveness. The truly assertive person always respects the assertive rights of others. In fact, this is a useful test of assertiveness versus aggressiveness.

QUESTIONNAIRE ON ASSERTIVENESS

To what extent do you agree or disagree with each of the ideas below? Do you strongly agree (1), agree (2), neither (3), disagree (4), or strongly disagree (5)?

	SA	A	N	D	SD
I. You should not make independent judgments about yourself and your actions. You must be judged by external rules, procedures, and authority wiser and greater than yourself.	1	2	3	4	5
II. You should explain your reasons for your behavior to other people since you are responsible to them for your actions. You should justify your actions to them.	1	2	3	4	5
III. You have an obligation to things and institutions greater than yourself which other groups of people have set up to conduct the business of living. You should sacrifice your own values to keep these systems from falling apart. If these systems do not always work effectively, *you* should bend or change, *not* the system. If any problems occur in dealing with the system, they are your problems and not the responsibility of the system.	1	2	3	4	5
IV. You should not change your mind after you have committed yourself. If you change your mind, someting is wrong. You should justify your new choice or admit you were in error. If you are in error, you have shown that you are irresponsible, likely to be wrong again, cause problems. Therefore you are not capable of making decisions by yourself.	1	2	3	4	5

QUESTIONNAIRE ON ASSERTIVENESS (continued)

V. You must not make errors. Errors are wrong and cause problems to other people. If you make errors, you should feel guilty. You are likely to make more errors and problems, and therefore you cannot cope properly or make proper decisions. Other people should control your behavior and decisions so that you will not cause problems; in this way, you can make up for the wrong you have done to them.   1   2   3   4   5

VI. You should have answers to any question about the possible consequence of your actions, because if you don't have answers, you are unaware of the problems you will cause other people and therefore you are irresponsible and must be controlled.   1   2   3   4   5

VII. You must have the good will of people you relate to or they can prevent you from doing anything. You need the cooperation of other people to survive. It is very important that other people like you.   1   2   3   4   5

VIII. You must follow logic because it makes better judgments than any of us can make.   1   2   3   4   5

IX. You must anticipate and be sensitive to the needs of other people if you are to live together without discord. You are expected to understand what these needs are without causing problems by making other people spell out their needs to you. If you do not understand without being   1   2   3   4   5

QUESTIONNAIRE ON ASSERTIVENESS (continued)

constantly told what other people want, you are not capable of living in harmony with others and are irresponsible or ignorant.

X. Because of your human condition,   1   2   3   4   5
you are base and have many flaws. You must try to make up for this humanness by striving to improve until you are perfect in all things. Being human, you will probably fail in this obligation, but you must still want to improve. If someone else points out how you can improve yourself, you are obliged to follow his direction. If you do not, you are corrupt, lazy, degenerate, and worthless, and therefore unworthy of respect from anyone, including yourself.

THE ASSERTIVE MANAGER

As an assertive manager, believe in yourself as a human being—responsible for your behavior, taking charge of your destiny, recognizing and expressing your feelings about things.

As an assertive manager, feel free to follow your desires, as long as they do not harm others or violate their rights.

As an assertive manager, be willing to take initiative, knowing that nothing will happen to further your development until you make it happen.

If every manager could be like this, think of what the organization would be like!

Another key distinction between assertive and aggressive people is that assertive people express themselves without violating the rights of others. Aggressive people tend to "rob" others of their ability and their opportunity to decide for themselves.

Nonassertive people allow their interpersonal rights to be violated by someone else. Figure 3.9 shows the distinctions between aggressive and assertive behavior, as well as non assertive behavior. NOTICE: Both non assertive and aggressive behavior differ from assertive behavior on basically the same factors.

The basic techniques of assertiveness can be mastered with a little practice. Here are five techniques for developing assertive behavior:

1. *Broken record.* Say what you want over and over again without getting irritated, angry, or loud.

2. *Fogging.* Agree with the truth in principle, and with the odds. As the term implies, throw a fog over the issue by agreeing with any truth in the statements people use to criticize you. The fog helps to diffuse the criticism. Verbally cope with your errors by saying, "Yes, that's correct—I goofed." By admitting it, you blunt the criticism.

3. *Self-disclosure.* Say what you think, feel, and how you react to the other person's information.

4. *Free information.* Recognize cues that show what is of interest or importance to other people.

5. *Workable compromise.* Look for a way out of a conflict and try to produce positive results for both parties. EXAMPLE: You disagree with another person on what a particular standard should be. Instead of arguing, try to arrive instead at a solution that meets the desires of both parties. CAUTION: Workable compromise does not mean compromising your ideals, principles, and feelings of self-worth.

A CASE-IN-POINT: This conversation demonstrates the various skills involved in assertiveness:

John: *Jim, I need to talk with you.*

Jim: *Sure, John, what's up?*

John: *I don't know about the other people in the depart-
            ment, but I'm just about snowed under. I cannot take
            the ten percent increase in workload that the budget
            calls for. I think that is just plain unfair to ask the
            department to take on the additional burden.*

Jim: *You're probably right, John. It is a very heavy load for
            the department. But, nevertheless, I still have to in-
            crease the workload.* (Fogging and Broken Record)

A COMPARISON OF NONASSERTIVE, AGGRESSIVE, AND ASSERTIVE BEHAVIOR

	Nonassertive Behavior	Aggressive Behavior	Assertive Behavior
Characteristics of the behavior:	Emotionally dishonest, indirect, self-denying, inhibited Allows others to choose for him	(Inappropriately) emotionally honest, direct, self-enhancing at expense of another, expressive Chooses for others	(Appropriately) emotionally honest, direct, self-enhancing, expressive Chooses for self
Goal of behavior	Doesn't achieve desired goal	Achieves desired goal by hurting others	May achieve desired goal
Your feelings when you engage in this behavior:	Hurt, anxious at the time, and possibly angry later	Righteous, superior, depreciatory at the time, and possibly guilty later	Confident, Self-respecting at the time and later
The other person's feelings about herself when you engage in this behavior:	Guilty or superior	Hurt, humiliated, defensive	Valued, respected
The other person's feelings about you when you engage in this behavior	Irritated, feels pity, disgust	Angry, vengeful	Generally respectful

FIGURE 3.9

A COMPARISON OF NONASSERTIVE, AGGRESSIVE, AND ASSERTIVE BEHAVIOR (continued)

ASSERTIVE behavior is that type of interpersonal behavior in which an individual stands up for his or her interpersonal rights in such a way that the rights of the other person are not violated. It is a direct, honest, and appropriate expression of one's thoughts, feelings, and opinions. It communicates respect for the other person as well as for oneself.

AGGRESSIVE behavior is that type of interpersonal behavior in which an individual stands up for his or her interpersonal rights in such a way that the rights of the other person are violated. The purpose of aggressive behavior is to dominate, humiliate, or put the other person down. It is frequently a hostile overreaction to a situation. It communicates a lack of respect for the other person.

NONASSERTIVE behavior is that type of interpersonal behavior that enables the person's interpersonal rights to be violated by someone else. It is often characterized by overapologizing and self-effacement. It often involves sending double messages.

FIGURE 3.9 (continued)

John: *That really puts us in a bind. Didn't you tell them that it wouldn't work in our department?*

Jim: *John, right now I am faced with a problem of having to follow the new directives if I want to remain in this job. (Free information) I intend to follow the instructions to increase production.* (Broken Record)

John: *OK, if that's the way you want it. I think you are going to have trouble on your hands.*

Jim: *I don't understand, John. Why is it that you think I will have trouble on my hands?* (Negative Inquiry)

John: *Because people can only take so much. And even though we enjoy working in this department, we also feel that there is a point when the company starts taking advantage of us, and we are not going to take it any longer.*

Jim: *I can certainly see how you would think that the company might be taking advantage of you. However, it is a decision made by the company, and I intend to follow it, and I want the workload to increase.* (Fogging and Broken Record)

John: *Well, OK. I don't know if I will be able to do it, but I'll try. Mind you, I can't guarantee anything.*

Jim: *I understand how it might be difficult for you, and I will be happy to assist you in any way that I can.* (Self-disclosure)

John: *Well, perhaps if I set aside the Adams's account, which can be postponed for a couple of weeks anyway, I could speed up on the other, more urgent, projects.* (Workable compromise)

Jim: *It sounds like a good idea to me, John. If there is a way that I can help you to work it out, let me know.*

Another aspect of assertiveness comes from the TA notion of "OKness." In order to be assertive, you must feel OK about yourself. According to modern psychological theory, behavior change can change attitudes as readily as changing attitudes can influence behavior. By exercising assertiveness skills, you can "get on with it" first and analyze later.

ANOTHER POINT: In order to be truly assertive, your Adult must be in control.

EXAMPLE: Two employees might sit around griping about how bad things are in the company. They may exchange a lot of feelings, but they do so out of the Parent or Child ego state. If, on the other hand, they discuss what to do about their problems, then their Adult takes over, and assertive behavior begins.

TEN BASICS OF ASSERTIVENESS

1. You have a right to your feelings. Feelings need no rational justification. Feelings don't have to be reasonable, rational, and capable of depending. You have the right to feel confused, ambivalent, and inconsistent as long as you blame no one else for your confusion, ambivalence, or inconsistency.

2. You must give yourself permission to feel things, even if they are negative or seemingly inappropriate.

3. You must take responsibility for your feelings. Instead of saying, "You make me feel," say, "I feel _____." Do not explain feelings away. There need not be any excuses given for feelings. They simply exist. .

4. It is important to make an attempt to get in touch with and explore feelings rather than avoid, deny, or suppress them.

5. It is important to be willing to express feelings spontaneously, without censoring or monitoring them.

6. Feelings must be expressed for the purpose of expressing and not for impressing, attacking, or attempting to change the other person.

7. You have a right to your beliefs and values. You have a right to hold beliefs and choose values that are meaningful, relevant, and workable for you, regardless of how unpopular they may be.

8. You have a right to a belief and to express your beliefs and values as long as you don't take away, trample, or deny others their rights to beliefs and values.

9. Conflict and confrontation relationships can be productive if dealt with properly; that is, directly and honestly.

10. There is a certain risk in being assertive. You must be willing to risk rejection for experiencing unpopular or negative feelings or feelings that are unacceptable to others. This risk decreases, of course, when you honestly own the feelings and make it known to others that the feelings are not blamed on them.

GETTING THE MESSAGE THROUGH ACTIVE LISTENING

Based partly on the works of Dr. Thomas Gordon, active listening is an approach that emphasizes listening *with* rather than listening *to* another person.[4] A listener participates in the situation and mirrors what the other person is saying in order to move toward solving the problem.

The foremost skill that a manager needs in communicating with employees is to recognize and deal with the messages that go on inside of people. The key to doing that is active listening, out of the Adult ego state. Remember that the Adult ego state is the only one that perceives reality clearly, with a minimum of filtering and bias.

The importance of the internal state cannot be overly emphasized. People behave on the basis of their feelings, and active listening attempts to understand and accept these feelings as legitimate reasons for behavior. Research shows that when people see that others truly understand how they feel and accept their feelings, they become less defensive. They gain insight that enables them to solve problems they previously either avoided or ignored.

The key is knowing and understanding your employee's frame of reference. Developing empathy is like any other skill—it requires practice. WHAT TO DO: Start with those who know and understand you, such as your spouse or your children. Then approach a problem by trying to see the situation through the other's viewpoint.

Empathy is not achieved without stopping long enough to learn about the other person. It takes time, effort, and energy. But unless you do so, you simply will not be able to appreciate another person.

---

[4] See Dr. Thomas Gordon, *Parent Effectiveness Training* (New York: *Psychology Today*, 1977), and Gordon, *Leadership Effectiveness Training* (New York: Wyden Books 1977).

WHO OWNS THE PROBLEM?

Two basic techniques involved in active listening are *reflective feedback* and *"I" messages*. The decision as to which method is most appropriate depends on who owns the problem.

If it is clear that the employee owns the problem, then it is equally clear that this person owns the solution. "You" messages are nonassertive and result in criticizing or passing judgment on another person or what they are saying. Some examples:

- You must stop doing this . . . (ordering and directing)
- You should try this . . . (moralizing and preaching)
- It would be best if . . . (advising and giving suggestions)
- Let me give you the facts . . . (persuading with logic)
- You'll feel differently tomorrow . . . (reassuring)
- You are acting foolishly . . . (judging and criticizing)

Active listening can be a powerful tool when you remain objective and nonjudgmental. WHAT TO DO: Keep yourself out of the problem and encourage the other person to solve the problem by reflecting back on what he or she is saying.

When you own the problem, you also need to find a solution. "I" messages state what you want in the situation and express personal responsibility for the feelings and problem interpretation that you have.

> EXAMPLE: Your employee has been absent five times in the past month. Of course, you could simply fine the person a day's pay. Instead, you decide to use an "I" message, "When you are absent, it causes me problems because I have to get a replacement, which usually results in not getting work done somewhere else. I feel strongly that our effectiveness is reduced by your absence, and I am very concerned about this behavior—to the point that I believe we must do something about it." You can safely predict that the employee will give more thought to his absences after this kind of assertion.

WHERE FEELINGS COME FROM

People experience at least three levels of awareness. (See Figure 3.10.)

1. *Subconscious.* Primarily nonverbal communication or feelings.
2. *Conscious.* Awareness of current reality.
3. *Superconscious.* Theologically referred to as the "soul."

LEVELS OF AWARENESS

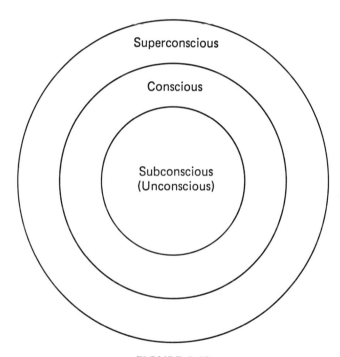

Superconscious

Conscious

Subconscious
(Unconscious)

FIGURE 3.10

People are influenced by their subconscious and the messages
that are in it. Eric Berne used the term "preconscious" because he
believed that these feelings and memories could be recalled given
the appropriate stimulus.

EXAMPLE: A great deal of activity occurs while sleeping, a
subconscious state. Whether you realize it or not, most people
have several dreams during the sleep period. By training your-

self to remember dreams, you can use them to help solve problems during waking hours.

The purpose of the subconscious level of thinking and activity is to express needs and to solve problems of a very basic nature. If you are in touch with this level and bring the subconscious to a level of conscious awareness, you can find a gold mine of information.

At the conscious level of awareness, you analyze data and information, examine goals, and observe the consequences of your behavior. In TA, this equates to the Adult level of functioning, although the Parent and Child are present in the conscious as well.

Philosophical thoughts often come from the superconscious. You can invite your employees to think such thoughts by expressing your own higher level needs and ideals. What are the practical results of higher level, superconscious communication? For one, this is an effective way to appeal to quality consciousness. Second, it is a nonmanipulative approach to getting people to cooperate through sharing of higher goals.

There is really no way to hide feelings. If they are not verbalized, they will be expressed in a person's behavior. For example, people "act out" anger every day by passive resistance, hostile attitudes and stares, rigid body posture, or vengeful activities. This "acting out" costs organizations enormous sums of money in poor products and service, labor problems, and, even more importantly, the human energy invested in destructive rather than constructive activities.

One of the most obvious forms of nonverbal communication has been popularized as body language. Here, expressions and gestures of the body communicate information and feelings.

> EXAMPLE: A stiff, erect posture indicates not only that the person is in the Parent ego state, but it also says the person is probably going to be critical when communicating with you.

The most effective way to deal with body language is to reflect back to the person what you observe. Say, "I see you scratching your ear." This objective observation invites the person to say more about what is going on. IMPORTANT: There are occasions when a person may be wanting to say something but doesn't for one reason or another. Body language and other nonverbal cues can be vitally important in establishing a communication situation. Figure 3.11 is a guide to picking up verbal and nonverbal clues.

VERBAL AND NONVERBAL CLUES TO PERSONALITY STATES

	Parent State		Adult State	Child State (full of feeling)	
	Nurturing	*Critical*		*OK Child*	*Not OK Child*
Voice Tones	Caring, loving, helpful	Accusing, impatient, disgusted,	Matter-of-fact, bright, pleasant, interested, enthusiastic, businesslike	Positive feelings— excited, gleeful, teasing	Negative feelings— whining, hurt, nervous
Words Used	You should, everyone knows that, always, never, I can't understand why, sonny, honey, dear		How, what, when, where, why, who, in my opinion, probable, I suggest, do you think	I wish, I want, it's my fault again, why me, wow, whee, hey great, do I have to	
Postures	Puffed-up, super-correct, very proper		Attentive, direct eye contact, listening and looking for maximum data	Slouching, playful, beat-down or burdened, self-conscious	
Facial Expressions	Frowns, worried or disapproving looks, chin jutted out, benign smile		Alert eyes, pays close attention, sincere smile	Pouting, downcast eyes, quivering lip or chin, moist eyes, excitement, surprise	
Body Gestures	Hands on hips, pointing finger, arms folded on chest, foot or finger tapping		Leaning forward in chair toward other person, moving closer to see and hear better	Wringing hand, pacing, withdrawing, squirming, nail biting, clapping hands, raising hand for permission	

FIGURE 3.11

You need to understand the real message that the other person is sending. Nonverbal communication does not lie. If you are unsure whether a verbal message is authentic, check the body clues. Then seek clarification.

WHAT TO DO: You might ask the person, "Am I hearing you correctly?" and then go on to repeat what the person is saying. Give the person ample opportunity to disclose his or her full meaning and feelings. Discretion is the best policy, and a degree of trust must be developed before openness can be achieved.

HOW YOU CAN IMPROVE YOUR WRITING SKILLS FOR BETTER MANAGEMENT

A cemetery monument producer wrote a customer to thank him for an order. In the letter, he used the old familiar close, "We hope to serve you again in the future—and often." This blunder, like many others when the writer uses stock terminology: "Pursuant to this request" or "I am in receipt of . . ." happens more often than you think. While these phrases may be harmless, they are totally uninteresting and lacking in crisp language that gets the reader's attention.

Written communication involves a set of principles similar to oral communication. The fundamental principle is clarity—of purpose, intent, and the basic message. Here are six principles for effective letter writing:

1. *The objective.* Define clearly the purpose of the letter or memo.

2. *The subject or theme.* Mention the theme directly, without ambiguity.

3. *Logical sequencing.* Put your thoughts in logical order. Give the reader an idea of where you are going.

4. *Conciseness.* Use one word in place of ten if it expresses what you want to say.

5. *Brevity.* Cut out whatever is unnecessary. Respect your reader's time and intelligence.

6. *Tone.* This conveys your attitude and establishes your relationship with the reader. Keep the tone straightforward and adult.

Figure 3.12 shows an example of a good letter. Notice how each principle is followed.

Memos are used for announcements, for clarification of particular points, or for the record. Whenever oral communication will not suffice, use a memo.

Figure 3.13 demonstrates proper use of a memo. It clarifies a point made in the policy-and-procedures manual and heads off questions and probable work interruptions.

When should you use a letter rather than a memo? Memos are basically for in-house use and are typically more informal. Use a letter when:

1. Official business is being conducted with an outside client or individual.

2. It conveys official business inside the organization that is of an especially permanent nature, such as a letter of recommendation.

3. The emphasis is on the official position of the writer, such as an open letter by a manager taking a position that is somewhat formal in nature.

Like letters, memos need not be stuffy. Use the same principles when you write memos as when you write letters.

THE THREE CRITICAL "P'S" FOR EFFECTIVE REPORT WRITING

Some memos essentially become reports, which are lengthy documents written for the purpose of supplying information. The major purposes of reports are (1) for the record, (2) for planning purposes, (3) to focus interest, (4) to solve problems, or (5) to inform. Problem-solving reports are among the most useful and normally require analysis and precision in arriving at recommendations and solutions.

Good report writing includes three "P's":

1. *Purpose.* States the writer's objective and gives the reader a notion of what to expect in the report. EXAMPLE: "The purposes of this report are to identify the sequencing problem in assembly #3, to determine its causes, to present alternatives, and to recommend a solution."

BIGFOOT MANUFACTURING COMPANY
Peoria, Illinois 69867

October 1, 1988

Mr. Jake Bartonis
Industrial Products Division
AP Corporation
Biloxi, Miss. 43789

Dear Mr. Bartonis:

The purpose of this letter is to reply to your September 12 letter and to help resolve your problems with the F-13 press. The letter will concentrate on our sales engineers' response to the problems you cited in your letter and will suggest possible follow-up actions, which we might discuss further by correspondence or on the phone.

In the two weeks following your letter, our sales engineers have looked into the problems you mentioned. They carefully examined the tolerances that are causing you the greatest problem. As a result of the testing, the tolerances were found to be the same as with the earlier model. Frankly, I am a bit puzzled over the contrast between our sales engineers' results and the operational results that you reported. There are a number of possibilities that would help explain the difference, but I am aware at this time that your main concern is to make the machine operational. With that in mind, I would like to have more information about the conditions under which the press malfunctions. This will help in our own testing as well as in determining what follow-up service we might perform.

I will call you within a week, assuming a week is enough time for you to gather the additional information. If our staff is unable to come up with an answer based on the additional information, I am ready to send the appropriate service personnel to assist you firsthand.

I look forward to hearing from you and to assisting you in any way I can to resolve this problem.

Sincerely,

Russell Dodge
Bigfoot Manufacturing Co.

RD/lh

FIGURE 3.12

2. *Plan.* Data gathering, analysis, and presentation. The most appropriate data sources will be determined by the situation, but be prepared to search in various places for needed information. Your analysis should be concise and precise. Analysis normally includes not only interpretation but also comparison and evaluation. The outcome of a good analysis should be an understanding of the problem, its causes, how it relates to other problems, how significant it is, and what remedies can be developed.

3. *Projection.* The plan leads to statements of the alternatives and recommendations. If the data collection is done thoroughly, the alternatives should flow logically out of the analysis. Options should be stated as precisely as possible, showing probable outcomes of each. In a good report, the recommendation will flow logically from the alternatives. IMPORTANT: A recommendation needs to be feasible more than it needs to be perfect. Be sure to allow for anticipated problems as you make your decisions.

TO: All Nonexempt Personnel

FROM: Jake Townsend, Personnel Manager

SUBJECT: Overtime pay for working on holidays

This is to remind you of the policy on overtime pay for holidays and to clarify the hours covered by the policy.

According to the contract, the overtime pay is two and one half times the regular hourly pay for all nonexempt employees. The period of time over which this policy applies is from 6:00 P.M. on the evening preceding the holiday until 6:00 A.M. on the day after the holiday. All hours worked within that time period will be compensated at two and one half times.

If there are any further questions about the policy, ask either your manager or myself. We will be glad to help resolve any questions that remain.

FIGURE 3.13

A proper report format will vary according to the organization and situation. Here is one useful format:

1. *Title page.* The subject of the report, for whom it was prepared, and by whom.
2. *Transmittal or introductory message.* A foreword or preface, including acknowledgments.
3. *Contents.* A table of contents, indicating headings and topics.
4. *Report body.* The three P's, obviously the most important section.
5. *Supplementary information.* An appendix, bibliography, index, glossary, or whatever else may be needed.

NOTE: If you have specific questions about style and format, refer to *A Manual of Style,* published by the University of Chicago Press.

Written or oral—what's best? Common sense suggests that the best medium depends on the purpose of the communication. You should choose the medium keeping in mind your record-keeping needs, the geographical distance involved, information needs, interaction needs, the avoidance of misinterpretation, and the time factor. RULE OF THUMB: Decide your most pressing need and then choose the medium that best fulfills it.

HOW TO FURTHER DEVELOP YOUR READING SKILLS TO SAVE VALUABLE MANAGEMENT TIME

What you read and understand is more important than how fast or how much. To develop reading efficiency, follow these guidelines:

1. Determine your priorities.
2. Screen your materials; that is, look through and select that which is most important.
3. Look for the main points in correspondence and other reading materials.
4. Skim by using headings and subheadings as cues and reading recommendations and conclusions.

Rapid reading is a technique that enables you to accomplish more reading in less time. IMPORTANT: What you're really learning is rapid understanding.

Comprehension is directly related to reading speed. By reading more rapidly, you place more emphasis on ideas and not the individual words that make up the sentence. So if you read an entire article fairly rapidly, make marks or checks in the margin, and go back over the confusing or difficult material, you will gain a higher level of comprehension in less time.

Here are the basic techniques for rapid reading:

1. *Skim.* You can skim 80 to 90 percent of most materials and still understand the message.

2. *Look for cues.* Paragraph headings and first and last sentences can give you a picture of the main ideas.

3. *Read groups of words.* Do not focus on a single word at a time but look at wider portions of sentences. Also, focus on the most important words.

WHAT TO DO: First, place your hand in such a way that the middle fingers are slightly spread and tips are just below the line you want to begin on. Then, move the fingers across the page at a steady rate, slightly faster than is comfortable, keeping the eyes moving with the fingers. At the end of the line, drop the fingers down to the next line and continue moving left to right. Do not stop to look at a word again but keep moving. Always go faster than is comfortable. Do not worry about losing the meaning; your mind operates a great deal faster than your eyes and fingers can.

Technical reports require another reading skill—*analytical reading*. Here, you are reading *with* the author, thinking, asking questions, and sometimes even challenging. Analytical reading requires active thinking to help you concentrate and understand. WHAT TO DO: You actually create a dialogue with the author by not only digesting the material but examining its significance.

REMEMBER THIS: Reading skills are forms of listening; that is, message receiving from others. How well you listen to oral messages relates directly to how receptive you will be to the written messages.

WHAT MEETINGS CAN ACCOMPLISH FOR YOU

Several interactions take place in meetings that would not normally take place in ordinary conversation or in a two-person gathering. Group dynamics forces people to take on various roles;

specifically, (1) *task roles,* where people attempt to accomplish the purpose of the meeting, and (2) *maintenance roles,* where people are concerned with social or nonobjective behaviors. The following summarizes specific roles within these categories:

Task Roles

1. *Initiating.* Setting the agenda and presenting the purpose of the meeting along with agenda items.
2. *Information giving.* Providing data or information that has a bearing on the situation.
3. *Information seeking.* Obtaining needed data or information.
4. *Clarifying or elaborating.* Explaining any matters that might not be clear to the group.
5. *Consensus taking.* Determining where the group stands on an issue.
6. *Summarizing.* Providing a perspective on where the group is at this point.

Maintenance Roles

1. *Encouraging.* Giving recognition to members of the group.
2. *Gatekeeping.* Making certain that everyone is heard.
3. *Expressing group feelings.* Expressing the underlying tone and mood of the members.
4. *Harmonizing.* Reconciling different viewpoints and verbalizing conflicts.
5. *Compromising.* Establishing a working agreement that everyone can live with.
6. *Standard setting.* Keeping the process consistent with accepted procedures.

In an effective group, roles are widely distributed throughout the members. Additionally, an efficient group has:[5]

1. A balanced distribution of tasks and social roles.
2. A clear set of objectives, understood by group members.

---

[5] Lippitt and Seashore, *The Leader Looks at Group Effectiveness* (Washington, DC: Leadership Resources, Inc., 1965).

3. A respect for minority views.

4. Flexibility in its procedures.

5. Willingness and capability to examine its own behavior and change it when necessary.

6. Achievable goals.

7. Cohesiveness.

8. Shared leadership among participants, in addition to the formal leader.

9. Appropriate size—most effective committees consist of five to seven members (outside range, three to nine).

Committees present useful forms of communication when the purpose includes coordination, getting a full spectrum of viewpoints, providing recommendations, or generating ideas. IMPORTANT: Be sure to convey clearly the purpose of your committee and see that it follows its mission.

ELEVEN RULES FOR GETTING RESULTS FROM COMMITTEES

- Stick to the agenda.
- Keep the agenda trim.
- Use the meeting for the intended purpose.
- Set your priorities.
- Set and follow time limits.
- Observe the principles of group interaction.
- Observe the limits of the committee's authority and responsibility.
- Distribute the agenda in advance.
- Use the appropriate physical arrangement.
- Rehearse and plan the meeting.
- Maintain Adult control.

The chairman is a first among equals. His or her primary function is to guide the group in achieving its objectives. In addition, the chairman:

1. Sets the agenda and distributes it.
2. Selects agenda items.
3. Notifies members.
4. Prepares follow-up and minutes.
5. Maintains the process established for the group.
6. Takes any votes or other official duties.
7. Maintains the committee functions as intended.

Whether you are a participant or a chairman, there are invariably follow-up responsibilities. These include carrying out the decisions and recommendations made at the meeting. HINT: Sit down after a meeting and go over your notes. By doing so, you can identify any particular follow-up action.

Regardless of your own position, the group's position must be implemented. You should remember to pass on information to the employees. SUGGESTION: It's best to give the facts in an Adult approach, then emphasize your plan and your desires for the future.

Actually, meeting roles and day-to-day management have much in common. Both require teamwork, and both involve conflict resolution. For example, your day-to-day experiences in scheduling, giving instructions, and meeting deadlines can help substantially in chairing meetings and participating in them. WHAT TO DO: Integrate in your own mind the two different roles and learn how each will apply to the other.

HOW TO GIVE EFFECTIVE PRESENTATIONS THAT GET RESULTS

Presentations can be persuasive or informational. With the former, you attempt to influence the listener, whereas the latter mostly provides information. CAUTION: With a persuasional presentation, it's best to say so at the outset.

A presentation should always begin with a plan.

Step One: Determine the objective. Ask yourself:

1. What do you want to get across?
2. What do people want to hear, and how do they want to hear it?
3. What do they want to go away with?

Step Two: Outline your presentation. Include any salient points that you want to make to achieve your objective. HINT: Keep in mind your overall time constraints. Sequence the points in terms of where you want to begin, proceed, and end up. The sequence should follow logically.

> EXAMPLE: You are giving a presentation on your department's progress under a new information system. You might begin by reviewing the old system. Then, you would identify particular milestones and problems along the way. You finish up by showing end-of-the-month reports on the progress of the new system.

The presentation normally opens with a comment that establishes rapport. Your tone of voice should be discussion oriented. It should be engaging, invite people to listen and to think, and light enough to get people to feel at ease. Use humor that is in good taste and appropriate to the situation at hand.

Stroke the audience whenever appropriate by recognizing something about them—their situation/geography, needs, and so on. Maintain their interest by varying the presentation, either with audio-visual aids, vocal inflections, or cadence.

> EXAMPLE: You might precede each point with an example. Or you might take several points and then show examples of each in sequence. Each way should help your listener understand the import of what you're trying to convey. REMEMBER: Make the points crisply, and then move on.

THE RULE OF THREE

"Good things come in three's." You can make as many points as you want, but make at least three. A speech with only two points seems unfinished in the minds of the audience.

As you conclude your presentation, keep in mind these three basic factors:

1. The conclusions should summarize the points made thus far.

2. Your own conclusions should be stated.

3. Sign off with a philosophical message or quotation that reflects the issues at hand.

HOW TO USE AUDIO-VISUAL AIDS FOR
BETTER COMMUNICATION

The use of media can help you emphasize the main point that you want to make. Basically, the media choice depends on availability, type of methods involved, the information you want to get across, the extent of audience participation, the need for audience contact during the presentation, and the overall impact desired. Here are some of the normal choices of visual and audio aids:

1. *Chalkboard.* Very useful for outlining your presentation. Use it when there are particular points that you want to hold in the forefront to capture in the minds of the audience.

2. *Film or Videotape.* Especially useful for illustrating up to three or four points. There are better for dramatization than for verbal information.

3. *The Overhead Projector.* Useful for technical presentations when you need to present voluminous information in a short period of time. CAUTION: Unless accompanied by discussion, the overhead projector can be perceived as tedious when the viewer is expected to take detailed notes.

4. *Slides.* Best used for pictorial purposes. Like films and videotape, three or four points are most appropriate when using slides.

5. *Slide-Tapes.* Add the audio dimension keyed to the visual. It can be very effective when you want the audience to examine another perspective or dimension and focus on that for a short time. If brief and to the point, slide-tapes can get a few points across very well.

THE GRAPEVINE AND OTHER LINES OF COMMUNICATION

Recent research has shown that regardless of the formal communications system, the most significant communications occur in many forms—formal and informal.[6] Communications follow the patterns and the flow of work. This is rarely shown on an organizational chart, neither is the flow of significant communications very obvious.

---

6 See P. Blau and W.R. Scott, *Formal Organization* (San Francisco, CA: Chandler Publishing Company, 1962).

As a manager, you're probably aware that the responsibilities you are expected to perform are not always clear, either in the way they are explained or because of a different perception. So, you turn to other ways by asking colleagues, staff people, friends, and even your subordinates.

Communication ropes are often tied to the grapevine. Since it knows no organizational boundaries, the grapevine is authentic. A WORD TO THE WISE: No manager has ever succeeded in destroying the grapevine. So, better join than fight.

Most communications can be visualized according to networks. There are basically five types, depicted in Figure 3.14 and as follows:

1. *Circle.* Highly satisfactory to participants but under some conditions lacks effectiveness in transmitting the message; used to provide discussion and clarification.
2. *Chain.* Transmits the message efficiently but does not yield much satisfaction for participants.
3. *Wheel.* Probably most effective for straightforward messages.
4. *"Y."* Like the wheel, except it originates from another party who in turn relays the message in a wheel fashion.
5. *Roundtable.* Not effective in straightforward messages; used mostly for a meeting network.

HOW TO COMMUNICATE WITHIN YOUR ORGANIZATION

Three major factors influence communications within the organization: (1) the atmosphere or climate, (2) structural factors, and (3) the organization's traditions.

Trust is the prime factor influencing organizational climate. In the final analysis, willingness to communicate is directly proportional to trust, which, in turn, relates to how information will be used. An organization committed to employee growth and development will encourage rather than discourage openness and sharing of ideas and opinions.

As with the "ropes," certain organizational traditions prevail that are not necessarily formal. If you look around, you'll find many such traditions. WARNING: You take a risk in breaking with traditions. Ask yourself, "What are the predominant influences at this

COMMUNICATION NETWORKS

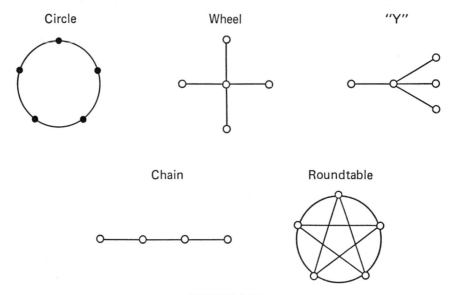

FIGURE 3.14

time? What can I do in the present system? If I need to change the system, how should I go about it without violating traditions?" The main issue, of course, is how you can accomplish your job, communicate what needs to be communicated, and get the information you need to perform the job.

As a manager, you are looked upon as a spokesperson for the organization. In social situations, your best bet is discretion. Avoid talking about employees and any other people on a personal basis. However, when you are at liberty to talk, do so candidly. You build trust when matters are addressed so that misunderstandings are avoided.

Remember this equation:

Knowledge = Power = Responsibility.

If you observe the rules surrounding each element, you'll enhance the image of the first-line manager.

CHAPTER 4

How to
Deal Effectively with
Others in the Workplace

*In order that people may be happy in their work,
these three things are needed: they must be fit for it;
they must not do too much of it; and they must
have a sense of success in it.*

—JOHN RUSKIN

IF there is any one bottom line for this chapter, it's *success*—acting, thinking, feeling, and being a successful person and manager in your relationships with others. Based on ideas set forth in Chapter 3, you are now ready to deal with communication barriers that must be overcome, as well as the concepts and techniques that promote sound relationships. Also, you'll come to understand and accept conflict as an everyday occurrence and a fact of life that must be and can be handled productively in order to become successful.

This chapter is designed to help you become aware of your own behavior and vulnerability, more conscious of the effects of your actions in others, and able to make better predictions about the consequences. You'll learn to confront yourself and others, to eliminate and overcome ineffective behavior patterns, and to develop a positive attitude toward yourself and your ability to solve problems. These are the building blocks of success. And they're yours for the taking.

CRITICAL THINGS YOU NEED TO KNOW ABOUT
YOUR SUBORDINATES

People relate with others in order to satisfy their basic needs. Within the modern organization, people need: (1) the approval and acceptance of others, (2) enhancement of their own self-esteem based upon how others see them, and (3) actualization of their own expectations of themselves.

Although people have these basic needs in common, they express them differently and are motivated to seek them in various degrees. On the job, a worker's motivation is affected by (1) the degree to which a job satisfies his or her needs, (2) the level of expectations he or she has toward a successful performance, and (3) his or her perception of fairness. The extent to which needs are met and fulfilled depends on their level of interaction with other people.

From Chapter 3, recall the definition of transactional exchange as the basic unit of communication. In a transaction, three things are exchanged: feelings, thoughts, and information. In the basic manager-subordinate transaction, you are responsible for giving instructions and your subordinates, for carrying them out.

The transactional exchange signals responsibilities as well as who controls what. Until these responsibilities are agreed upon by *both* parties, the relationship will not be compatible. Remember this principle: *Everyone* is motivated; maybe not to do what you want them to do, but they *are* motivated to do something. It's your job to unlock that motivation and direct it toward your organization's objectives.

WHAT TO DO: When you initiate a transactional exchange, try to predict how your subordinate will behave. By doing so, you can determine the right approach to use as well as the likely success of your efforts.

Three common misunderstandings about employees:

1. There is a tendency to judge the capabilities of a subordinate by the job he or she is performing. But the job may not be an accurate index. It's easy to underestimate people, and in so doing, treat them with less regard than those with higher levels of skill and training.

2. People who appear apathetic are often assumed to feel likewise about their job. To the contrary, apathy is actually a disguised form of aggression. The person usually cares a great deal.

3. It's wrong to assume that the needs of employees follow some preconceived stereotypes. Given the opportunity, employees are nearly as interested in higher level needs as are managers.

Figure 4.1 depicts three possible ways employee and organizational goals can relate. They can be mildly different, very close, or nearly opposite. WHAT TO DO: Your job is to keep them as close together as possible. To do that, you must assume your employees are

1. Motivated.
2. Sharing the same needs as others.
3. Capable of being influenced by you.
4. Willing, given the choice, to select the course of action they believe is right for them.

EMPLOYEE AND ORGANIZATIONAL GOALS

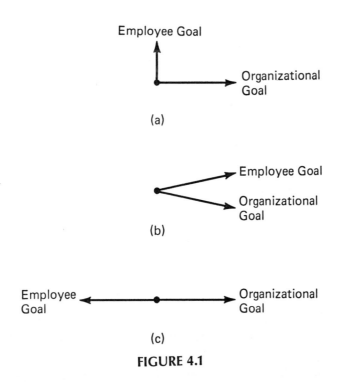

FIGURE 4.1

Whenever one person relies on another for his or her thinking or direction, this type of dependency is called *symbiosis*. Many employees are symbiotically dependent on their bosses.

Two kinds of symbiosis can be found in the workplace:

1. When an employee sees himself or herself as a Child and depends entirely on others to take responsibility for his or her situation.

2. When each one tries to get the other to assume the Child position. This is competitive symbiosis and can lead to a nonproductive relationship until someone "gives in."

A healthy relationship occurs when each perceives his or her role as interdependent. That is, both parties get something by cooperating with the other. BE PATIENT: Interdependency may take some time to achieve, especially when old patterns are being broken. It's a good idea to prepare yourself for a lengthy episode.

WHAT TO DO: To find out if you are in a symbiosis with your subordinate, determine if you can deal from all three ego states (Adult, Parent, Child). To break the symbiosis, begin dealing from a different state. Try again, until you can deal from all three. Adult functioning is the quickest way to break a symbiosis. Why? Because the Adult thinks and uses all three states.

Every relationship implies contractual responsibilities. The *50–50 Rule* says that whenever you make about 50 percent of the effort and carry out about 50 percent of the responsibility, the relationship will have a reasonably good chance of being balanced and productive. Try to keep your relationships within this parameter.

SIX WAYS PEOPLE SPEND THEIR TIME AND ENERGY

Whenever people get together in an ongoing relationship, they structure their activities in relation to its level of intensity. Here are six such levels:

1. *Withdrawal.* When there is no authentic communication.

2. *Rituals.* Greetings, partings, meetings, and so on. Some "stroking" takes place by the participating persons.

3. *Activities.* Work, party games, athletic contests, and so on. Here, the risks, strokes, and closeness occur on a higher level than rituals.

4. *Pastimes.* Areas of mutual interest; usually more intense than activities.

5. *Games.* Ongoing series of transactions having ulterior motives and predictable outcomes. Here, closeness and energy investment are at a high level.

6. *Intimacy.* The highest form of communication. It's what happens when you're not doing any of the other five.

As a manager, you will be involved in any number of structures requiring different approaches to relating to people. Remember this basic observation: If feelings are not expressed verbally, they will be expressed in action. Your goal is to encourage openness in communication. WHAT TO DO: If you want your employees to express their feelings and give you information freely, the best place to start is by expressing your own and sharing them with your employees.

HOW FEELINGS GOVERN A RELATIONSHIP AND AFFECT MANAGEMENT

Remember that feelings govern attitudes, and they, in turn, determine a person's willingness to cooperate and produce. Referring to transactional terminology, the less "OK" you feel about yourself, the more trouble you will have in relationships. Friction and trouble begin when you deal with people from a position of low esteem. Here are three points to keep in mind:

1. At any given time, the most important aspect is OKness, regardless of the ego state from which you operate.

2. When you operate out of the Not-OK side, you are apt to be playing games. Since games detract from work and goal attainment, they are inherently nonproductive.

3. Regardless of your ego state, the OK side of your personality produces a positive climate for relations with your employees. It leads to healthy interactions and productive and cooperative efforts.

AN IMPORTANT POINT: Belief in yourself can overcome any barrier. In order to get into the OK position, you must stroke yourself and others regularly. HERE'S A SUGGESTION: Instead of criticizing your employees, look at their positive potential and try to encourage them to unlock it, even while giving necessary negative information.

HOW TO BUILD TRUST THROUGH INTEGRITY

Trust is absolutely necessary for meaningful relationships. It develops from actions that respect and maintain the dignity of people involved. In order to build trust, you must be able to communicate freely and honestly with your employees.

Contractual agreements, while important and necessary, do not take the place of good communications. In fact, a contract can become a limitation to behavior rather than a positive influence. RULE: Never let a contract be the sole basis for trust.

WHAT TO DO: Become a role model to your subordinates. This is one way to develop trust and build cooperative relationships with your employees. Role modeling accomplishes what speeches and other appeals cannot always do—it puts your actions in proper perspective by conveying your real interests and intents.

Effective role modeling depends on a clear idea of your own responsibilities.

> A CASE-IN-POINT: Henry was in charge of training tire inspectors in a tire factory. Contrary to the way he showed the trainees what to look for in their inspection routines, Henry penciled in some items rather than actually inspecting them. He explained that he could take some liberties because he'd seen "a lot of tires in his day." What happened? Henry's employees took his example, and shortly thereafter, customer complaints about tire defects started to roll in. This led to an investigation that subsequently focused on the inspection department. Henry eventually lost his job.

As a manager, you must be able to say no. Otherwise, you'll find yourself harnessed with requests and pressures that could have been prevented. Your goal is to be able to do so and still live with yourself—to master your behavior and emotions in addition to your job.

FOUR VITAL STEPS TO TAKE TO IMPROVE YOUR INTERPERSONAL SKILLS

Step one: Assess your present skill level. A useful way to analyze your present skill level is to answer the questionnaire in Figure 4.2.

WHAT TO DO: First, complete the questionnaire. Then, go back and analyze the results. As a general guideline, the greater the percentage of time that you indicate for each item, the greater your skill level in interpersonal relations.

Step Two: Know your role. The key following the questionnaire lists the most important skill areas that you need to develop as a manager. Once you have assessed them, you'll want to consider your role and how you behave in it.

A management role consists of all the behaviors that are expected of a manager as part of his or her position. Every manager has a number of significant other people (SOPs) who influence this role. These are the role senders, and they comprise your role set. When you and/or the senders do not agree on expected behaviors, conflicts result.

Here are four types of conflicts that can occur:

1. *Inter-sender conflict.* When the senders do not agree on a behavior expected in a role. In order to resolve this conflict, you'll need to reconcile the different expectations.

2. *Person-role conflict.* When the employee sees his or her role differently from one or more of the role senders.

3. *Ambiguity.* When you are not clear about what is expected. To resolve this situation, you need to seek out more information.

4. *Role incongruity.* When one person plays several roles that may be very different from each other. When you experience someone having difficulty in making the appropriate adjustment in his or her behavior, you'll need skills in handling the problems that are likely to arise.

Step Three: Assert yourself constructively. Maintaining a relationship must be based on common *work* goals. As a manager, you must have firm grasp of what needs to be done organizationally. When you combine an accurate picture of your role with assertiveness, active listening, and other human skills, you'll be able to proceed confidently, emphatically, and firmly.

Sometimes relationships break down, and you might not want to deal with that person, but you must as part of your job. WHAT TO DO: Separate as much as possible the behavior from the person.

EXAMPLE: Take two people—one of whom you like personally and the other whom you dislike. Suppose both are tardy three

INTERPERSONAL SKILLS INVENTORY

Instructions

Imagine you are a close friend, observing your behavior. How would you describe *yourself* and *your behavior?*

	You Are This Way What Percent of the Time			
	0–20	21–40	41–60	61–100
1. Accepts other people—warts and all—as deserving of respect.				
2. Has a deep down feeling of positive self-worth—high positive self-esteem.				
3. Says no (when appropriate) without feeling guilty.				
4. Makes choices—does not behave compulsively.				
5. Sees self as having the internal resources to do or handle just about anything.				
6. Asks for what he/she wants in a straightforward way.				
7. Is working toward a worthwhile, predetermined goal defined by self.				
8. Separates behavior he/she dislikes from the person doing the behaving; can condemn the behavior while not condemning the person.				
9. Accepts the approval of others without embarrassment or denial.				
10. Communicates *appreciation* to people.				

11. Communicates *approval* to people.				
12. Ignores, even refuses, opportunities to give negative criticism.				
13. Accepts and even encourages negative criticism of self.				
14. Takes the credit for successes—doesn't blame them on luck.				
15. Takes the credit for the failures—doesn't blame them on luck, or other people.				
16. Takes a very active approach to listening.				
17. Dwells on the rewards of success, not the penalties of failure.				
18. Believes "I am good at what I do; tomorrow I'll do even better."				
19. Rehearses (repeatedly) the win, not the loss immediately after failing.				
20. Believes she/he will succeed at every undertaking.				
21. Is in touch with feelings of anger, resentment, etc. at the time these are being felt.				
22. Shares feelings with others at the time these are being felt.				

FIGURE 4.2

INTERPERSONAL SKILLS INVENTORY (continued)

You Are This Way What Percent of the Time

	0–20	21–40	41–60	61–100
23. Lives in the present—deals with current reality, rather than fantasizing about past or future.				
24. Expects others to succeed at everything they do.				
25. Sees every conflict as a problem to which there is an "everybody wins" solution.				
26. Assumes that others can solve their own problems and encourages them to do so.				
27. Believes there is a solution to every problem and looks for it.				

FIGURE 4.2 (Continued)

KEY TO EXERCISE: INTERPERSONAL SKILLS INVENTORY

	Statements
Positive self-esteem	2, 5
Accepting responsibility	14, 15
Positive reinforcement	10, 11
Belief in oneself and abilities	18, 20
Awareness of one's feelings	21
Solution-oriented	19, 15, 27
Dealing with reality	4, 23
Doesn't blame others for own faults	15
Focus on rewards	7, 17
Acceptance of others	1
Assertiveness	3, 6
Accepting criticism	13
Active listening	16
Openness in communication	22
Accepts others' capabilities	26
Expects others to succeed	24

(In addition to the list)

Self-acceptance	9
Separating behavior from the person	8
Esteem for others	12

FIGURE 4.2 (Continued)

days consecutively. Can you truly deal with both in exactly the same way and with the same feelings? Rarely can your answer be yes. Yet, to do so is a challenge and a good test of your assertiveness.

One more point. There are some "basket cases" who will resist you no matter what you do. Do not invest undue time and energy in this person but rather deal matter-of-factly and continue to apply your interpersonal skills.

Step Four: Develop a constructive attitude. A constructive attitude begins with yourself. You must develop positive self-esteem and positive self-expectancy. The former is based on an evaluation of your worth; the latter by deciding how you will increase it. In other words, you must decide to be a winner, not just in external accomplishments but in your own self-image.

A CASE-IN-POINT: Suppose you have the self-image of an average manager. You make some mistakes, but you do enough to keep your job and stay in good standing with your boss. Now suppose you performed particularly well on your last assignment. Given your current self-image, your performance will probably be lower on your next assignment. Why? Because your self-image regulates your behavior just like a thermostat. But if you want to raise your self-image and likewise your performance level, you need to reevaluate yourself and decide that you are really a high-level achiever and nothing else will do.

STROKES: HOW TO GIVE AND GET RECOGNITION

Reinforcements (stroking) are necessary for effective interpersonal relationships. Here are four principles to keep in mind:

1. Any kind of recognition is better than none at all. Everyone needs strokes and, if necessary, will seek negative reinforcement rather than none at all.

2. The behavior you reinforce is the behavior you will get. Positive strokes bring positive attitudes and behaviors, while negative strokes bring just the opposite.

3. All things equal, you usually reinforce what you like in other people.

4. Negative strokes reinforce undesirable behavior.

EXAMPLE: Chronic absentees usually seek negative strokes. So, after you apply all the penalties and punishments for absenteeism, it's not surprising that these persons still persist in being absent.

WHAT TO DO: Apply the penalty expeditiously, spending very little time and energy on the case. The message will get across to your employee without the attention the behavior is demanding. Also, remember to give due recognition to desirable behaviors.

Strokes can be either *conditional* or *unconditional*. Unconditional strokes give a person direct recognition, regardless of extenuating circumstances. The other applies only when a person does something or carries out some agreement. Both are necessary in an effective relationship. Unconditional strokes enhance self-esteem, but conditional strokes can influence a person to produce. KEEP IN MIND: Without unconditional recognition, the relationship will not achieve authentic communication.

A COMMON MISCONCEPTION: Traditionally, people have felt that recognitions are scarce and must be given out carefully. Of course, this is false. When you give strokes, you don't lose them; there are more to go around. Managers who make a habit of giving positive recognition find their reservoir of recognitions almost limitless. Positive energy builds upon itself.

Sometimes positive stroking is not enough for building productive relationships. A person may be in the Not-OK position as a result of belief structures or "injunctions" learned earlier in life. Often they stand in the way of healthy interactions.

To get rid of crippling injunctions, give permission to change them; that is, tell the person that it's OK to disobey the injunction. WHAT TO DO: Actively and reflectively listen to the conflicts and problems that are occurring within your employee. Say such things as, "It sounds like one part of you wants to try a new way but another part is afraid." Your employee may not immediately respond, but you are at least providing an open invitation to examine his or her behavior and become more productive. More on this in Chapter 7.

HOW TO TURN IT ON THROUGH MOTIVATION

There is no royal road to motivating people. But if you understand the factors that affect motivation, you at least have a good start.

Frederick Herzberg has developed the motivation–hygiene theory of behavior. This concept states that two factors affect the work situation: hygiene and motivators. The former surrounds the job and includes pay, physical working conditions, benefits, and so on. It satisfies primarily physiological and security needs. On the other hand, motivators are part of the job itself and bring a higher level of satisfaction.

Research shows that some individuals are oriented toward and seek out motivators; others look for hygienic factors. Either way, *people motivate themselves.* Managers influence the direction and awareness of this motivation, but the real source of the motivation lies inside the individual.

> EXAMPLE: A "lazy" worker is motivated—but to be lazy. Your job is not to motivate the employee but to get him to redirect his energy toward productive work. How? Through another basic

factor; namely, hunger for recognition.

Often what passes as motivation is actually what Frederick Herzberg calls KITA (Kick in the A____).[1] Herzberg insists that KITA can get movement but not motivation. He's right. Almost without exception, the great coaches in sports owe their success to their ability to trigger the internal force within players that makes them excel—not just to win, but to *excel*. By the same token, a KITA manager can get movement by threats and persuasion, and people will respond. However, KITA does not prepare them for the long haul—it doesn't encourage employees to use their capabilities in a way that develops pride and a feeling of accomplishment.

Recognition concerning job performance is one of the most important techniques you can use. When you tell an employee, "That was a really good job, it helped us cut two days off our deadline," the consequence is likely to be continued high performance.

Recognition involves more than face-to-face encouragement. What is needed, first of all, is a set of guidelines to correctly diagnose the situation. A good starting point is to concentrate on your areas of opportunity for influencing the motivational climate. Here are three:

1. *Competency.* Behavioral research studies have shown that competency motivation is a major performance factor. That is, the sense of competency brings satisfaction, especially to skilled professionals. It bolsters one's self-image, self-confidence, and self-importance. This, in turn, will stimulate a person to operate at a higher level of motivation.

2. *Achievement.* People like to see the contribution their work is making to the overall effort. EXAMPLE: Perhaps the custodial worker is not cleaning the floors conscientiously. So you explain the importance of cleanliness in the building. That person will likely feel that his or her job is a real contribution and will be more willing to undertake the responsibility of doing a better job.

3. *Personal growth and challenge.* This means more than enlarging or varying the work. One way it can be accomplished is by delegating more responsibility. In addition to "growth-on-the-job," personal fulfillment can be achieved through advancement, particularly to positions offering greater challenge.

---

[1] W. J. Paul, Jr., et al., "Job Enrichment Pays Off," *Harvard Business Review* (March–April 1969).

The key element in developing and, especially, maintaining high motivation is *reinforcement*. Basically, it involves a response from you that strengthens the employee's behavior. Reinforcement can take many forms, including:

1. Complimenting the employee on a job well done.
2. Listening to the employee talk about what he or she did.
3. Active listening. EXAMPLE: "Sounds like you're really proud of what you did."
4. Recognition of the outcome. EXAMPLE: "Because of your output this week, we've been able to reduce costs by ten percent and the department bonus pool was increased by fifteen hundred dollars."

Another way to maintain and build motivation is to look at the job itself. What barriers, if any, exist to block motivation? Here are some of the common items to look for as you uncover problems in the job that block motivation.

1. Is the work unhealthy or are conditions unsafe (dust, fumes, hazards, noise.)?
2. Does the job produce high scrap?
3. Are there frequent interruptions where the worker must stop to locate materials, supplies, or equipment?
4. Does this job compare favorably to others in utilizing time, people, materials, supplies, money, and equipment?
5. Is there a quality problem in this work?
6. Do workers find this job fatiguing?
7. Is the work synchronized with other jobs—are there periods where the operator waits or has to go fast to catch up?
8. Is the workload predictable? Does it fluctuate a great deal?
9. Is the next higher job grade or level clearly identified or is it confusing to the employee? Is this a dead-end job?

An effective manager is one who can step on people's toes without removing the shine. Nowhere does this apply more directly than to motivation. Experience has shown that certain practices will help bring about desired results on the job. These are outlined in the checklist following. In general, they form the basis for healthy human relations in today's organizations. By observing them, you not only learn to understand people but to influence positive responses in other people. If you fail to observe them, you perpetuate the "victim" image of a manager who is at the mercy of the situation and who conveys negative attitudes toward workers.

As a manager, you are not usually in a position to bring about cooperation at the overall company level. But your dealings with employees individually and in groups will make them more or less willing to see common goals and cooperate in meeting them.

CHECKLIST FOR EFFECTIVE MOTIVATION

What is expected of your employee?

- Take the time to explain the nature of the work, provide guidance and training as required, and be available when your employee needs help.

- Encourage suggestions on how the work can be performed. Where there is no preestablished way of doing the work, let your employee help decide which way to proceed.

- Discuss changes in duties and procedures with your employee. Give reasons behind the changes.

- Provide your employee with instructions, information, and access to the information necessary to do a good job.

- Provide the necessary supplies and equipment to get the work done.

- Introduce new employees to other employees as well as to the work.

- Give directions that are clear and complete. Give them yourself, preferably face to face.

- Avoid giving the same assignment to more than one individual, unless the assignment involves team effort.

What are the rewards for good performance?

- Explain the wage or salary structure and any incentives tied to work performance. Include also supplementary benefits such as vacation, sick leave, holidays, overtime policy, health insurance, and other benefit programs.

- Help the employee to understand the organization's career opportunities and how to pursue them.

- Explain the importance of the job to the work unit and how it contributes to department and organization goals.

How well is your employee doing?

- Review the work with each employee on a regular basis and be sure that the employee participates in the discussion.

- Be sure your employee knows the standards and measurements used in evaluating his or her performance.

- Hold evaluation sessions on a regular basis.

- Use disciplinary action as a last resort.

How do you like the way your employee handled the job?

- Take a genuine interest in the employee as a person and not just as an instrument for getting the work out.

- Treat employees impartially.

- Be consistent in your treatment of employees.

- If you make a mistake in the treatment of an employee, don't be afraid to admit it. Tell the employee right away; then get on with the business at hand.

- Avoid careless remarks or gossip about employees to other employees.

- Handle complaints promptly. Give and get answers as soon as possible.

HOW MANAGERS HANDLE CONFLICT

In order to understand conflict, first examine its foundation. People cope with potential confrontations in four ways: (1) fight, (2) flight, (3) withdrawal, or (4) assertion. Of these, assertiveness holds the most promise.

Conflict produces frustration which, in turn, produces stress. Psychologists Thomas V. Bonoma and Gerald Zaltman say there are five common responses to frustration: (1) regression, (2) repression,

(3) aggression, (4) withdrawal, and (5) fixation.[2] All five result in further stressful situations for you. WHAT TO DO: Take steps to recognize them when they occur and prepare for a planned response using problem solving.

As a manager, you will be concerned with two levels of conflict: internal and interpersonal.[3] The first involves differing tendencies within a person. Its sources include competing internal messages, confusion over values, closemindedness about certain options, self-doubt, or lack of confidence. The second involves two persons and can be caused by poor communication, threatened identity and status, differing value systems, different attitudes and so on.

The following describes four types of internal conflicts:

1. *Approach–avoidance.* When a positive and negative reaction coincide. EXAMPLE: You want to take on a new job, but you are afraid the new challenge will be too difficult.

2. *Avoidance–avoidance.* When both aspects of the conflict are negative. EXAMPLE: You must give a low rating to your employee or else face a reprimand from your own boss.

3. *Approach–approach.* When two desirable situations present themselves but only one is permissible. EXAMPLE: Given a choice between hiring additional staff or purchasing new equipment but not both.

4. *Double approach–avoidance.* When positives and negatives coexist and no clear-cut solution can satisfy all. Here, you must weigh the pros and cons and search until you find a solution that resolves conflict at least to the point where frustration and stress are relieved.

KEEP THIS IN MIND: As you near a goal, avoidance conflicts will tend to overshadow the approach, and negative aspects will tend to dominate your thoughts. The closer the goal, the greater the avoidance.

Recall Figure 4.1 Each situation shows a division between personal and organizational goals. The level of conflict will likely correspond to the extent of their compatibility.

A conflict of goals is not as serious as one of basic values, because the latter are difficult to change except over a long period of

---

[2] Lillian E. Gilbreth, *Psychology for Management*, (Easton, PA: Hive Publishing Company, 1973).

[3] Group and organizational conflicts will arise, too, but this is not a matter here.

time. As a manager, try to recognize shifts in basic values and consider them when discussing problems.

Interpersonal conflicts, like internal conflicts, imply choices about eventual outcomes. Between two persons with conflicting needs, you can take four possible approaches:

1. Win–lose   (you win/they lose)
2. Lose–win   (you lose/they win)
3. Compromise (each gives up something he or she wants)
4. Win–win   (both get what they want)

In all but the last, you're likely to continue conflict in some way or another. By finding a workable solution through collaborative efforts, you can resolve conflicts and increase self-esteem and productivity. HOW TO DO IT: You must think creatively beyond your present limitations. And you must believe that a solution *is* possible to find.

Your main concern is to develop and design a strategy for dealing with conflict. Here's how:

1. In the case of interpersonal conflicts, clarify each person's *wants* and *feelings*. In an organizational conflict, clarify personal, group, and organizational goals.
2. Identify issues, problems, and objectives. In organizational conflict, clarify expectations, roles, and work contracts.
3. Determine your options.
4. Test the best option(s).
5. Decide.
6. Implement your solution.

IMPORTANT: Secure a meeting of the minds about each party's commitment to resolving the conflict. Without that, you're likely to need disciplinary action, arbitration, directives, and so on.

ANOTHER SUGGESTION: Collaboration and consensus are helpful when a group is involved. When you have reached a consensus, people will likely invest their energy and resources in a joint effort.

WHEN TO USE MUTUAL PROBLEM SOLVING FOR HANDLING RELATIONSHIPS

The essential first step in mutual problem solving involves moving to your and your employee's Adult ego state. Second, use lots of stroking. If you stroke solutions—not intentions—you'll get results.

WHAT TO DO: Emphasize outcomes that you want. For example, say "I expect the matter to be concluded by the end of the week and implemented next Monday." This brings the focus on results.

KEEP IN MIND: There is *always* a workable solutuon. If there's no solution, then the parties involved may as well accept the situation as it is and get on with what they're doing. Then, there's really no problem after all.

Many conflicts and problems in interpersonal relations stem from confusion over responsibility. Ask yourself, "Who owns the problem?" RULE: Whoever owns the problem is also responsible for the solution. Figure 4.3 depicts the problem-ownership situation.

WHO OWNS THE PROBLEM?

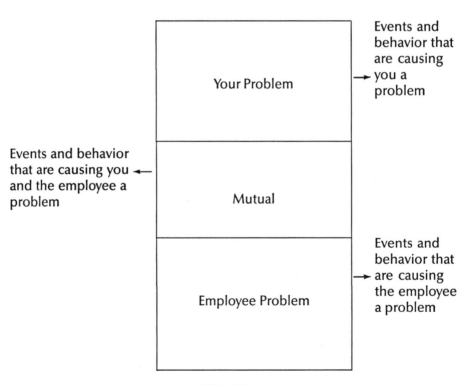

FIGURE 4.3

The *employee* owns the problem when it is of a personal nature and stems from conditions outside of work. *You* own the problem when the department's work is not getting done. Your problem is *mutual* when the employee's relationship with other employees interferes with the department's work.

WHAT TO DO: Here are guidelines for handling interpersonal problems:

1. Be a listener and a counselor.
2. Try to help the other person solve his or her problem.
3. Be a sounding board.
4. As a helper, you facilitate the other person to find a solution but do not find the solution for the person.
5. Accept the solution that the other person arrives at.
6. You don't need to be personally satisfied, as long as the other person is satisfied.
7. Make your primary interest the other person's need.
8. Keep your role more neutral and less active.

When you own the problem:

1. Rather than a listener, you are a sender.
2. You influence the solution.
3. Your need is to help yourself.
4. You may find it necessary to sound off.
5. Your solution must satisfy you.
6. Your needs are primary.
7. Be more assertive.

When the problem is mutual:

1. Sort out individual responsibilities and treat them as in the above guidelines.
2. Find a solution through collaboration.
3. Use "I" messages and active listening to arrive at mutually acceptable solutions.

It has been estimated that in some organizations, upward of 70 percent of time spent is spent in game playing. Without replacing this with something more constructive or by not trying to eliminate those that are going on, game playing will escalate.

Game playing usually results in wasted time and bad feelings. Yet people continue to play them because they provide structure to their time and offer emotional kicks such as negative recognition and negative reinforcement. Games allow people to avoid closeness, collect their favorite bad feelings, and maintain their chosen life position.

All of us are vulnerable to playing games. This is because games allow us to take a role in what is commonly called the Drama Triangle. Three roles are common in all games:

1. *Victim* gets crossed up in the game.
2. *Persecutor* takes the one-up position.
3. *Rescuer* tries to bail out one of the parties involved, either through excuses or in some other way.

Here's an example that illustrates typical game playing: Jane is chronically late for work. One day, the conversation went like this:

Jane: *I'm afraid I'm late again.*
Manager: *That's the third time this month. I'll have to take action.*

Subconsciously, Jane was saying, "I messed up. Kick me." The manager obliged, and Jane got her payoff.

The most important thing in learning about games is to learn how to stop them. The most effective way, of course, is not to get involved in the first place. However, if you find yourself in game playing, here's what to do:

1. Recognize the game.
2. Get in touch with your feelings.
3. Actively listen and assertively communicate what you feel and want.
4. Give positive recognition and reinforcement.

Dealing with employee problems is like fine tuning a TV. Bring the relationship into clear, crisp focus and keep it there by active use of your interpersonal skills and techniques.

THE FORMAL APPROACH: HOW TO DEAL WITH GRIEVANCES AND CONTRACTS

Grievances are ways employees formally communicate complaints to management. Ask yourself, "What is the person really saying with this grievance?" Rarely is the stated grievance the real issue. The real issue could be any number of things, including retaliation or some extraneous circumstance.

WHAT TO DO: Follow the grievance procedure as it is formally stated. At the same time, consider the possibility of resolving the grievance at the first level. Use active listening, reflection, assertiveness skills with Adult control to bring about a nonthreatening environment. Here's an example of how a potential grievance situation can be resolved productively:

Employee:	*You let Sally take a twenty-minute break. I got only ten minutes. I'm going to get the steward.*
Manager:	*I understand how you might feel this is unfair. What is it that you want from me?*
Employee:	*Well, I want you to treat me like you treat Sally. If she gets twenty minutes, so should I.*
Manager:	*Are you saying that under every circumstance you should have the same amount of break time as Sally?*
Employee:	*Well, when you put it that way, not every time.*
Manager:	*What occasions might the break time be different?*
Employee:	*Well... some days one of us comes in earlier, or when we take more frequent breaks.*
Manager:	*Yes. What might be some other kinds of situations?*

Maybe this seems unrealistic, but your persistence with this approach will eventually succeed.

A contract is essentially an argument or a commitment to do or not to do something. Contracts can be made with anyone and need not be in writing.

EXAMPLE: You can decide to listen to others and to the feedback you recieve. This is an unwritten contract.

The basic qualities of a contract are mutual consent, competency, and consideration. You'll find this to be true in both legal and interpersonal situations.

Any contract situation will be complicated by other factors. Often, you a manager will be required to interpret a contract to the fairest extent possible. WARNING: Many contracts are not explicit and involve terms that contain ulterior motives. It's in your best interest to strive for clarity whenever you involve yourself in a contractual agreement.

GROUP DYNAMICS: IS THERE SAFETY IN NUMBERS?

Sometimes people seem to act strangely when they are part of a group, and this differs from how they act individually. To understand this, it may be necessary to put yourself in the shoes of a group member—let's say a managerial group. Suppose you heard a rumor that certain managerial positions are going to be demoted. What will be your reaction as a group member? Will you look at this from the organization's logic? Or will you band together more closely as managers and try to protect your jobs?

Groups have their own logic. What others think is irrational the group may see as quite rational.

> EXAMPLE: When workers strike for three months and never recover their economic losses, people look at this and call it irrational. To the workers of the union, it's not irrational at all. It's the principle of the matter that is most compelling, and they feel it's perfectly logical to sustain economic losses in order to win recognition, their cause, or whatever it is they really seek. Some people would do this individually, but in a group, ideas become solidified and people behave so as to keep the group together.

People behave the way they do because of their special needs. Here are six commonly acknowledged needs:

1. *Coordination.* When they need to share information about what each person is doing, about the work, and the organization.

2. *Common goals.*

3. *Perpetuation.* When the group wants to continue as a group.

4. *Belonging.* Feeling, experiencing, and getting accepted as part of the group.

5. *Solidarity.* Unity that makes people feel secure and supported by their peers.

6. *Strength.*

Once you recognize these group needs, you can understand why employee groups band together so closely and so frequently. The degree to which they band together depends on any or all of these factors:

1. *Norms.* Standards of behavior set by the group.

2. *Syntality.* How much the group members have in common.

3. *Cohesiveness.* The degree to which the group members stick together.

4. *Leadership.* Either *social* or *task* (that is, to maintain social roles or accomplish the group's purpose).

5. *Sanctions.* Approval and/or disapproval of certain actions.

6. *Status.* A member's relative standing in a group.

7. *Roles.* Sets of expected behaviors.

8. *Groupthink.* The degree of "sameness" of thinking on particular issues.[4]

9. *Purposes.* Formed to meet member needs, be they self-esteem, security, and so on.

The presence of group members has an impact on every major area of work performance. Here are four major effects that groups can have:

1. *Employee know-how.* Groups can have a positive or negative effect on informal as well as technical knowledge of a job.

2. *Stimulation and arousal.* The presence of others can stimulate and arouse certain emotions, which in turn decrease or increase commitment to work.

3. *Strategy.* Presence from other members of a work group can modify a worker's strategy for doing a job.

---

[4] Symptoms and problems that occur as a result of groupthink are discussed in Irving L. Janis, *Victims of Groupthinks*, (Boston: Houghton, Mifflin, 1972).

4. *Motivation.* The overall effort an employee is willing to expend, strongly influenced by expectations of success and the degree to which needs are satisfied.

Do people perform better outside of or as part of groups? The answer is both yes and no, and there are compelling arguments on both sides. Many problems occur as a result of group membership, such as loss of individuality, diminished sense of responsibility, excesses in group leadership, and so on. On the other hand, groups can be more effective in producing ideas, analyzing choices, and building strength of commitment.

How can you determine when groups are more effective than individuals? RULE OF THUMB: If the tasks are relatively simple and the choices clear, a group works better. But as the tasks become more complex, individuals are more effective.

Your decision to participate in a peer group organization depends on your own needs. Of course, you'll be subject to the deleterious effects of group behavior and influences. But you'll also reap major benefits by having the opportunity for positive contributions and actions that you believe are needed. SOME POINTERS: You are the only person responsible for your own self-esteem. Avoid pitfalls like groupthink but instead emphasize the opportunities available from a group rather than the individuals in the group.

HOW YOU CAN WORK WITH GROUPS SUCCESSFULLY

The group leader's situation is not unlike your own. He or she reflects the values of the group and can influence the constituency only insofar as members are willing to change. Recognizing this, here are four guidelines for you to follow:

1. Give the group leaders information they need in order to develop their own arguments and rationale, but avoid "planting" the arguments with them.
2. Be aware of their need to save face, and give them a chance to arrive at solutions themselves.
3. Be aware that groups often change informal leaders. Be conscious of other group members and the possibility that one will emerge as an informal leader in the future.
4. Assert your position and feelings candidly. In the long run, your candor will improve your status and relationship with the group.

When conflicts arise, there are two levels with which you must deal: (1) between you and the group and (2) among group members. In the first case, follow these guidelines:

1. Recognize differences in goals and methods.

2. Invite the group (or group leaders) to participate in resolving the issue.

3. State your position clearly; present your goals and wants. SUGGESTION: You might want to use a contract that spells out what you and the group expect.

4. Be willing to share in the solution even if it means sacrifices.

A CASE-IN-POINT: In one company, top management unilaterally decided to cut their own salaries in order to improve the company's economic distress. When they asked employees to take a pay cut also, their argument was very strong. Predictably, although unionized, the employees agreed, and the company prospered. Management kept faith and awarded them accordingly as soon as they began to turn a profit again.

Conflicts within the group are best solved by the group itself. WHAT TO DO: Encourage members to find their own solution. If they can't, then you'll need to take a more active role. For example, when new employees experience friction with a group, you may need to interfere. Encourage the new employee to maintain his or her standards. Provide support and reinforcement for the employee's performance. Assert your standards, and remind the other group members of them as well. Remember, the new employee is caught in a contest for loyalty between the work group and you, the manager.

You may find youself in a position where you must deal with adversary groups. Apply the same general guidelines for resolving conflict when you deal with them as with all other groups. Ask yourself these questions:

1. Who are the group leaders and other prominent members?

2. What is the basis of the group's hostility?

3. Are group norms being threatened?

4. Is there some disagreement with the organization?

5. Is outside agitation involved?

WHAT TO DO: Establish a common superordinate goal; that is, common grounds that underlie your relationship. Then, firmly set standards and expectations and stick to them. Carry them out through positive assertive action.

It's important to recognize that in any work group there is usually more than one leader. This need not be upsetting to you because it's a rather natural situation. The manager who tries to eliminate the "other" leader is inviting serious trouble.

The informal leader is not a threat to your position. His or her skills are useful to the group but not necessarily to the organization. He or she often has human and technical skills but lacks conceptual skill. Research shows that informal leaders do not necessarily make effective managers, and managers tend to lose their effectiveness and stature if they become informal leaders. CONCLUSION: The best strategy is to recognize and work with the informal leader in mutual cooperation.

Several positive consequences can result from working in tandem with informal leaders. You can get:

1. Better mutual understanding of each other's role.
2. Feedback about employee concerns and their reactions to management decisions.
3. Cooperation from the group.

CAUTION: Do not single out the informal leader and shower him or her with recognition. Work groups are wary of manipulation and might interpret your behavior as an attempt to win the group's favor. Also, informal leaders tend to change often, so it's best to remain evenhanded.

HOW TO BE A TEAM PLAYER EVEN WHEN IT HURTS

Just as there exists interdependency between you and your subordinates, there exists interdependency between you and your boss. Making the boss more effective is part of your job, and your support is critically needed.

It's important to recognize that bosses also have needs and rights. Conflict most often occurs over competition for resources, position, performance, and jurisdictional disputes. Here, collaboration is essential for a win–win resolution.

Assertiveness, when expressed properly with understanding and empathy for your boss's frame of reference, is appropriate for handling conflict. Remember, your boss is closer than you to the major decisions about goals and policies, and you are closer to implementation. If your boss also takes an assertive approach, conflict will likely end up in a workable compromise.

> A CASE-IN-POINT: One boss prefers and expects cooperation among managers, but because of how the system is designed, the managers find themselves in competition with each other. After a year of fierce competition, the boss decided to emphasize cooperation by getting the managers together into a group. After thrashing out the problems, they were able to resolve issues among themselves. The result: Decision making returned to the proper level, and cooperation was rewarded by a more productive system.

Differences of opinion between you and your boss are virtually unavoidable. When the situation arises, follow these suggestions:

1. Discuss the issue with your boss by being prepared to convince him or her of your approach.
2. Find out the basis for your boss's disagreement with you; identify the associated assumptions.
3. Seek out the common goals. Emphasize the benefits, mention the shortcomings of your approach, and be willing to take responsibility for any part of it.

SEVEN WAYS TO MAKE YOUR BOSS LOOK GOOD

1. Avoid upward delegation. Handle your own responsibilities rather than depending on your boss for decisions you should be making.

2. Complete your work, present solutions and recommendations, and point out problems you feel should be handled by your boss.

3. Keep your boss informed both in positive and negative situations. Do not wait until asked.

4. Avoid scapegoating. If someone else is causing you problems, take it up with that person. Go to your boss only when you get poor results.

5. Use the communication bridge to relate to someone outside your unit. Keep your boss informed as you proceed.

6. Make an effort to understand your boss's frame of reference and his or her need for peer acceptance.

7. Use your assertiveness principles to express your needs. Avoid the traditional Parent–Child/Boss–Subordinate relationship and communicate on an Adult–Adult level.

Of course, cooperation brings the best results when working with your peers, too. However, competition often can find its way into the workplace. This can trigger game playing in the form of ulterior transactions, put-downs, and other tricks. But competition can also stimulate departments to achieve the organization's goals. WHAT TO DO: Steer the competition toward performance and away from personality. Establish working ground rules with your colleagues and "let the best manager win."

The first question to ask yourself in a peer conflict is, "What is this problem about?" If it's a personality conflict, identify specifically what's involved—mannerisms, appearance, expressions? Specifically, what is it about you or that person that dominates the relationship? There may be something that can cause you to slip into the Not-OK position.

The second question: "How can we both get what we want?" It may seem impossible, but both parties *can* be satisfied if you reach out to find a common interest. When you find it, follow it persistently. The result: The most effective relationship possible.

REMEMBER THIS: It's possible to simultaneously keep your self-respect, manage your unit, and work well with your boss and your peers.

CO-OPTION: HOW TO WORK WITHIN THE SYSTEM

The management system consists of all policies, rules, and structures under which you operate. Two variables, structure and authority, measure the extent to which you experience restrictions on your freedom and activities and can make decisions. Normally, low structure results in high authority delegation, but any combination can exist within an organization.

EXAMPLE: A research scientist may have low structure and high authority to make decisions. His or her manager has low structure and low authority because the decision usually rests with the scientists themselves.

As you chart your course through whatever system you are part of, you may find certain aspects unappealing. *Co-option* can help you work within the system. This means you take on the characteristics of the system that most benefit you.

KEEP IN MIND: The system was not designed to benefit you alone but rather to achieve the purposes of the organization. Unless your self-esteem is jeopardized, you can stay within a system, co-opt the positive aspects, and contribute positively to the system and those who work with you.

There will always be frictions between you and your organization. According to a study by Dr. Norman George, the values of first-line managers do not always correlate with those of upper management, but the difference does not usually affect their performance.[5] In other words, you can differ from your superior and still be effective.

What you need to do is identify areas of compatibility and emphasize them. Give yourself permission to accept a less-than-perfect work situation. Meanwhile, work to improve the system. RULE OF THUMB: Keep your options open. Once you close your options, you'll not only rob the organization of the benefit of your ideas, but you'll also feel like something less than a winner. And this could affect your own self-esteem.

TEN KEY QUALITIES OF A WINNING MANAGER

There are several attitudinal qualities of a winning person that are also qualities of a winning manager. Here are six:

1. Positive self-image
2. Positive self-esteem
3. Positive self-motivation
4. Positive self-direction
5. Positive self-expectancy

---

[5] Norman George, "Supervisors' Identification with Management—A Study of Comparative Values and Job Effectiveness," dissertation (Ohio State University, 1962).

6. Positive self-awareness

Along with these, the winning manager:

1. *Listens*—actively and patiently.
2. *Takes personal responsibility* for his or her own behavior and response to others'.
3. *Stays physically fit* as well as emotionally trim.
4. *Asks for what he or she wants;* doesn't beat around the bush.
5. *Visualizes his or her goal.*
6. *Engages in self-talk;* says "I can."
7. Is *effectiveness oriented* rather than efficiency oriented; focuses on what is needed at the right time, in the right place, and in the right amount.
8. *Separates the person from the behavior;* that is, maintains respect for an employee while dealing with that person's undesirable behavior.
9. *Looks for solutions* in problem solving.
10. *Truly believes in a win–win solution;* focuses on problems that can be solved rather than those that must be solved at another level.

WRITING YOUR INTERPERSONAL SUCCESS STORY

The ten qualities of a winning manager constitute a blueprint for change. Now visualize your desired self-image and behavior. Then follow these five steps:[6]

1. Become aware of the need for a new approach or need.
2. Identify the behavior involved.
3. Practice the behavior by rehearsing, engaging in self-talk.
4. Get feedback on the effectiveness of your new behavior.
5. Desensitize yourself to fears. TRY THIS: Visualize a fear-producing situation in a relaxed state of mind such as meditation. If you can do this, you'll be dealing with a traumatic situation under more rational terms.

---

[6] From Janis Day, *A Working Approach to Human Relations* (Monterey, CA: Brooks/Cole Publishing Co., 1981).

Finally, integrate your new behavior into your repertoire. Form a habit *and* develop a new self-awareness, then build your self-image upon the new behavior.

Developing personal qualities for success requires appropriate permissions and the self-esteem to maintain your behavior. Once you set a goal, get permission (from yourself) to acomplish it, and feel that you are doing something worthwhile.

HERE'S A HINT: You need not be perfect to be satisfied. For example, your goal may be to improve unit performance by 50 percent over the next two years. To do this, you set another goal of 100 percent conflict resolution by year-end. However, you only reach 75 percent. Does this mean failure? No. After all, your goal may be a little unrealistic, and partial success deserves credit, too!

There are four dimensions of total success:

1. *Being* successful—maintaining a sense of presence that says "I'm a winner."
2. *Feeling* successful—experiencing deep-down self-worth.
3. *Doing* successful things—achieving winning solutions, accomplishing goals, and feeling satisfied in their accomplishment.
4. *Thinking* successfully—visualizing goals, developing strategies, and being aware of self-worth.

Fit these ideas together to form the four components of success: self-esteem, knowledge, confidence, and enthusiasm.

Feeling good about yourself plus know-how in handling your job will make you ready to meet any challenge in your job:

SELF-ESTEEM + KNOWLEDGE = SELF-CONFIDENCE

Self confidence, spirit, and excitement about what you do multiplied by a high self-image and self-standard yield the successful realization of goals truly worthwhile to you!

SELF-CONFIDENCE + ENTHUSIASM × PRIDE = SUCCESS

TSF³ FOR SUCCESS

Bad feelings can impede the way you perceive overall success. To deal with this situation on the spot, try TSF³ the Think System for Feeling Fine Faster.[7] It goes like this: Right now I feel ___ that if I ___ I will ___, so I ___ and end up ___; instead, I can feel good about the situation if I ___ because this will then ___."

As you fill in the blanks, you become aware of what's happening. Get in touch with your feelings and take control of the present. Give yourself options; you'll have a much better chance to succeed if you do. WHAT TO DO: apply TSF[3] when confronting people and situations at home, play, or at work. Making yourself feel OK is not just an uplifting experience. It is, after all, the most productive way to operate.

What you can vividly conceive and sincerely believe, you can inevitably achieve. If you really buy this message *with no reservations*, you are far along on the path to success.

---

[7] Based on a similar system by Transactional Analyst Pamela Levin.

CHAPTER 5

Why Performance Is the Manager's Bottom Line

The very first step toward success is to become interested in it.

—SIR WILLIAM OSLER

IN a sense, performance is your bottom line. According to some experts, the U.S. economy currently bumbles along at perhaps 25 percent of its potential, in terms of the human and natural resources invested. Fortunately, numerous examples of individual organizations that far exceed this norm demonstrate the dramatic improvement to be achieved through more efficient management. The way is open for any manager who wants to master these techniques to achieve significant improvements in the performance and productivity of his or her organization.

How do you as a manager get and maintain optimum performance from employees? First, you need to develop skills and approaches necessary to build and sustain performance. This chapter will help you understand clearly what makes people perform, develop, and use an effective performance system, and it will help you know and apply the techniques that will maintain good performance and increase productivity. And, as you see yourself improve, so too, will your bottom line.

HOW TO EVALUATE WORK PERFORMANCE

Work is your window to the world and, as such, is a major opportunity to find a purpose in life. Simply put, workers want to feel useful. They want to know that what they do is worthwhile and appreciated. For example, take your lowliest skilled employee and tell him, genuinely and sincerely, that you appreciate the job he does, and tell him why. You can be sure this person will give you an extra effort when you need it.

The key components needed to achieve maximum performance can be summarized in the following equation:

Performance = Motivation + Ability + Environment

All three work together in combination to produce the level of effort and results that you see.

You are actually the main day-to-day influence on your worker's skill and will to work—and these are the direct determinants of performance. REMEMBER: Only the employee has the power to decide what level of effort to extend. But you can influence his or her decision.

As a manager, you are the catalyst who transforms people into a productive work force. You take on various roles, many of which were described in Chapter 1. Lately, the "keystone" role has become more and more accepted. Through it, you have the opportunity to develop both perspectives and skills, the human and the conceptual. You become more and more a manager of performance.

Performance situations vary a great deal. In some organizations, performance guidelines are clearly spelled out and accepted by employees, so the manager can attain the desired results simply by applying the system. In others, the manager is left to his or her own resources in achieving the needed performance. There are also cases when a fully developed system exists, such as a piecework system, but it is not accepted by employees. Then, the manager acts as buffer between the system and employees. So in order to discuss performance in a meaningful way, it's necessary to identify the different conditions and to look at how you might respond to your particular situation.

HOW PERFORMANCE SYSTEMS AFFECT EMPLOYEES

There are three kinds of systems that affect employee (and manager) performance:

1. *Work System.* The design of the job. Is it routine? Complex? Does it have a lot of variety? Responsibility?

2. *Reward System.* The compensation scheme, including both economic and noneconomic rewards. A *merit-based* system ties the amount of reward to the level of performance, as in a piecework system. A *maintenance-based* system is concerned more with maintaining an equitable compensation plan overall, with no variation for high or low performance. An example would be a straight hourly wage or salary.

3. *Management System.* The way in which management gets decisions made and controls operations. A *centralized* management system restricts most decision authority to upper level management. Lower level managers and employees implement decisions and relay information. In a *decentralized* management system, managers and employees have greater decision-making authority.

Figure 5.1 shows the performance requirements of different systems:

This figure shows that high performance can be achieved in each situation if appropriate actions are taken. However, even when conditions are most favorable for high performance—when the work system is varied, the reward system is merit-based, and the management system is decentralized—certain actions still must be taken to assure high performance.

THREE KEYS TO IMPROVING EMPLOYEE PERFORMANCE

Everything you do has an effect on employee performance. In this section, let's focus on impersonal approaches to building performance: goal setting, job design, and reward systems.

1. *Goal setting.* Research has shown that people work more productively when they understand and are committed to a goal. However, achieving work goals brings satisfaction to the employee *only* when those goals are related to the employee's own needs. When they are not—when the employee can see no connection between better work output and improving the quality of his or her own life—problems will result. But the fact remains that in many cases the two—personal needs and work goals—are indeed related or can be; but the employee does not perceive that fact. It's your responsibility to clarify this relationship.

GETTING HIGH PERFORMANCE UNDER DIFFERENT SYSTEMS

When the Work System Is:	High performance can be attained if:
Routine	Appropriate recognition is given and other opportunities are permitted for maintaining interest, such as peer interaction.
Varied: enriched or enlarged	Appropriate reinforcement is given for greater effort and responsibility.

When the Reward System Is:	High performance can be attained if:
Merit-based	Reward serves as a positive reinforcement; merit is related closely to performance.
Maintenance-based	Positive reinforcement is given in nonfinancial forms— recognition, support, good relationships.

When the Management System Is:	Performance can be attained if:
Centralized	Upward communication is maintained and management listens to employees; employee's contribution is appreciated and rewarded; tangible rewards are important.
Decentralized	Unit-level decisions are coordinated with higher level goals and decisions. Reinforcement is given for participation, decisions, problem resolution at the first-line level.

FIGURE 5.1

A CASE-IN-POINT: Sally, who was a cheerleader in high school, has a strong need for visibility, personal contact, and recognition. However, after graduation, she finds the employment market tight; so she settles for a job as stock clerk in a department store, with virtually no opportunity to deal with people. You can predict that Sally will not be satisfied with her work and will perform at a minimal level (and probably not stay with the job) unless some means can be found to relate performance on her current job to satisfying her need to be with people.

2. *Job Design.* "Job enrichment" and "job enlargement" are words often heard in the world of work today. They represent a major strategy for making work more interesting and increasing the linkage in the employee's mind between successful performance and the satisfaction of personal needs for achievement and growth.

EXAMPLE: In manufacturing, a worker or team of workers would be assigned to an entire assembly process, including final testing, rather than breaking the job down into specialized operations, as has been the custom in the past.

3. *Reward System.* When a job is redesigned to make it more challenging and to make the employee contribution more meaningful, employees expect appropriate compensation. The compensation system, in turn, can provide further recognition and motivation to perform.

When a direct-incentive system, such as piecework, is used, the employee can see a clear-cut connection between output and the money reward. WHAT TO DO: In this situation, your main task is to make sure the employee is supplied with resources and whatever is necessary to keep the path clear for achieving the worker's (and the unit's) performance goals.

The *periodic-incentive system* uses merit pay increases based on performance appraisal. This system can also supply the link between performance and need satisfaction. CAUTION: This is tougher and more challenging to you than a direct-incentive system because it requires greater interpersonal skills as well as the skill of matching job requirements with individual need.

A word to the wise: Regardless of the system, you must be careful about putting too much emphasis on external rewards. Holding up the promise of a fatter paycheck in return for better performance can bring short-term improvement, but it does not increase the worker's sense of doing meaningful work or fulfilling his or her potential. It can easily backfire!

HOW TO APPROACH EMPLOYEES ABOUT PERFORMANCE

There are three basic approaches for improving employee performance:

1. *A Developmental Approach* emphasizes planning, goal setting, and direction. It focuses on the employee's longer range interests and aspirations, and concentrates on working toward possible promotion and greater responsibilities. The employee holds a high degree of control over how to carry out the job. And, the employee's own performance provides direct feedback once goals and standards are established and agreed upon.

> EXAMPLE: If the standard output is fifty units an hour, an employee can obviously measure his performance once he knows that standard. Your role then becomes a supportive one that concentrates on problem solving and stimulating the goal aspirations of the employee.

2. *The Maintenance-Oriented Approach* is used with employees whose upward mobility is limited. The focus here is on acceptable performance; that is, meeting standards. In this case, the goals are usually predetermined and well defined. Your aim here is to get good performance consistent with the technology at hand.

> EXAMPLE: Machine limitations on productivity usually imply standard procedures to follow, along with conventional performance-rating forms. It would be unrealistic to encourage the employee to strive for higher output; however, giving recognition for meeting the job demands would help to maintain the employee's level of commitment and morale.

3. *The Remedial Approach is used for the low achiever.* Lagging performance is the reason for a remedial program. In such a program, performance goals are usually strictly imposed on the employee. The focus should be on improvement and rehabilitation. The appraisal process must deliver the following:

(a)   clear feedback, with ample instances and examples of bad performance.

(b) a highly structured program of corrective action, with clear performance goals and targets.

(c) frequent review sessions and monitoring.

(d) provision for "graduation" to a higher performance status in a less-structured program if the employee improves.

(e) preparation for termination if the employee does not respond.

IMPORTANT: You must recognize that the alternatives may be termination or transfer. Procedures are important here. Documentation is essential for legal and related purposes.

PPRS: A PROVEN METHOD FOR DEVELOPING PERFORMANCE

The Performance Planning and Results System (PPRS) is a performance management technique that has been used successfully in a variety of work situations. PPRS is useful primarily in situations when managers have an *active, direct* role in performance appraisal. It focuses on developmental and internal reinforcements, regardless of the reward system. It addresses all important areas and brings the employee into the mainstream of company concerns.

First, PPRS must be viewed as a *total* system. It combines aspects of the different appraisal systems in a format that can be applied formally or informally, whether the rest of the organization uses it or not. The system framework is shown in Figure 5.2.

SYSTEM FRAMEWORK

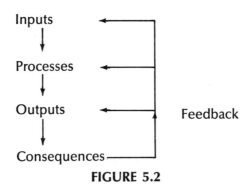

FIGURE 5.2

Here's how the framework fits together:

Input   = employee effort.

Process   = the duties and tasks that the employee performs.

Output   = how much. How will performance be compared to the targets?

Consequences = goals achieved or not achieved; department efficiency rating, product acceptance, and so on, to include any consequences that result from the output.

The major events that are part of PPRS may happen roughly in this chronological order (although this is not a requirement):

1. *Identify needs*, which, in the system framework, means identifying the needs for inputs, the needs in the process area, the output needs, and the consequences. They can be identified further as personal or organizational needs.

2. *Express needs* in terms of goals that are worthwhile to the employee and the organization.

3. *Discuss goals* for the employee's performance for the next planning period (whatever the appropriate time frame is in your organization—three months, six months, one year, and so on).

4. *Resolve any disputes* about the goals, conflicts between personal and organizational goals, and the feasibility of the goals.

5. *State these performance goals specifically* and in written form. HINT: The contract method can be helpful here.

6. Once the goals are agreed to and the disputes settled, *set specific target objectives*, stated in such a way that they will serve as measurable standards for performance. Also, determine the plan of action to accomplish the goals.

7. *Compare performance results* for the period with the expectations for that period and discuss this in the perspective of the new goals (which could be extensions of previous goals). Also discuss unintended results.

8. At this point, the employee works to *achieve the new targets* for the period; your role is that of an ongoing coach and a monitor of results.

9. *Hold review sessions* at appropriate points during or at the end of the current planning period.

10. *The planning is repeated*, as in Step 1.

PROS AND CONS OF PPRS

Pros

- It gives you a logical framework for performance assessment.

- It ensures that all bases are covered.

- It reviews the past, which is important, but it focuses mainly on the future, which is even more important.

- It allows you to manage and influence performance rather than be managed by it.

- It is a doorway to building good relationships with employees.

- It focuses on results, and results are where the most important action is.

- It is a ready basis for feedback for employees.

- It provides a supportive role for the manager, and this is healthy.

Cons

- It is time consuming. You must be willing to commit a substantial amount of time—always a critical resource.

- It requires effort and skill. You may need to develop new skills and improve old ones in order to conduct PPRS effectively.

- It may require a reorientation of your priorities. You will have to shift from watching employees to monitoring their results.

- You are not always free to do the things in the PPRS because of the present system of doing things in the organization.

- PPRS may seem overly formal and appear awkward at first, especially where no system exists and the performance assessment is informal and nonprogrammed.

The "how-tos" of PPRS provide much of the remaining subjects of this chapter. As a suggestion, take a look at the PPRS Worksheet shown in Figure 5.3. It will prove helpful as you learn how to implement the system.

Guidelines for allocating your time: The first planning sessions should take 30 minutes to an hour. Subsequent sessions could take 15 to 30 minutes. In all, allow about 5% of your time for discussing performance.

NOTE: Coaching is a key part of PPRS. Review the section on Chapter 2 before you proceed.

Step One: Assess Performance Needs

Performance needs determine goals. Since goals are what we aim for, needs are the reasons for having the goals in the first place.

The first thing to do in PPRS is to decide what the needs are. Here are some useful guidelines:

1. Identify the horizons; forget about barriers at this point and focus on what you really need.
2. Discuss openly your feelings about what should be done. Invite your employees to do likewise.
3. State accurately where you are presently and measure the gap in terms that you and the employees can understand.
4. Take a critical look and give all the reasons that something may not be feasible.
5. Filter out what is reasonable and realistic.

The results of the needs analysis should be a clear idea of the priorities on which you and the employee will focus. WHAT TO DO: Determine which needs are more important than others and how important each is relative to others.

The most effective and quickest way to spot performance problems is direct observation—watching output rise or fall. However, some problems may be difficult to spot. For example, even though output might be acceptable, a morale problem could be developing that is not so obvious.

WHAT TO DO: Try the input-process-output-consequences model as a way of spotting performance problems.[1] Observe each phase of the model and determine whether or not a real or potential problem exists. Then confirm your observations by checking the criteria and communicating them to employees.

---

[1] You can find information about this in Chapter 9.

PPRS WORKSHEET

	Needs	Goals	Target Objectives	Performance Standards
Personal				
Unit				
Organization				

FIGURE 5.3

Step Two: Set Goals and Objectives

During the planning session, the next step is to identify goals. SUGGESTIONS: Consider the atmosphere, the physical and psychological climate of the setting. Reserve enough time—at least an hour for the initial session and at least a half hour for follow-up.

Goals are the overall intended results—the mission you want to accomplish. They usually can be stated qualitatively. EXAMPLE: Make the inventory system as effective and efficient as possible.

Objectives are specific statements of what you want to accomplish—the means to achieving goals. Objectives are usually stated quantitatively, as shown for example in Figure 5.4. Standards, or criteria, specify the level or type of result to be achieved and make the goals and objectives more concrete.

Step Three: Take a Problem-Solving Approach

The skills that are useful in problem solving are also useful in PPRS. Once you have identified the needs and set goals and objectives, the problem-solving process looks like this:

EXAMPLES OF NEEDS, GOALS, AND OBJECTIVES

Needs	Goals	Objectives
Organizational Need:		
to have optimal inventory system	efficient & effective stock system	improve system within a year
Personal need:		
satisfaction	development of personnel capability	encourage and support efforts to modify the system
etc.	etc.	etc.

FIGURE 5.4

1. Select solution strategies, methods, and so on.

2. Implement, decide, delegate, actuate, and initiate.

3. Observe and determine performance effectiveness.

4. Revise as required.

Plans represent solutions to a problem. Once the plans are established, problems of implementation must be resolved. Thus, the planning and problem-solving process is a continuous cycle.

USING A SAMPLE CONTROL SYSTEM FOR MONITORING PERFORMANCE

Evaluation is an on-going activity. It's easy to "gunnysack" by saving up criticism and observations and then unloading them at formal evaluation time. But timely, on-the-spot evaluation is best. Remember the principle of reinforcement: It should follow behavior as quickly and directly as possible. So, too, prompt, on-the-spot evaluation ensures a more effective evaluation conference.

Following the input-process-output approach, the control system framework, as shown in Figure 5.5, describes the different roles people take in the process.

During the control process, you function mainly as a monitor and decision maker. You compare output results to standards and relate these standards to goals when necessary. If the output is not up to standard, you might report these findings to your superior who, in turn, will make decisions about the standards themselves.

This control process is universal. It applies to all kinds of activities.

> EXAMPLE: If you are coaching a softball team, you will monitor input, output, and process. The inputs are the players; the process is how they play; and the outputs are runs and wins.

There are three types of control:

1. *Preliminary control.* Control before the fact, also referred to as feedforward control. (See Chapter 2, page 58.) It is concerned mainly with inputs—personnel, materials, resources of all sorts. Orientation and planning are especially important here because

TYPICAL CONTROL SYSTEM

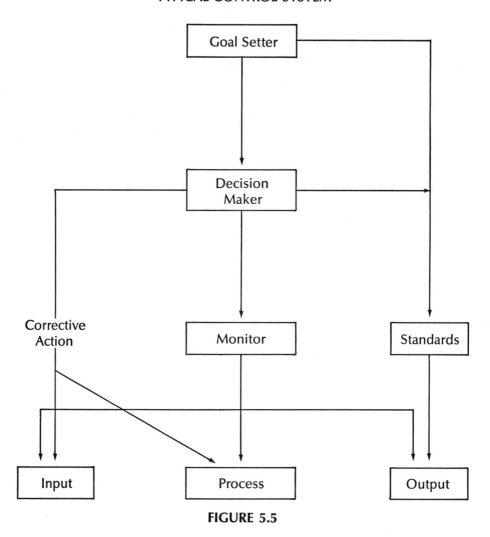

FIGURE 5.5

they seek to prepare the inputs in such a way that they will produce the desired results.

2. *Concurrent control.* Control at the time that the activity is happening. The manager watches the on-going process. The computer is often used here. Managers who exercise concurrent control are sometimes perceived as being close to their workers. Plan on spending a lot of time working alongside employees and keeping up with their progress. Coaching is, in a sense, concurrent control.

3. *Post-control.* Relies on data after the fact. The output is the

main thing that is monitored. By reviewing output, you make assumptions about the inputs and processes. So if output is not up to standard, you might make assumptions about bad parts, machines needing adjustment, or employees using the wrong methods.

PPRS is not only a planning system, but it can also be used as a control system. It employs pre-, concurrent, and feedback control. NOTE: The trend today is more toward concurrent and precontrol. They reflect the principle that prevention is best.

Here are eight guidelines for a good control system:

1. Know the standards; develop them if necessary.
2. Make sure employees know the standards and understand them.
3. Coordinate the standards with others; be consistent.
4. Watch for feedback and actively seek it.
5. Interpret feedback accurately and carefully.
6. Time your actions to the needs of the situation.
7. Practice "management by exception." You can't control everything, so focus on the important things and handle others by exception; that is, deal with them when there is a noticeable deviation from normal practice.
8. Follow up; use reinforcement to reward and build behavior patterns.

HOW TO READ AND UNDERSTAND REPORTS

An important element in effective control in PPRS is the ability to read and understand reports. Why? Because much of what you need to know is contained in them. Most managers receive two or three kinds of reports. These normally include financial/budget, production, and personnel reports.

Financial reports often seem hard to read because of the detail and complexity of the data presented. Also, interpretation usually must be extracted from the report. WHAT TO DO: You must determine what is important and what is not. On your budget printout, what does certain information mean? Details about understanding financial data are found in Chapter 9.

Production reports often contain more than cost and unit data. They may also include sales data and projections. HINTS: Look for trends. Projections are often based on past performance and should be interpreted with a grain of salt. Look at past history and make your own judgment. Also, know the source of reports and how the reports impact your area.

Personnel reports include such information as personnel cost data, overtime, seniority information, safety, utilization of personnel, absence records, sick time taken, vacation, and so forth. While not as quantitative as production and financial reports, personnel reports provide important information and require interpretation.

As you monitor employee performance, you can observe two types of behavior patterns: *emerging* and *persistent*. The former requires a very timely response—catch it right at the beginning! Persistent patterns call for a similar strategy; but you need more discussion, coaching, reinforcement, and patience. HINT: Try active feedback as an effective tool.

Oftentimes, your actions can produce unintended results, which can be desirable, undesirable, or neutral. The best way to deal with them is to anticipate and put them in perspective. Ask yourself, "Do the advantages of the positive results outweigh the disadvantages of the negative results? Do you want the unintended results to continue?"

> A CASE-IN-POINT: Bill is a fast worker but burns up his equipment because he does not attend to it. Burning up the equipment is an unintended result, and you will want to discuss it with Bill. But it may come down to a choice of either getting high output or having a well-maintained machine. The choice may not be so easy.

HOW TO MEASURE PROGRESS THROUGH THE PERFORMANCE EVALUATION

Performance evaluation is a central element of any program aimed at improving and maintaining employee performance. The evaluation process accomplishes three important objectives:

1. It helps both you and the employee gain a clear picture of how the employee has performed during the period under review.

2. It provides a basis for planning for the future, both in terms of the employee's work and the work of the organization.

3. It provides a formal record of performance. In a case where an employee faces discharge for poor performance, the record should contain the reasons. On the other hand, if an employee has established a good record over a period of years, this should be so reflected. If this employee leaves the company and later asks to return, the record will serve as his or her recommendation.

Performance evaluation is best used when it is part of a system like PPRS. It involves higher level management, the personnel department, and employees. Basically, the system should incorporate the following:

1. Objectives and standards

2. Job descriptions

3. Evaluation procedures

In the PPRS system, performance review comes as Step No. 7, after establishing goals, objectives, standards, and agreements on these. YOUR RESPONSIBILITIES: Your job, basically, is to conduct the review as needed and render an accurate evaluation. You also have an active part in maintaining the system and providing information useful for keeping up or improving upon the system.

Performance review is normally a two-stage process. First, you prepare a written evaluation of the employee's performance. Then, you discuss the evaluation with the employee during an evaluation interview.

HOW TO MEASURE ACTUAL PERFORMANCE

The most common method of measuring employee performance is the *absolute standard*. It's also used to measure student performance in school, using grades such as A, B, C, D.

The advantage of measuring employee performance by an absolute standard is its simplicity. An employee's performance rating for a given time period can be calculated, recorded, and compared to the ratings for earlier or later periods, or to those of other employees. The disadvantage is what educators call "grade inflation." Many managers tend to be lenient in their evaluations, giving most people passing grades because they want to be "nice guys."

Often they don't want the extra work involved or the hard feelings associated with criticizing their subordinates.

Figures 5.6 and 5.7 are two examples of forms used by the Globe Tool and Engineering Company of Dayton, Ohio, to evaluate the performance of employees. The first is used to evaluate hourly workers. It contains a few words of explanation, both of the qualities being measured and of the standards used to measure them. The second is used by the same company to evaluate the performance of salaried employees. Because of greater work complexity and the difficulty of measuring exact output, this form includes much more detail than the other.

In an effort to force managers to be more realistic and honest in their evaluation of employees, some companies have adopted various methods of *comparative measurement*. For example, you might list members of a work team and rank them in order of their overall performance. The advantage of this approach is that it forces you to differentiate among employees. The disadvantage is that, in some cases, there may be no significant difference in performance among them. In a high-performing department, this artificial method of comparison can be misleading and demoralizing.

In an effort to avoid the disadvantages of either the absolute standard or comparative techniques, personnel specialists have developed methods of evaluating performance on the basis of the specific activities required for success on a particular job. This is called the *critical incidents* method.

The performance evaluation form for the job in question would list a number of such activities, and you would be asked to indicate how regularly and reliably the employee performs them.

> EXAMPLE: When materials come into the workroom, the employee checks the list for accuracy, inspects the materials, and places them on the conveyor in proper order with no damage to the material.

A variation on the critical incidents approach is the *weighted checklist*. A list might be prepared containing some items that describe the employee being evaluated. A typical checklist would look like this:

EMPLOYEE MERIT RATING SHEET
GLOBE TOOL & ENGINEERING COMPANY

Employee Name _____ Job Title _____ Job No. _____ Date _____

Factor	Descriptive Levels					Substantiation	Points
Quality	Ability to work to specifications						
	<u>Excellent</u> Always works to specs & under difficult conditions	<u>Good</u> Rarely does poor work	<u>Fair</u> Occasionally does poor work	<u>Poor</u> Frequently does poor work	<u>Very poor</u> Very often does poor work		
Reliability	Compliance with company policies, procedures, attendance, promptness, conventional appearance, personal hygiene, safe work habits						
	<u>Excellent</u> Always in compliance with all requirements	<u>Good</u> Rarely fails to comply	<u>Fair</u> Normal compliance	<u>Unreliable</u> Often undependable	<u>Very unreliable</u> Completely undependable		
Quantity	Productivity level of acceptable quality						
	<u>Excellent</u> Consistently turns out top quality	<u>Good</u> Frequently turns out more than called for	<u>Fair</u> Occasionally turns out less than expected	<u>Poor</u> Frequently turns out less than expected	<u>Very poor</u> Consistently turns out very little work		

FIGURE 5.6

Factor	Descriptive Levels					Substantiation	Points
	Willingness to comply, cooperate, get along with supervision and fellow workers						
	<u>Excellent</u>	<u>Good</u>	<u>Fair</u>	<u>Poor</u>	<u>Very poor</u>		
Attitude	Always cheerfully complies with manager's objectives; gets along with fellow workers	Usually complies, cooperates and gets along	Occasionally complies begrudgingly or has problems with fellow workers	Frequently reacts begrudgingly; does not get along well with fellow workers	Generally un-cooperative; difficult to work with		
	Knowledge, experience, skills levels						
	<u>Excellent</u>	<u>Good</u>	<u>Fair</u>	<u>Low</u>	<u>Very low</u>		
Job Knowledge	Performs all aspects of job; very rarely requires assistance	Performs most aspects of job; very rarely requires assistance	Quite often requires assistance when performing complex functions	Performs limited functions, or requires close supervision	Normally requires close supervision		
						TOTAL	

Rater _____ Job Title _____ Dept. _____
Date For Employee Review _____ Date Accomplished _____ By S/S _____

Courtesy of Globe Tool and Engineering Co., Dayton, Ohio

FIGURE 5.6 (continued)

GUIDE TO EMPLOYEE PERFORMANCE APPRAISAL
AND
PERFORMANCE DEGREES

Performance Factors	5 Far Exceeds Job Requirements	4 Exceeds Job Requirements	3 Meets Job Requirements	2 Needs Some Improvement	1 Does Not Meet Minimum Requirements
Quality	Leaps tall buildings with a single bound.	Must take running start to leap over tall buildings.	Can only leap over a medium or short building with no spires.	Crashes into building when attempting to jump over it.	Cannot recognize building at all, what's more jump.
Timeliness	Is faster than a speeding bullet.	Is as fast as a speeding bullet.	Not quite as fast as a speeding bullet.	Would you believe a slow bullet?	Wounds self with bullet when attempting to shoot gun.
Initiative	Is stronger than a locomotive.	Is stronger than a bull elephant.	Is stronger than a bull.	Shoots the bull.	Smells like a bull.
Adaptability	Walks on water consistently.	Walks on water in emergencies.	Washes with water.	Drinks water.	Passes water in emergencies.
Communication	Talks with God.	Talks with the angels.	Talks to himself.	Argues with himself.	Loses those arguments.

FIGURE 5.6 (continued)

SALARIED PERFORMANCE REVIEW
(Nonexempt)
GLOBE TOOL & ENGINEERING COMPANY

Name	Department	Date
Position	Appraised By	

Statements descriptive of your performance are grouped on the following pages in blocks of four. To the right of each statement is a row of squares (numbered from 0 to 9). You are asked to mark an X in one of these squares to show how well the employee's performance coincides with each statement. (An X in square #0 means that the statement is a very poor description of the individual's performance. An X in #9 means that the statement applies very well. The squares between represent intermediate degrees of fit.)

Read all four statements in each block before marking any item in that block. Select from the four the one that is most descriptive of this individual's performance. Mark it along the (0 to 9) scale in the square that you believe to be most appropriate. Then select the next most descriptive statement, mark it along the (0 to 9) scale—except that it must be one or more degrees lower than your previous statement. Continue to mark the third and fourth statements in the block, ensuring that each is lower than the preceding one.

Should you feel that one of your four evaluations is in fact equal to one already marked, you will be allowed one equal or "tied" evaluation to occur. Please do not skip any statements.

MARGINAL   —A provisional zone for inexperienced newcomers and others whose performance is *clearly below the acceptability level.* Incumbents should either move up in the range or out of the position in a relatively short time.

ADEQUATE   —*Adequate progress* being made from "marginal" to "competent" zone.

COMPETENT   —Zone for *consistently satisfactory* performance of job as defined by job description.

COMMENDABLE —Zone for seasoned employees whose performance is *noticeably better* than "competent."

DISTINGUISHED —This zone is normally reserved for those individuals whose *outstanding* performance is *clearly obvious to all.*

FIGURE 5.7

			M	A	CPT	CBL	D				
			0	1	2 3	4 5	6 7	8 9			

1. A Keeps talks on discussion level and above
   argument level. ( ) ( ) ( ) ( ) ( ) ( ) ( ) ( ) ( ) ( )
   B Performs assignments efficiently and
   speedily. ( ) ( ) ( ) ( ) ( ) ( ) ( ) ( ) ( ) ( )
   C Performs duties with a minimum of
   supervision. ( ) ( ) ( ) ( ) ( ) ( ) ( ) ( ) ( ) ( )
   D Assumes his share of blame when things
   go wrong. ( ) ( ) ( ) ( ) ( ) ( ) ( ) ( ) ( ) ( )

	M	A	CPT	CBL	D
	0 1 2 3 4 5 6 7 8 9				

2. A Follows works schedule closely. ( ) ( ) ( ) ( ) ( ) ( ) ( ) ( ) ( ) ( )
   B Has good work habits. ( ) ( ) ( ) ( ) ( ) ( ) ( ) ( ) ( ) ( )
   C Is a credit to his department. ( ) ( ) ( ) ( ) ( ) ( ) ( ) ( ) ( ) ( )
   D Makes decisions promptly. ( ) ( ) ( ) ( ) ( ) ( ) ( ) ( ) ( ) ( )

	M	A	CPT	CBL	D
	0 1 2 3 4 5 6 7 8 9				

3. A Insists on good housekeeping. ( ) ( ) ( ) ( ) ( ) ( ) ( ) ( ) ( ) ( )
   B Is determined to make good. ( ) ( ) ( ) ( ) ( ) ( ) ( ) ( ) ( ) ( )
   C Is good at developing better
   ways to do a job. ( ) ( ) ( ) ( ) ( ) ( ) ( ) ( ) ( ) ( )
   D Is well liked by others. ( ) ( ) ( ) ( ) ( ) ( ) ( ) ( ) ( ) ( )

	M	A	CPT	CBL	D
	0 1 2 3 4 5 6 7 8 9				

4. A Has a good attendance record. ( ) ( ) ( ) ( ) ( ) ( ) ( ) ( ) ( ) ( )
   B Is considered one of the team. ( ) ( ) ( ) ( ) ( ) ( ) ( ) ( ) ( ) ( )
   C Is well suited for his type of work. ( ) ( ) ( ) ( ) ( ) ( ) ( ) ( ) ( ) ( )
   D Views the bright side of things. ( ) ( ) ( ) ( ) ( ) ( ) ( ) ( ) ( ) ( )

	M	A	CPT	CBL	D
	0 1 2 3 4 5 6 7 8 9				

5. A Always takes the lead. ( ) ( ) ( ) ( ) ( ) ( ) ( ) ( ) ( ) ( )
   B Can take criticism without getting angry. ( ) ( ) ( ) ( ) ( ) ( ) ( ) ( ) ( ) ( )
   C Goes out of his way to help others. ( ) ( ) ( ) ( ) ( ) ( ) ( ) ( ) ( ) ( )
   D Promotes high working morale ( ) ( ) ( ) ( ) ( ) ( ) ( ) ( ) ( ) ( )

	M	A	CPT	CBL	D
	0 1 2 3 4 5 6 7 8 9				

6. A Is eager to accept any assignment. ( ) ( ) ( ) ( ) ( ) ( ) ( ) ( ) ( ) ( )
   B Keeps work output up to schedule. ( ) ( ) ( ) ( ) ( ) ( ) ( ) ( ) ( ) ( )
   C Remains calm even under heavy pressure. ( ) ( ) ( ) ( ) ( ) ( ) ( ) ( ) ( ) ( )
   D Spends his workday on company
   business. ( ) ( ) ( ) ( ) ( ) ( ) ( ) ( ) ( ) ( )

FIGURE 5.7 (continued)

		M	A	CPT	CBL	D				
		0	1	2	3	4	5	6	7	8	9
7.	A Can take a joke well.	( )	( )	( )	( )	( )	( )	( )	( )	( )	( )
	B Has plenty of initiative.	( )	( )	( )	( )	( )	( )	( )	( )	( )	( )
	C Likes things clean and orderly.	( )	( )	( )	( )	( )	( )	( )	( )	( )	( )
	D Makes a good impression on others.	( )	( )	( )	( )	( )	( )	( )	( )	( )	( )

		M	A	CPT	CBL	D				
		0	1	2	3	4	5	6	7	8	9
8.	A Has the knowledge to carry out this job.	( )	( )	( )	( )	( )	( )	( )	( )	( )	( )
	B Is neat and orderly in his work.	( )	( )	( )	( )	( )	( )	( )	( )	( )	( )
	C Likes to take on responsibility.	( )	( )	( )	( )	( )	( )	( )	( )	( )	( )
	D Seeks all available information on a problem.	( )	( )	( )	( )	( )	( )	( )	( )	( )	( )

		M	A	CPT	CBL	D				
		0	1	2	3	4	5	6	7	8	9
9.	A Approaches tense situations calmly.	( )	( )	( )	( )	( )	( )	( )	( )	( )	( )
	B Has effective leadership ability.	( )	( )	( )	( )	( )	( )	( )	( )	( )	( )
	C Has training and experience necessary for the job.	( )	( )	( )	( )	( )	( )	( )	( )	( )	( )
	D Is loyal to superiors and to company.	( )	( )	( )	( )	( )	( )	( )	( )	( )	( )

		M	A	CPT	CBL	D				
		0	1	2	3	4	5	6	7	8	9
10.	A Has prepared himself for the work he is doing.	( )	( )	( )	( )	( )	( )	( )	( )	( )	( )
	B Is glad to tell of the accomplishments of others.	( )	( )	( )	( )	( )	( )	( )	( )	( )	( )
	C Is systematic in his approach to his work.	( )	( )	( )	( )	( )	( )	( )	( )	( )	( )
	D Sticks to job even when not closely supervised.	( )	( )	( )	( )	( )	( )	( )	( )	( )	( )

		M	A	CPT	CBL	D				
		0	1	2	3	4	5	6	7	8	9
11.	A Backs up company decisions when made.	( )	( )	( )	( )	( )	( )	( )	( )	( )	( )
	B Carries out policies established by superiors.	( )	( )	( )	( )	( )	( )	( )	( )	( )	( )
	C Cooperates with others in getting the job done.	( )	( )	( )	( )	( )	( )	( )	( )	( )	( )
	D Is levelheaded in tense situations.	( )	( )	( )	( )	( )	( )	( )	( )	( )	( )

FIGURE 5.7 (continued)

		M	A	CPT	CBL	D
		0 1 2 3 4 5 6 7 8 9
12.	A Has orderly work habits.	( ) ( ) ( ) ( ) ( ) ( ) ( ) ( ) ( ) ( )
	B Has outstanding ability in the type of work he does.	( ) ( ) ( ) ( ) ( ) ( ) ( ) ( ) ( ) ( )
	C Is a consistent performer.	( ) ( ) ( ) ( ) ( ) ( ) ( ) ( ) ( ) ( )
	D Thinks well on his feet and in emergencies.	( ) ( ) ( ) ( ) ( ) ( ) ( ) ( ) ( ) ( )

		M	A	CPT	CBL	D
		0 1 2 3 4 5 6 7 8 9
13.	A Is willing to accept varied responsibilities.	( ) ( ) ( ) ( ) ( ) ( ) ( ) ( ) ( ) ( )
	B Likes to help people.	( ) ( ) ( ) ( ) ( ) ( ) ( ) ( ) ( ) ( )
	C Looks after the company's interests.	( ) ( ) ( ) ( ) ( ) ( ) ( ) ( ) ( ) ( )
	D Strives to do a better job.	( ) ( ) ( ) ( ) ( ) ( ) ( ) ( ) ( ) ( )

		M	A	CPT	CBL	D
		0 1 2 3 4 5 6 7 8 9
14.	A His personality invites the confidence of others.	( ) ( ) ( ) ( ) ( ) ( ) ( ) ( ) ( ) ( )
	B Is easy to get along with.	( ) ( ) ( ) ( ) ( ) ( ) ( ) ( ) ( ) ( )
	C Is right on hand when needed.	( ) ( ) ( ) ( ) ( ) ( ) ( ) ( ) ( ) ( )
	D Plans his work.	( ) ( ) ( ) ( ) ( ) ( ) ( ) ( ) ( ) ( )

		M	A	CPT	CBL	D
		0 1 2 3 4 5 6 7 8 9
15.	A Does extra work in order to learn.	( ) ( ) ( ) ( ) ( ) ( ) ( ) ( ) ( ) ( )
	B Follows through on tasks assigned.	( ) ( ) ( ) ( ) ( ) ( ) ( ) ( ) ( ) ( )
	C Handles people well.	( ) ( ) ( ) ( ) ( ) ( ) ( ) ( ) ( ) ( )
	D Is optimistic in his approach to problems.	( ) ( ) ( ) ( ) ( ) ( ) ( ) ( ) ( ) ( )

APPRAISAL INTERVIEW COMMENTS _____

_____

_____

_____

_____

_____

Employee's Signature

FIGURE 5.7 (continued)

Courtesy of Globe Tool and Engineering Company, Dayton, Ohio

THIS EMPLOYEE TYPICALLY:

_____ Gets his/her reports out on time.

_____ Reports to work late.

_____ Talks with co-workers.

_____ Solicits donations among co-workers.

_____ Gives a lot of suggestions.

_____ Cooperates with others.

_____ Completes tasks on time.

_____ Runs above standard.

_____ Criticizes the company unnecessarily.

_____ Bickers and argues with the manager.

_____ Does exactly what he/she is told.

_____ Has a pleasant personality.

The approach is relatively painless because you are not required to be critical of an employee but merely describe his or her behavior. The interpretation of your response is then left up to the personnel department or whoever is responsible for the evaluation system.

Most of these approaches utilize quantitative techniques; that is, the rater gives an assessment that can be converted into a number figure. By using a scale, the degree of variation can be measured. The most common quantitative technique is the *conventional scale*, where you rate a person on several characteristics according to some numerical value or description such as Excellent, Very Good, Good, Fair, Poor, and Very Poor. By and large, these scales are easy to work with, and they yield a quantitative score that can be discussed with the employee in specific terms.

Another type of scale developed in recent years is the *behaviorally anchored scale*. Here, a predetermined importance is established for each description. Figure 5.8 shows an example of a behaviorally anchored rating scale for a stock clerk. This scale focuses on behavior and requires you to base your rating on actual, observable behavior rather than interpretations. For this reason, it is becoming increasingly popular in industry.

BEHAVIORALLY ANCHORED RATING SCALE
STOCK CLERK EFFICIENCY IN FILLING ORDERS

Outstanding	10	Knows where items are, how much is on stock, and gets them quickly.
Commendable	8	Knows where items are, how much is on stock, and gets them in reasonable time.
Good	6	Checks the right sources on what is in stock; gets items without undue delay.
Fair	5	Customer delays of 15 to 20 minutes are common on nonstandard items.
Substandard	4	Sometimes caught in bottleneck; gets help from other clerks.
Poor	3	Usually is at station but finds things only when other clerks help. Sometimes absent or away from station and finds things after searching for 30 minutes.
Unacceptable	1	Sometimes not available and gets in the way when present.

FIGURE 5.8

HOW TO CONDUCT THE EVALUATION INTERVIEW SUCCESSFULLY

When conducting an evaluation interview with an employee, you can use one of three approaches:

1. The traditional approach, or *tell and sell*. You simply inform the employee how his or her performance has been evaluated, then try to persuade the employee that your evaluation is valid.

2. *Tell and listen*. You inform the employee of the evaluation, then listen and attempt to tune in on the employee's feelings and thoughts about the situation.

3. *Tell and listen with problem solving.* The frame of mind is analytical—wanting to search out problems and get to causes. This approach especially stimulates growth and is the most productive way to handle the interview.

Success depends on your attitude. If you see the evaluation as a distasteful job to get out of the way as quickly as possible, the employee will see it that way too. On the other hand, if you see the evaluation interview as a means of accomplishing something positive for both the employee and the company, the chances are good that the result will be positive.

Obviously, both you and the employee should be prepared for the evaluation interview. WHAT TO DO: Go over the employee's records and jot down or keep in mind the points to be covered. Establish a time for the interview sufficiently in advance, enabling the employee to prepare also.

Set aside sufficient time for the discussion and try to eliminate interruptions. Of course, the evaluation interview should be done in private.

An informal, open atmosphere usually is best for a meaningful exchange. SUGGESTION: An effective way to open the interview is to ask the employee's opinions and to encourage him or her to talk by asking appropriate questions. A good manager is invariably a good listener. Many employees have some idea about what they are doing well and where they can improve. Most are willing to discuss their performance if you give them a chance.

The performance review should begin on a positive note. Discuss employee strengths first. If you use an evaluation form, you can address the evaluation item by item, starting with favorable items and proceeding to less favorable ones. HINT: Try the sandwich technique here. The idea is to sandwich the bad things between the good things, thereby keeping the overall atmosphere positive.

The employee's work is, of course, the central theme of the discussion. Discuss results in specific terms, not generalities. The employee has to know exactly what it is that needs improvement. Otherwise, he will just think you don't like him. This is harmful to self-confidence and can cause various reactions, mostly bad.

After the session, you should:

1. Record the important points.
2. Evaluate *your* performance.

3. Follow up.

Even if there is a formal record, you should still record anything that occurred during the session. This information can be helpful for future sessions and for ongoing coaching. Once an improvement plan is in place, it must be implemented. It's your responsibility to make sure the plan is carried out and to assist whenever appropriate. Coaching, then, becomes an important part of follow-up, guiding the employee and ensuring that the plan is carried out.

KEY ISSUES TO AVOID IN PERFORMANCE EVALUATIONS

Here are four common errors managers tend to make in evaluating employees:

1. *The "Halo" and the "Horns" Effects.* You may evaluate an employee low or high by a general impression you have of the person. Something the employee has done stands out in your mind and you base your evaluation on that. For example, an open, friendly, and very cooperative attitude may make a favorable impression on you. So you lean on these traits in making the evaluation. However, to be more objective, you should concentrate on such factors as the quality and quantity of the employee's work.

2. *Leniency.* You may rate an employee higher than the performance justifies because you want to be nice, to avoid unpleasant situations, and to remain "friends." Leniency is one of the most common evaluation errors. The opposite, of course, is undue strictness.

3. *Average Tendency.* Some managers tend to rate people as "average," particularly if they do not know them well. They play it safe. Often, this is a convenient way for you to avoid your responsibility.

4. *Opportunity Bias.* There is tendency on the part of managers to give a higher rating to the more visible and a lower rating to the less so.

EXAMPLE: A machine operator working on a certain project may be more visible than other machine operators. The evaluation should, of course, relate to a person's role. But if the role contains more opportunity to show specific results, you should be on guard for potential opportunity bias.

Everyday work problems are difficult to keep up with on a regular basis. Yet if you do not deal with the problems on the spot, there is a tendency to develop the "black book approach." This occurs when the manager makes notes in his or her little black book and unloads everything at the performance appraisal. By not correcting and telling employees on the spot, a lot of time and energy is wasted in work problems that go unresolved. Performance appraisal then becomes an exercise in "heapmanship," where the manager heaps one event on top of another, then unloads the whole pile in a dramatic gesture to point out to the employee the problems he or she is having. Not only is this poor management; *it's not cricket.*

The performance review session should reveal very few surprises. It should sum up the problems that should be known by the time of the appraisal session. If the work problems are monitored regularly, the employee will already know what to expect and what the problems are.

HOW TO EFFECTIVELY JUDGE PERFORMANCE OVER THE LONG HAUL

It's not too difficult to get top performance for a day or two. The real challenge is to sustain it. Simply put, there's no shortcut for building the good performance habit. It requires a deliberate effort and skill in reinforcing and maintaining performance.

WHAT TO DO: Follow the "logic of the line." That is, relate present tasks to the larger picture. Then you and your employees will understand your jobs better and probably be better at it. It's been demonstrated over and over that the knowledgeable worker is also the committed worker. SUGGESTION: Try briefings and seminars about different facets of the operation. Other ideas include tours of the facilities, job rotation, newsletters, product testing, and evaluation. These simple approaches can provide a spark that renews enthusiasm and commitment to the job.

Above-average performance is, of course, the ideal situation. Your main concern here is to maintain performance at the present level. The best approach is positive reinforcement, where recognition and other reinforcements are given for the exceptional performance.

When performance is *average*, you need to stimulate and challenge the employee to set and reach new goals. Dealing with average performance is more difficult than it sometimes seems because there is always the possibility that performance will drop once people plateau at a certain level. Their self-image as an average performer can easily slip to the margin where their performance barely meets standards.

The *below-average* performer creates the greatest problems and, unfortunately, usually gets the most attention. Below-average performance calls for remedial action. This may be in the form of punishment or positive and negative reinforcement. Feedback must be given so the worker knows where he or she stands. Disciplinary action is and should remain a final resolution. It is a last resort if all other attempts fail.

HOW TO ENFORCE AND MAINTAIN DISCIPLINE

The first thing needed in disciplinary action is a system that follows the principles of behavioral change, especially the ones that work in your situation.

Disciplinary action should progress systematically through a series of steps, such as: (1) oral reprimand, (2) written reprimand, (3) probation, (4) punishment, (5) dismissal or transfer. Many times the procedure is defined by the organization. The following checklist will help you develop and follow a systematic procedure.

CHECKLIST FOR DISCIPLINARY PROCEDURE

☑ GATHER YOUR FACTS. Find out exactly what happened: why, when, where, and under what circumstances.

☑ ARRANGE A DISCUSSION WITH THE EMPLOYEE. Hold a meeting in accordance with your system. If a union is involved, follow the procedure specified in the contract.

☑ REVIEW THE FACTS WITH THE EMPLOYEE. Emphasize behavior and results.

☑ USE POSITIVE REINFORCEMENT. "Here's what I would like to see." "You did that job really well last month. I'd like to see you do that again. Let's look at how you might get back on track."

☑ NEGATIVE REINFORCEMENT IS NEXT. If the employee is not responding to positive reinforcement, use negative reinforcement. "If you get this problem resolved, I won't have to reprimand you." Remember: *negative reinforcement removes* the negative consequence; it is much different from *punishment*, which *applies* the negative consequence.

☑ IF NEGATIVE REINFORCEMENT FAILS, USE PUNISHMENT. Follow your disciplinary penalty system in this regard, perhaps using a progression as shown above.

☑ DISCUSS CORRECTIVE ACTION. Regardless of where you are on this checklist, focus on action that will correct the problem behavior. Be constructive even when administering punishment. "The rule says that this calls for a three-day layoff, and I am enforcing the rule. However, when you return, I'd like to review things with you and plan what you'll do to improve."

☑ KEEP A RECORD OF YOUR DISCUSSION. Take notes. Outline your session and strategy in advance.

☑ INFORM THE EMPLOYEE OF ALL ACTIONS TO BE TAKEN.

☑ IF ALL OTHER STEPS FAIL, SEVER THE EMPLOYEE. PREPARE FOR DISMISSAL. Process the necessary paperwork. A transfer might be appropriate in some circumstances, but it is too often an easy way out for you but unloads a problem employee on some other manager. Do unto others————! Bite the bullet and be decisive. Do not look back and do not waffle the decision with if's, or's, maybe's, possibly's, and other postscripts. On the other hand, you may want to arrange for further departure counseling once your decision is made to sever the employee.

When behavior is out of line, it's best to begin with feedback. If that action restores discipline, so much the better. But what if the worker does not respond? Then you need to use positive reinforcement. Emphasize the positive aspects of what the worker is doing. In fact, try using it along with feedback. If positive reinforcement does not work, then negative reinforcement is your next choice. When this does not work, punishment is probably needed. If this does not get results, the last resort is termination or transfer.

Discipline is more than punishment. By the time punishment is needed, discipline has failed. Maintaining the quality of discipline means using all the tools at your disposal.

Here are six guidelines for you to use:

1. Keep your focus and energy on objectives—results.
2. Recognize when discipline is failing.
3. Give positive recognition, reinforcement, and appreciation.
4. Use active feedback; show interest and understanding of employee problems.
5. Share your enthusiasm. Is something worth doing well? Say so and show it.
6. Apply the incentive system to provide need satisfaction. Influence and support attempts to improve the incentive system.

When actual job results, objectives, and accomplishments do not coincide with predetermined standards for success, this calls for a disciplinary interview. Your purpose here is to determine the problem and who owns it. Then, both parties can work on a solution plan.

To achieve the main objectives of the disciplinary interview, use these basic guidelines:

1. *Focus on actual performance results.* Do not approach the problem as a personal failure on the part of the employee.
2. *Be sure the employee understands* the performance you are concerned about and how it leads to desired results and objectives. Be specific and give examples.
3. *Identify possible causes of the problem.* It's important to have a mutual and realistic understanding of the problem and who owns it.
4. *Develop goals and action plans.* The plan must be specific, detailed, and in writing.

The main purpose of disciplinary action should be to restore self-discipline while avoiding the need for dismissal. WHAT TO DO: Use techniques that will get information across while getting the employee's commitment to improve performance. Here are some suggestions:[2]

1. *Keep the matter private.* Managers should never discipline or be disciplined in the presence of peers or subordinates.
2. *Be involved.* Take pains to show the employee that he or she is uppermost on your mind at the moment.
3. *Take one point at a time.* Don't confuse the employee by letting loose with all the complaints you've kept pent up for weeks and months.
4. *Focus on constructive steps.* Feedback must be specific and provide the employee with information needed for good performance.
5. *Be consistent everytime.* Do not ignore rule violations, especially in the beginning.
6. *Avoid saying "always."* Reserve the word for those rare cases when it is really true.
7. *Face facts squarely.* Try this sequence: First, strengths, second, weaknesses; and third, improvement plans.
8. *Don't joke about it.* A light touch can seem very heavy to the employee.
9. *Attack the act.* Tell subordinates what is wrong with the work, not with them.
10. *Criticize without comparison.* People compete more effectively and productively when competing against themselves rather than with others.
11. *Recognize your power and role.* Your job is not to make friends; it's to get the work done. So state your feedback clearly and emphatically.

PROVEN TECHNIQUES FOR DEALING WITH WASTE AND ABSENTEEISM

Waste is a matter of attitude and knowledge. Some workers simply do not understand the economics of waste; they need information.

---

[2] Based on G.G. Alpander, "Training First-Line Supervisors to Criticize Constructively," *Personnel Journal,* 59, no. 3 (March 1980).

A CASE-IN-POINT: Consider a grocery store. One case of ketchup dropped and broken means twenty cases need to be sold to recoup the loss. In a department store, one dress ruined or stolen means thirty must be sold to make up the loss. This kind of information can impress people.

WHAT TO DO: Accentuate the positive. Equate efficient and economic use of material with more bonus wages, incentives, profits, and improved competitive position and job security. Your own attitude is going to be of utmost importance. When workers see you using resources efficiently, they will get the message.

Absenteeism is a special case of discipline that, like waste, also reflects attitudes. Encouraging good attendance is often a matter of making the employee feel needed. One of our strongest needs is to feel worthwhile and appreciated. Convey this to the worker, and you can turn absenteeism around.

It's also important to recognize that there are different kinds of absenteeism, and each type must be dealt with in a slightly different way:

1. The *chronic absentee* has a weak ego and little self-discipline. This person doesn't really feel needed and believes "they can get along without me." WHAT TO DO: Stress the importance of the person's presence in the operation. You might mention what happened as a result of that person's not being there: "We had to double up. We had to borrow an employee from another section, which created problems in that section, and we had to put people on overtime because of your absence." Stress the fact that you need to count on that person being there.

2. The *escapist* is often bored on the job, doesn't really feel much challenge. Whenever such a person faces problems that appear trivial, he or she tries to escape from them, setting them aside for another time. WHAT TO DO: Provide challenge. Delegate responsibility and emphasize the opportunities the person has in the organization; even though this job may seem boring, it's a step that will open doors. In the meantime, have the person take on more responsibility.

3. The *immature absentee* does not understand his or her role in the organization. He thinks that work is a game and would rather spend time going hunting or in some other kind of leisure activity. This person needs more orientation about the world of work. Immature absentees are often young and inexperienced. They do not

deliberately intend to hurt the organization, but they are careless and unthinking as far as consequences are concerned.

4. The *abusive absentee* thinks the organization owes her something and takes off because it's a matter of right as far as she is concerned. The abusive absentee usually has some excuse, whether it's a sick horse or an uncle in the hospital; but the real reason is to rip off the organization. WHAT TO DO: You must be direct, firm, and assertive. Do not get drawn into the excuses that the abusive absentee will give you. Hold your ground and even issue threats if necessary: "One more absence and I will have to let you go." The abusive absentee needs to know, in no uncertain terms, that you are upset and concerned and that the behavior must stop.

5. The *legitimate absentee* is not really a problem. This person has a good reason for being absent and does not abuse the policy. It's best to simply take this absence in stride and show your appreciation of normally good attendance.

WHAT HAPPENS WHEN YOU'RE SUCCESSFUL AS A MANAGER?

You can be sure that others, notably peers and superiors, will learn about any unusual performance or activity. Peers, especially, may find it threatening. WHAT TO DO: Be aware of this problem and do not flaunt any successes you have achieved. Also, stay focused on your own goals. Be willing to share your methods, techniques, and insights with other managers. Invite them to observe your operation if they want.

The effect of your unit's performance on the system is even more important than the performance itself. Disrupting the system can booby-trap your efforts. SUGGESTION: The principle here is one of "gradualness." Make progress in steps rather than in leaps.

> EXAMPLE: If your department suddenly unloads 20 percent more finished units on the next department, the other manager will likely react negatively. Find a way to buffer this situation. Talk with the other manager and explain how you are working on performance improvment and that more units will likely be shipped than usual.

PERFORMANCE, JAPANESE STYLE

Thirty years ago, "Made in Japan" had derogatory connotations; it was taken to mean the product was cheap or flimsy. Today, the opposite is true. Japanese industry is admired because of the high-quality products it makes and markets. American managers grumble about the competitive advantage of Japanese industry. The fact is, the Japanese are more productive than their competitors. Customers around the world prefer to buy Japanese products on the basis of their quality, innovation, and relatively low price. Why? The answer to that question can be an instructive lesson for American managers.

The father of the modern Japanese quality control philosophy is Dr. W. E. Deming, an American.[3] Many years ago, Dr. Deming taught his philosophy to Japanese managers. Today, many American companies have finally adopted it. The Deming philosophy of quality control starts with some very basic ideas. For example:

1. It's not enough for everybody to do his best. Being effective requires direction. People can be made to do better through proper direction, and statistical techniques can furnish that direction.

2. It is not enough that top management commit itself to quality and productivity. Managers must know to what they are committed; they must know just exactly what quality and productivity mean in terms of their product.

The Japanese philosophy has little regard for top management quality control committees unless these committees actually practice these principles:

1. *Innovate and plan for the future.* Behind this is the idea of allocating resources for the long-range needs of the company and the customer. Dr. Deming emphasizes training managers and other personnel in the skills that are required for quality control.

2. *Learn the new philosophy.* This philosophy simply does not accept such things as defective material, defective workmanship, shoddy products, or equipment that is out of order.

3. *De-emphasize mass inspection for quality.* Rely on vendors who use statistical techniques in quality control. Quality by inspection is outmoded. Why? The final inspector is not there to sort out the good from the bad but rather simply to reaffirm product

---

[3] In 1951, the Japanese industry honored Dr. Deming by creating the Deming prize, which is awarded annually for innovation in quality control. This is one of the most cherished awards in Japan, and it goes to the firm that has made the most significant achievements in quality control.

quality. There should be no surprises by the time of final inspection, and the Japanese do not rely on final inspection to do the job.

4. *Reduce the number of suppliers for the same item.* Demand that suppliers use statistical process control and to furnish evidence of this.

5. *Use statistical techniques to identify the sources of waste.* Encourage managers to use statistical methods to identify problems and defects.

6. *Eliminate fear throughout the organization.* Tremendous economic losses result from a fear to ask questions or to report trouble.

7. *Help to reduce waste.* Put people together in teams that combine the perspectives of design, research, sales, production, and so forth. Japanese workers are much more versatile and less specialized than American workers. Japanese workers move around from job to job; it's common to find committees and groups made up of workers from the various areas mentioned. Also, engineers are not detached from production, as they are in American companies.

8. *Eliminate slogans and gimmicks for increasing productivity.* An example is "zero defect." Quality control simply does not happen by exhorting the work force to better performance. Rather, it results from management's expertise in engineering and creating conditions needed for good quality control and productivity.

9. *Take a close look at work standards in production.* Work standards ought to be established from the ground up—from market need and product requirements.

10. *Launch statistical training on a broad scale.* Many people throughout a plant must learn simple but powerful statistical methods. The average Japanese worker is extremely well informed in quality control and statistical techniques—better educated in this regard than his American counterpart.

11. *Retrain people in new skills.* Keep up with changes in materials, methods, product design, and machinery.

12. *Make use of the talent and knowledge on your staff.* Dr. Deming traces one of the obstacles to quality improvement to the executive suite, where senior managers have little idea of what quality control actually involves.

AN AMERICAN COMPANY EXPERIENCE

Can Japanese principles be applied in the United States? Consider the example of a company in Des Moines, Iowa, whose productivity is so high that 120 people do what 400 to 500 employees accomplish in most companies. Employees work a four-day week. Management and workers get along very well. There is almost zero turnover. Employees, management, and their families get together in recreational activities and vacation trips. Does this sound like some utopia? Not at all. The company is called Townsend Engineering. It makes the machines that put the smoke into smoked ham and the basting in a self-basting turkey. True, Townsend is not a conventional assembly-line company. But neither are most industries. Management, according to Townsend engineering, bears a responsibility to employees for their highly productive efforts and for the special attitudes that support the company. Where a company normally gives employees raises in the year following a productive year, Townsend gives employees bonus checks immediately following a job well done. He spontaneously calls meetings to thank employees. The company has a gymnasium and offers company-sponsored vacation trips. Circuses, wiener roasts, softball, and picnics are typical of the outings that Townsend Engineering has for its employees, and management participates along with everyone else. As Ray Townsend says, "Our people are better than average, so we treat them better than average. We grew up as a family in this business, and we are going to stay a family." The Townsend company shows many of the characteristics of Japanese industry. There is a lack of class distinction between management and workers. Employees are versatile on their jobs. There is a high degree of automation, employing the latest technology. And there is the assumption that if you treat people well, they will respond accordingly. Japanese management obviously places high priority on treating people well. So does the Townsend Engineering Company.

CHAPTER 6

Why a New Employee
Is Always a
Management Challenge

*In a free country, it is not always enough to care
about mankind. We must also, sometimes, care for
human beings.*

—DAVID LAWRENCE

"THE challenge of a new employee" has many meanings to first-line managers. Some may think of the hassles and disruptions that come with breaking in a new employee. Others think about what it will do to productivity, or the amount of time that will have to be spent working with the new employee. Yes, the challenge of the new employee can mean problems and sometimes pain. But the *real* challenge is the opportunity to work with someone new, to have a positive influence in developing him or her, and to help that person learn the job and the company. There's a special feeling that goes with knowing you have helped someone become a part of the operation and because of you that employee has developed into a productive, self-confident individual. *This* is the challenge of the new employee, and it's unique to you because only you have direct responsibility for guiding and leading that employee.

The challenge can turn either to gold or dust, depending on how you handle it. This chapter is designed to help you find the gold and mine it.

WHAT'S NEW ABOUT A NEW EMPLOYEE?

When comparing new versus old employees, you'll find differences in at least three areas: proficiency, confidence, and commitment. The new employee lacks all three simply because experience and success have not yet had their turn. You'll also find a fourth difference—attitude. New employees are frequently more open and have fewer preconceived notions of how to do things.

WHAT TO LOOK FOR: Your new employee typically needs assistance, is open to suggestions and guidance, and needs basic information about what you and the company expect. At this point, the new employee doesn't have a strong attitude toward the department and to you. But he or she will soon look for support, as it relates directly to the need for self-esteem. It's important that you recognize your new employee as a person who wants and needs to feel important and worthwhile.

The first and most important thing affecting the new employee is his or her *frame of reference*. As described in Chapter 3, this includes all the influences—past and present—that play upon behavior. For the new employee, the present environment is not yet sufficient to counteract past influences. So what you see is behavior that is influenced a lot by the immediate past.

> EXAMPLE: Often while job hunting the new employee is involved more than at other times with family, friends, school influences, even church. This is because these influences tend to be supportive, and the person turns to these facets of life at a time of need.

The previous job experience will still have an impact on the person's present behavior. If the job had a high-recognition value for the new employee, the influence of that job in the mind of the person at present will still be high.

Many present influences can quickly shape the new employee's attitude. These include orientation procedures, first contact with other employees, and you. WHAT TO KEEP IN MIND: By knowing how the employee's frame of reference affects present attitudes and abilities, you'll be equipped to deal with him or her effectively, and you'll show understanding with which to build support and get cooperation.

THE NEW EMPLOYEE AND YOU

Your basic responsibility to a new employee is to prepare him or her for productive work. This includes:

1. Giving needed information about the job, department, and organization.
2. Training the employee as needed in order to perform the job properly.
3. Assuring fair treatment of the employee.
4. Providing support and job-related guidance.
5. Referring the employee to Personnel and other sources, as needed, when a matter can better be handled by specialists.

The indoctrination process can vary from a brief orientation to an extensive training program. Whatever you do, your role involves more than just giving information. You convey attitudes, too.

EXAMPLE: Even though you may have rush orders to get out, if you don't stop and assist your new employee, you'll lose respect. The employee will turn to others for help and see you mainly as a taskmaster interested only in output and nothing else.

REMEMBER THIS: You are there to assist, and that means having a good attitude. Use this checklist to help you develop the attitudes and skills you need.

CHECKLIST FOR BUILDING GOOD ATTITUDES AND SKILLS

Attitudes

- Are you willing to help?
- Do you take a personal interest?
- Are you sensitive to problems and dilemmas encountered by the new employee?
- Do you foster positive attitudes toward succeeding on the job?
- Do you put yourself in your worker's shoes?

Skills

- Do you listen and speak with empathy, tact, and assertiveness?

- Do you set expectations and models of behavior?

- Do you promote a new employee's career opportunities?

THE PAYOFF PROCESS: HOW EFFECTIVE MANAGING PAYS OFF

With a new employee, it's best to stay with immediate and mid-range objectives rather than elaborate goals. Long-range career development should take place after the employee has mastered the job and is ready to think further ahead. Contrary to popular opinion, career planning is not intended for those who do not know what they want; rather, it is for those who know their interests and capabilities and are ready to make longer term commitments.

TRY THIS APPROACH: Set challenging goals but build them gradually as performance improves.

A CASE-IN-POINT: For a new billing clerk, setting a target of eighty-five customer orders per hour by the end of the first week might be a bit overwhelming. Rather, set the goal in steps: begin with ten orders per hour at 90 percent accuracy (nine out of ten acceptable); then increase that a little bit more each day. It may very well happen that eighty-five orders per hour can be reached sooner than if the entire "dump truck" set of goals were unloaded all at once.

A systematic orientation process uses the following principles:

1. Get employees off to a good start.
2. Provide information and support that will help the new employee build confidence and competence.
3. Understand the new employee and provide opportunities for his or her development.
4. Get the employee acquainted with the organization through a positive first impression that will earn the loyalty and commitment of the employee.

The orientation process should be done in a systematic and comprehensive manner, as will be discussed further in this chapter. What is the payoff? For one, it makes good first impressions; and these, in this case, are lasting. Your efforts will yield cooperation, loyalty, and productivity. And you'll experience lower turnover and increased satisfaction among new employees.

HOW TO ESTABLISH YOUR ROLE IN THE STAFFING PROCESS

Staffing is essentially a process that begins with the creation of a position and ends by filling it with a qualified person. You may not be involved at every step, but nonetheless it's important to be aware of what is involved. Figure 6.1 depicts the staffing process.

Your role will most likely begin by either requesting a new position or filling a vacant one. Occasionally, you may be involved in the initial development of the position; for example, when you analyze the workload in the department and determine a need for another position.

The scenario usually goes like this: The manager requests a position; the superior determines whether it is economically and organizationally possible and in the process may implement a further study of job needs. Then, if the study shows a valid need, approval is granted and Personnel is asked to develop a description and specifications in consultation with the manager. Also, Personnel will set the compensation rate based on whatever system the organization uses. Personnel then advertises the position, screens applicants, and interviews the best prospects. At this point, the manager may become involved in the interviewing, especially for highly skilled hourly or salaried positions.

Who does the hiring? For unskilled and semi-skilled jobs, this is usually left to Personnel. Ideally, each manager should have control over selecting resources used in the department. Realistically, however, there are other parties involved. What's important is that you take charge of the resources at hand and forego the temptation to pin the responsibility on other parties. KEEP THIS IN MIND: Perhaps you cannot hire or fire, but the more you work with those who do, the more influence you will have over these processes.

Personnel typically helps you select the best qualified employee. While you may be required to do paperwork for Personnel, this should not overshadow the basic services and assistance they can provide. Their services are substantial, and if you utilize them properly with a cooperative attitude, you can benefit immensely.

HINT: Maximize the benefit to you by providing input that will help in selecting a proper person for the job.

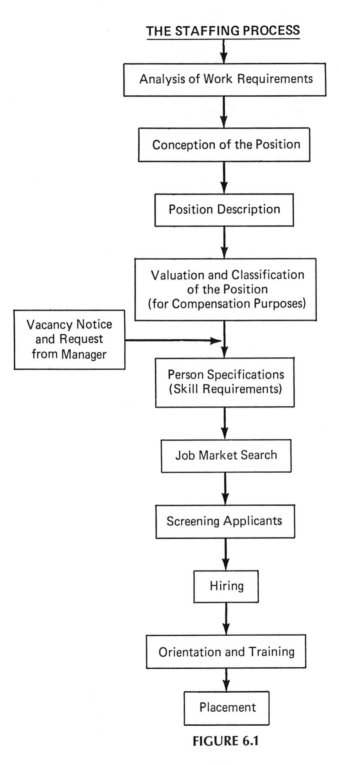

FIGURE 6.1

HOW TO KNOW AND GET WHAT YOU NEED

Before filling a position, the first thing you must do is determine your job needs. This requires knowledge of your department's productivity compared with current and projected demand. Use these steps when you make you assessment:

Step One: Learn the demand for your product/service for the foreseeable future from expert opinion/information, market trends, and your own interpretations and intuitions.

Step Two: Convert this into job needs by taking your present rate of productivity and projecting it into the time frame of the forecast. Determine to what extent it will fill the demand. Compare the difference and convert that into the number of jobs needed to meet the demand.

Step Three: Take inventory of your current personnel (adjusting for turnover), their skill levels, and expected growth in productivity and efficiency. Assess their ability to fill the needs of the future. Consider also the loss of skills due to turnovers.

Step Four: Identify the position and jobs needed after adjusting for expected growth in productivity and efficiency.

Step Five: Get authorization from your superior or from personnel, whichever is the appropriate authorizing agency.

Once you gain approval, the next step is to complete a job analysis for purposes of evaluation and salary determination. This is usually done by Personnel, but through your input, you can help to decide a job's worth.

There are several techniques for analyzing and interpreting the basic job information. One useful approach is to describe the activities involved according to people, data, and things. (See Figure 6.2.) This will help you quickly sort out skills needed on the job. CAUTION: This technique must be used only as a guide; it does not spell out exact requirements.

A position description will show in detail responsibilities and duties in the job, the reporting relationship, and the qualifications needed for the job. (See Figure 6.3.) KEEP IN MIND: For new jobs, much of the information may not be readily available. It's best, then, to list only essential information and allow some room for interpretation.

WORK ACTIVITY ANALYSIS

Data	People	Things
0 Synthesizing	0 Mentoring	0 Setting up
1 Coordinating	1 Negotiating	1 Precision working
2 Analyzing	2 Instructing	2 Operating– controlling
3 Compiling	3 Supervising	3 Driving– operating
4 Computing	4 Diverting	4 Manipulating
5 Copying	5 Persuading	5 Tending
6 Comparing	6 Speaking– signaling	6 Feeding– offbearing
	7 Serving	7 Handling
	8 Taking instructions– helping	

Basic Activities { (bracket grouping Data items 0–6)

Source: U.S. Department of Labor, Manpower Administration, *Handbook for Analyzing Jobs* (Washington, DC: U.S. Government Printing Office, 1972), p. 73. Reprinted in Gary Dessler, *Personnel Management: Modern Concepts and Techniques* (Reston, VA: Reston Publishing Co., 1978), p. 44.

FIGURE 6.2

SAMPLE POSITION DESCRIPTION
Job Description for a Production Control Manager*

TITLE:	Production Control Manager
REPORTS TO:	Assistant Plant Manager
SPECIAL REQUIREMENTS:	High school graduate, college degree preferred. Background in production classes, construction, machine capacities. Ability to understand specifications. Ability to coordinate and manage.
SUPERVISORY RESPONSIBILITY OVER:	Assistant Production Control Manager, Production Control Supervisor, Production Control Schedulers, Clerks, Hourly employees, and such other operations as designated by Plant Manager.
JOB SUMMARY:	Directs the activities of scheduling plant production; procuring raw materials; and maintaining inventory for production and shipping.

*Some items may violate fair employment practice legislation.

DUTIES: Receive, review, enter, and promise all orders. Schedule
                     machinery, manpower, and materials in such a way that
                     the maximum amount of efficiency is obtained from
                     the operating departments. Prepares production sched-
                     ules in accordance with customer requirements and
                     applicable specifications. Coordinates production con-
                     trol with technical and production operations and
                     maintenance. Supervises procurement and raw mate-
                     rials and inventory control. Responsible for all produc-
                     tion schedules, including machine operation,
                     overtime, vacation, etc. Prepares forthcoming sched-
                     ules and advises Plant Manager, Production Manager,
                     and Department Managers of these schedules. Super-
                     vises and coordinates packing, shipping, traffic, freight
                     consolidation operations to ensure most economical
                     freight rates and best delivery. Confers with sales of-
                     fices. Follows up rush and delinquent orders. Confers
                     with Plant Manager, Production Manager, and Plant Ac-
                     countant in maintaining accurate backlogs by product
                     class. Assists in operations report. Receives, reviews,
                     and compiles daily production reports of plant's pro-
                     gress per department. Performs special projects as re-
                     quired. Has authority to hire, fire, promote, demote,
                     train, discipline, and supervise employees under his
                     jurisdiction. Responsible for plant safety, housekeep-
                     ing, scrap, and usage where applicable to his sphere of
                     plant influence. Implements cost reduction and effi-
                     ciency improvement programs. May be responsible for
                     execution of Union agreement.

Developed by U.S. Department of Labor and illustrated in Gary Dessler, *Personnel Management: Modern Concepts and Techniques* (Reston, VA: Reston Publishing Co., 1978), p. 47.

FIGURE 6.3

Once the job description is prepared, the person specifications or "job specs" are developed. These describe the knowledge, attitude, and skills (KAS) needed in the person to be hired. (See Figure 6.4.) Note that KAS are based directly on the duties involved.

The job specs are what management and personnel use for official documentation, advertising, screening, and interviewing.

JOB (PERSON) SPECIFICATIONS

Job Analysis Record Sheet

Identifying Information
Name of incumbent:	A. Adler
Organization/Unit:	Welfare Services
Title:	Welfare Eligibility Examiner
Date:	11/12/88
Interviewer:	E. Jones

Brief Summary of Job
Conducts interviews, completes applications, determines eligibility, provides information to community sources regarding food stamp program; refers noneligible food stamp applicants to other applicable community resource agencies.

Tasks
1. (Task 1 has been developed above.)

2. Decides (determines) eligiblity of applicant in order to complete client's application for food stamps using regulatory policies as guide.

   Knowledge required
   Knowledge of contents and meaning of items on standard application form.
   Knowledge of Social–Health Services food stamp regulatory policies.
   Knowledge of statutes relating to Social–Health Services food stamp program.

   Skills required
   None.

   Abilities required
   Ability to read and understand complex instructions such as regulatory policies.
   Ability to read and understand a variety of procedural instructions, written and oral, and convert these to proper actions.
   Ability to use simple arithmetic: addition and subtraction.
   Ability to translate requirements into language appropriate to laymen.

   Physical activities
   Sedentary.

   Environmental conditions
   None.

Typical work incidents
Working with people beyond giving and receiving instructions.

Interest areas
Communication of data.
Business contact with people.
Working for the presumed good of people.

3. Decides upon, describes, and explains other agencies available for client to contact in order to assist and refer client to appropriate community resource using worker's knowledge of resources available and knowledge of client's needs.

Knowledge required
Knowledge of functions of various assistance agencies.
Knowledge of community resources available and their locations.
Knowledge of referral procedures.

Skills required
None.

Abilities required
Ability to extract (discern) persons' needs from oral discussion.
Ability to give simple oral and written instructions to persons.

Physical activities
Sedentary.

Environmental conditions
None.

Typical work incidents
Working with people beyond giving and receiving instructions.

Interest areas
Communication of data.
Business contact with people.
Abstract and creative problem solving.
Working for presumed good of people.

4. Explains (describes) policies and regulations appropriate to applicant's case in order to inform applicants of their status with regard to agency's eligiblity guidelines using regulations and policies.

Knowledge required
Knowledge of agency eligibility guidelines, regulations, and policies.

Skills required
None.

FIGURE 6.4

Abilities required
Ability to read and understand moderately complex instructions, such as guidelines, regulations, and policies.
Ability to apply written instructions such as guidelines, regulations, and policies to a variety of situations.
Ability to give simple verbal explanations of applicable guidelines, regulations, and policies.
Ability to express orally simple mathematical calculations.

Physical activities
Sedentary.

Environmental conditions
None.

Typical work incidents
Influencing people in their opinions, attitudes, or judgments about ideas or things.
Working with people beyond giving and receiving instructions.

Interest areas
Communication of data.
Business contact with people.
Abstract and creative problem solving.
Works for the presumed good of people.

5. Evaluates information gained from home–visit interview and observation in order to decide if home conditions are consistent with information given on original application using original application and agency's housing standards as guide.

Knowledge required
Knowledge of agency housing standards.
Knowledge of information contained on original application form.

Skills required
None.

Abilities required
Ability to read and understand written standards.
Ability to make accurate observations.
Ability to apply written standards to a variety of observations.

FIGURE 6.4 (continued)

Thus, it should be as specific as possible. Also, once set, the specs cannot be readily changed.

> EXAMPLE: You decide to require the employee to lift twenty-five pounds about every half hour. If you change that to every five minutes, you'll suddenly disqualify several people from the job. CAUTION: Affirmative action looks dimly on incorrect job specs, so make sure all significant skills are included at the beginning.

STEP-BY-STEP GUIDE TO SELECTING, SCREENING, AND INTERVIEWING

Your role in selecting, screening, and interviewing will vary among organizations. Usually, your main inputs are in stating the person specifications and job requirements and in interviewing the candidates once they've been screened by personnel. Here's how the process normally works:

Step One: Personnel takes job specs, draws up the profiles, and advertises the position. If there's no advertising, the application process may begin simply on a first-in, first-review basis.

Step Two: Personnel brings in likely prospects for testing and initial interviewing. Reference checks are usually done by personnel and can occur before, during, or after the testing and interviewing.

Step Three: Personnel refers the most likely candidates to the manager for interviewing and recommendations. Sometimes with unskilled and semi-skilled workers, the manager does no interviewing.

Step Four: The manager advises Personnel of his or her choice, and usually alternative preferences.

Step Five: Personnel hires the person and gives instructions on reporting time, date, physicals, and so on.

Step Six: The new employee reports, and the orientation begins.

The main purpose of the interview, of course, is to select the best person for the job. To do this, you need the right information, and this requires certain skills on your part. Your most important skills are listening and asking the right questions. WHAT TO DO: Use active listening, such as "sounds like you want to apply your experience to a more challenging job." Listen for feelings to get a true picture of the applicant's self-confidence, attitudes, and interests.

Since the interview is the most common tool for selecting employees, knowing and using good interview procedure will lead to better selection. Here are some basic considerations:

1. Minimize subjectivity in the selection process and the criteria.
2. Maintain consistency throughout the interview process.
3. Obtain information that assesses skill and ability needed on the job.
4. Maximize effectiveness of the interview.
5. Help the applicant decide whether this job is right for him or her.

These goals can be reached only with a well-defined perspective of the job. As a manager, you fit perfectly into the interview process at this point.

You can minimize subjectivity and maintain consistency by structuring the interview to a specific set of information needs. SUGGESTION: Break job requirements into "critical levels" and conduct the interview based on these requirements. Figure 6.5 shows how this process might unfold.

Basically, you are responsible for controlling the interview. This involves preparation for the mood, tone, and timing, as well as the evaluation process. In order to avoid serious problems in communication, try to avoid these common errors:

1. *Impatience.* Don't make hasty judgments without obtaining sufficient information.
2. *Talking too much.* At least half the interview should be spent listening to the applicant.
3. *Inconsistency.* You need to ask consistent questions that reveal whether or not an applicant is qualified to do the job.
4. *Central tendency errors.* Don't rate applicants around a hypothetical average.
5. *The "Halo effect".* There's a tendency to view the applicant in terms of a dominant characteristic.
6. *Contrast effects.* Sometimes a mediocre applicant gets high ratings simply because the others are even worse.

7. *Stereotyping.* Fixed and inflexible images of applicants are not valid.

8. *Personal bias.* Of course, this is illegal and unethical.

9. *Playing psychologist.* You are probably not a qualified psychologist, so don't play these kinds of games.

10. *Inappropriate questions.* Avoid questions relating to race, religion, sex, sexual preference, national origin, age, or marital status.

11. *Projecting.* This happens when you assign others your own qualities. It leads to faulty assumptions; such as, the applicant will get bored with the job because you would (or did).

**LEVELS OF CRITERIA
FOR EVALUATING APPLICANTS**

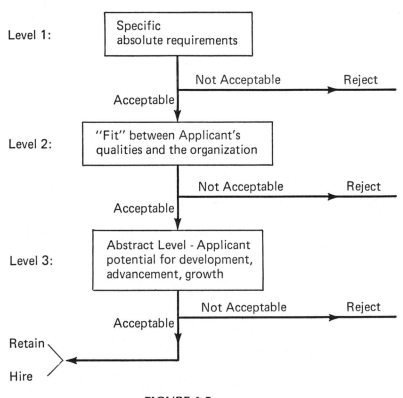

FIGURE 6.5

Here is a step-by-step procedure for accomplishing a successful interview process:

Before the Interview

Step One: Plan the interview

1. Review the applicant information.
2. Prepare your questions.
3. Talk to others who know the applicant.
4. Contact references.

Step Two: Arrange a suitable location for the interview

1. Avoid distractions and interruptions.
2. Have a comfortable place to talk.
3. Have convenient access.

Step Three: Arrange the time

1. Schedule the interview.
2. Let Personnel know when it is scheduled.

Step Four: Rehearse the interview

1. Visualize; go over it in your mind.
2. Think about the questions you will ask.
3. Concentrate on your goals; have them firmly in mind.

During the Interview

Step One: Establish rapport

1. Relax; keep on the Adult level. Be neither solicitous nor abrupt. Be friendly and businesslike.
2. Maintain an open, comfortable environment.
3. Set the person at ease and encourage him or her to talk about himself.
4. Avoid rude and/or preoccupied behavior.

Step Two: Begin

1. Get right into the interview; do not spend time shooting the breeze.

2. Guide the applicant systematically to get the information you need.

Step Three: Exchange information

1. Let the applicant know what the job requires.
2. Seek information that is important to your main purpose. Make sure your questions are clear, understandable, and unambiguous.
3. Avoid questions that can be answered with a simple yes or no.
4. Practice active and passive listening. Let silence happen.
5. Retain objectivity; let the applicant respond the way he or she wants.
6. Recognize responses that conflict with the job criteria.
7. Let the applicant know how you perceive his qualifications. Be frank with negatives.
8. Give the applicant a chance to select himself in or out.
9. Inform the applicant concerning your decision timetable and by what procedure the applicants will be informed.
10. Take notes throughout (do not use a tape recorder unless the situation requires it *and* the applicant consents to it).

After the Session

Step Five: Interpret and follow up.

1. Review the key points in your notes and from your memory.
2. Reflect back on the job requirements. Visualize this applicant at work.
3. Question yourself concerning biases and stereotypes. Bring them out in the open.
4. Decide. After each applicant, make comparisons. After all are interviewed, *decide.*
5. Convey your decision/recommendation through the appropriate procedure.

When you interpret interview data, a systematic analysis of the information will be most useful. Begin by relating specific requirements of the job to the answers you received. IMPORTANT: Remain objective and avoid conclusions that you cannot support.

CHECKLIST OF INTERVIEW QUESTIONS

Here are fifteen questions that will prove useful in the interview process:

- Tell me about your performance on your most recent job. What were your accomplishments?
- To what do you attribute your success?
- What difficulties or barriers did you overcome?
- What did you learn on the job that would be useful on this one?
- What did you like about your position? Dislike?
- If you could have changed anything about the position, what might it have been? Why?
- How did you contribute to your work unit or organization?
- How do you plan your job duties?
- How do you organize your time? Equipment?
- What are examples of decisions you made on the job?
- What decisions seem easiest? Most difficult?
- How do you feel about your development in this area?
- Tell me about times when you've felt more confident in your work? Proud of your work?
- Where and how do you see yourself in three, four, or five years?
- Describe interactions with fellow employees and past managers. What circumstances made you feel good or bad?

The final choice is often difficult. Nearly always, it requires your good judgment peppered with some of your own feelings. SUGGESTION: You might try rating a person, say from one to five, for each area you consider important. This can only be a first step. Ultimately, you must make a judgment. Never sell yourself short— and trust your good sense.

Regardless of how you make your selection, for legal and other purposes, it's essential to be able to explain yourself and describe how you made your decision. Qualitative judgments can and should be made, but you must be prepared to explain the process.

HOW TO ORIENT THE NEW EMPLOYEE SO YOU GET QUICK BENEFITS

Think back to your first day on the job. Your excitement and anticipation were probably mixed with anxiety. First-day jitters are not uncommon, and they leave a bad taste at an otherwise exciting time.

Why the anxiety? You're literally among strangers in a pretty serious situation. Your livelihood depends on how well you are accepted. Did you pass muster by midday? Did someone invite you to have lunch? Are you embarrassed about not being able to do some fairly simple task?

A good orientation program will address many of the needs that go along with first-day woes. When conducted properly, the orientation should:

1. Leave the employee in a secure, relaxed frame of mind.

2. Introduce the job and the co-workers.

3. Help the new employee, manager, and other employees to accommodate one another and make the adjustments needed for a productive relationship.

The purpose of the orientation is to allow the employee and the organization to get to know each other, and to do so on a positive note. It's also a time to let the employee learn about you. This way you can understand each other better and work together more effectively.

Developing a good job orientation program will pay off. Studies show how companies have reaped impressive results by training and rewarding managers in their employee orientation role.

A CASE-IN-POINT: Company A launched a training program when it became evident that employees were not developing well. Managers were taught to conduct the orientation, and they were monitored closely. As a result, training time was reduced by 30 percent, new employee productivity increased by 10 percent, and the number of new employees remaining with the company increased by 300 percent. New employee job satisfaction increased; a cost–benefit analysis showed an estimated savings of $300,000 annually!

HOW TO DO IT: Try informal methods first. Create a relaxed atmosphere and begin an informal discussion. Get the employee to talk freely about himself, his family, hobbies, interests, experiences. This is a good opportunity to find out what the employee wants from the job and his or her plans for the future. CAUTION: Especially with people just out of school, a reality adjustment is inevitable. These people often come in with an idealized picture of the job and of their careers. They may be shocked to learn how things really are done. So it helps to warn the employee in advance and provide him or her with a down-to-earth picture of what to expect.

New employees come in with a blank space—like an empty chalkboard waiting to be filled. This is why new employees are more easily influenced by ideas, attitudes, and suggestions than old employees. Besides the blank space, there are also mental and psychological images that exist about the job, organization, or department. Your informal acquaintance will help the new employee talk about these attitudes, and this will in turn affect his or her attitude.

Most job failures and turnovers are not caused by lack of technical know-how but rather by faulty social adjustment. By far, psychological and social aspects of work are the most neglected yet most needed areas in orientation programs today.

> A CASE-IN-POINT: In a large department store, employees who identified least with society and with its specific work values were also the least productive and committed to the store's objectives. A management consultant noticed this and recommended behavior and value training as a part of the orientation, to be added to the formal, technical orientation that already existed. The store did so, and the dropout rate decreased noticeably.

WHAT TO DO: Try to teach these six principles as part of your social orientation program.

1. *Success is within reach.* Emphasize success a great deal, as if it were the normal expectation.

2. *Ignore hall talk.* Tell the new employee to expect some sort of hazing or initiation from fellow workers. Try to keep it all in good humor.

3. *Be assertive in your communications; ask questions; go to your manager.* Encourage openness.

4. *Get acquainted with the manager.* Describe yourself, your likes, and dislikes. Are you strict? What do you expect?

5. *Know what the organization stands for*—what its values are.

6. *Think about consequences.* Make the new employee aware of how he or she affects co-workers, the manager, and the organization.

HOW A TYPICAL ORIENTATION PROGRAM WORKS

The typical orientation program begins with a welcome and proceeds to cover the job, the conditions, company background, benefits, facilities, the new employee's probationary status, introduction to co-workers, and the initial on-the-job training. WHAT TO INCLUDE: Pay attention to details such as figuring paychecks, information about sick leave, first aid, restroom locations, and housekeeping. Figure 6.6 shows a checklist that can be useful to you. By using it, you can make sure that you will cover all important areas in the orientation.

Sometimes a handbook or similar handout is given out to supplement the orientation. Figure 6.7 shows the table of contents of a typical employee handbook.

Your role in the orientation will vary according to the organization. You might be called upon to conduct any part of the orientation, although usually others share the responsibilities.

A note about the psychology of orientation. Many experts believe that the success of the recruit is tied directly to the expectations of the manager. This is known as the Pygmalion effect. Your contact with the new employee is the single most significant thing influencing his or her performance and attitude. So you would do well to master the art and science of orientation.

MANAGER'S ORIENTATION CHECKLIST

Employee's Name:	Discussion completed (please check *each* individual item)
1. Word of welcome.	
2. Explain overall departmental organization and its relationship to other activities of the company.	
3. Explain employee's individual contribution to the objectives of the department and the starting assignment in broad terms.	
4. Discuss job content with employee and give a copy of job description (if available).	
5. Explain departmental training program(s) and salary increase practices and procedures.	
6. Discuss where the employee lives and transportation facilities.	
7. Explain working conditions.: a. Hours of work, time sheets b. Use of employee entrance and elevators c. Lunch hours d. Coffee breaks, rest periods e. Personal telephone calls and mail f. Overtime policy and requirements g. Paydays and procedure for being paid h. Lockers i. Other _____	

FIGURE 6.6

8. Requirements for continuance of employment—explain company standards as to: a. Performance of duties b. Attendance and punctuality c. Handling confidential information d. Behavior e. General appearance f. Wearing of uniform	
9. Introduce new staff member to manager(s) and other supervisors. Special attention should be paid to the person to whom the new employee will be assigned.	
10. Release employee to immediate superior who will: a. Introduce new staff member to fellow workers. b. Familiarize the employee with his workplace. c. Begin on-the-job training.	

If not applicable, insert N/A in space provided.

_____	_____
Employee's Signature	Manager's Signature
_____	_____
Date	Division

Form examined for filing:

_____	_____
Date	Personnel Department

Source: Joan Holland and Theodore Curtis, "Orientation of New Employees," in Joseph Famulare (ed.), *Handbook of Modern Personnel Administration* (New York: McGraw-Hill Book Co., 1972), Chap. 23.

FIGURE 6.6 (continued)

TABLE OF CONTENTS FOR AN EMPLOYEE ORIENTATION HANDBOOK

FIGURE 6.7

A CASE-IN-POINT: Ray Scheid, head food buyer at a Kroger Company branch, invested a lot of energy and time in training new people. Many of the people he mentored were promoted. He had virtually no turnover. And he was recognized within his organization. How did he do it? He uplifted his recruits, respected their inherent human dignity, gave them challenging assignments, and worked right along with them in a supportive role. His formula will work for you every time!

At some point in the orientation, you will discuss work and work experience. Begin by stressing the positive aspects of the work goals, objectives, and what doing a good job means.

The single biggest factor that will motivate the employee to do a good job is to know how his or her performance will affect the end result. So if you want to get the employee off on the right foot, start by talking about how his or her contribution affects the end product and the customer's use of the product. Technical details can wait. Make this mental connection first, and the rest will follow.

Another way to get workers' commitment very quickly is to talk *seriously* about the future. What lies on the horizon; what changes do you expect? This triggers interest and gets the new employee to think about the job and its future.

When introducing the job, you should demonstrate the essential operations. Let the employee try, and then observe the work. Ask the employee how he or she likes it. What did it feel like? What concerns are there?

SUGGESTION: When machinery is involved, use vestibule equipment away from the line. This way, the employee is not competing with others and will not be embarrassed.

THE FUSION PROCESS: HOW TO BRING PEOPLE TOGETHER

The co-worker is, of course, part of the job situation, and this introduction is necessary both to develop teamwork and for getting acquainted. The new employee will naturally be curious about his or her co-workers, so you should brief the new employee about the group, its likes and dislikes, and the way it operates.

New employees are dependent on their co-workers for approval, acceptance, and recognition. They perceive co-workers as more capable and more confident than themselves. They also may very well fear co-workers because of what they can do, that is, hazing, initiations, sanctions. In short, the co-worker can have an important influence on the success of the new employee.

From Chapter 1, you learned about the odd–even number negative phenomenon. This stated that people and attitudes are in balance when there is an even number of negatives or no negatives at all in the relationship. Suppose the new employee likes the manager but the co-workers do not. There are at least four options available to the new employee:

1. Begin to dislike the manager, too.
2. Begin to dislike the group.
3. Begin to like the manager (unlikely).
4. Make attitudes about the manager unimportant.

Realistically, the only option most likely to occur is Number 1. Why? Because of the group influence. Individual needs for recognition and structure involve group influences and therefore make the individual very susceptible. THE RESULT: Peer group influence can become a very powerful force.

WHAT TO DO: Since the employee needs both the manager and the company, you need to create the proper fusion between the employee and the job on one hand and the employee and other work situations, including the work group, on the other.

The fusion process, so named by social scientist E. Wright Bahke, describes the adjustment that takes place among the new employee, the work group, and the organization. As shown in Figure 6.8, your main concern is to focus the employee toward the job—on performing his or her role in the organization. At the same time, the group seeks loyalty to its own values: ideas about quality, performance standards, dependability, initiative, responsibility, and so on. In order to accomplish a successful fusion between the worker and the organization, you must mold what the workers perceive and expect to what the organization and the group wants and expects.

FUSION PROCESS

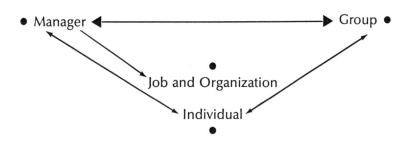

FIGURE 6.8

A fusion analysis will provide you with a basis for bringing about a satisfying and productive adjustment. The process identifies the forces at work in each party and develops strategies to handle each one, thereby bringing about an integration of values and perceptions. REMEMBER THE WATCHWORD: Harmony. Here's what to do:

Begin with the characteristics of the employee that promote cooperation and harmony. Call these "plus" factors. Then identify the factors that encourage friction. Call these "minus" factors. Do this for the work group, the organization, and for yourself. Figure 6.9 shows how to diagram this.

After analyzing each influence separately, determine your strategy for revising the negative factors. Once this is done, a productive fusion results. The positive forces combine to produce a harmonious integration of new employee, manager, organization, and work group. Each will have adjusted in the interest of common goals.

WINNING EMPLOYEE LOYALTY

Loyalty follows trust. Once the new employee can trust you and the organization, you will earn his or her loyalty. HOW TO DO IT:

FUSION ANALYSIS

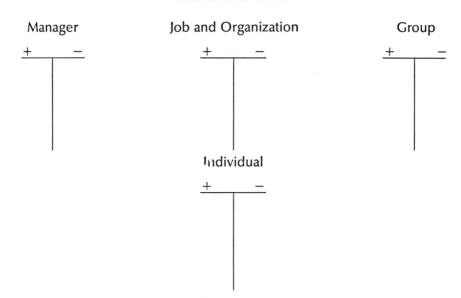

Manager

Job and Organization

Group

Individual

EXAMPLE: Let's identify the plus/minus factors for a hypothetical employee:

+   Employee   −

+	−
Attitude	Training different
Job Inherent	Experience on a past job
Enthusiasm	Union membership
Family response	Productivity to group pressure
Ability	Former manager's expectations

The same analysis can be done for other influences in the fusion process; the result might look like this:

+   Manager (You)   −

+	−
Interest in new employee	Busy schedule; impatient
Basic capability	Work pressure
Past record of cooperation	Loyalty to management
Good technical skills	Communication skills
Genuine concern for organization's future	Lack of authority

+   Job/Organization   −

Challenging; responsible	No incentive pay
Good benefits	Little promotion opportunity
Good hourly pay	Seniority bound
Pleasant working conditions	Strenuous visual requirement
Steady employment	Bureaucratic practices

+   Work Group   −

Cohesive	Cliquish
Fairly high standards	Resistant to changes
Helpful to new worker	Strict sanctions for nonperformance
Peaceful union relations	Demanding of worker loyalty

FIGURE 6.9

Do what you say you will do; make sure the employee has the right information, orientation, and training; and build the right rapport.

Remember that the new employee usually begins with wanting to do the right thing. This is the best time to begin gaining loyalty.

A CASE-IN-POINT: Joe was oriented to his new job and then given his first assignment. During the morning break, he went to the vending area but found no one there. When he returned, the other employees asked him where he was. They then told Joe that nobody goes to the vending area. Instead, they go to the locker room where they've hidden a small refrigerator with beer. Soon Joe learned how "things are done around here." To counteract, the manager continued by developing pride, quality consciousness, and so on. Soon, Joe decided to forego the beer.

REMEMBER THIS: Loyalty will not automatically result from a good orientation program. But by applying the principles behind it with personal integrity, your chances of winning employee loyalty are very good.

HOW TO USE WORK GROUPS IN ORIENTATION AND TRAINING

Work groups need not be your adversary. In developing the new employee, they can also serve as a catalyst, particularly in apprenticeship programs. HERE'S THE KEY: The work group must be *productive:* otherwise, the influence will be negative.

Work group participation in orientation varies a lot from one organization to another. Generally, you have some latitude on this. HINT: The social orientation by the group will be done whether or not you schedule it. If you include it as part of your orientation, you can have a more positive influence.

Here are recommended guidelines for deciding how to involve the work group in orientation:

1. Examine your orientation checklist (page 208).
2. Decide which items can be better handled by the group and by which members of the group.
3. Determine how you would use the group members and what preparation would be required.
4. Approach the group and those you want to help handle the orientation. Explain their purpose and role. Ask them if they will participate.
5. Build into the program a social orientation by group members.
6. Brief the participating group members specifically on their task in the orientation.
7. Give appropriate recognition to participating members.

SUGGESTION: Do not pressure employees to participate. It should be voluntary and done with a positive attitude.

In many organizations, and in some countries such as Japan, new employees are placed under the protective wing of experienced senior employees. Such "buddy" or "mentor" systems provide the new employee with an influential "friend" who will guide him or her in learning the job and the ropes.

The mentor can help you considerably by reinforcing productivity and loyalty. A mentor also saves you considerable time. You may find, too, that the new employee will listen to a peer more readily than a manager and feel more comfortable being trained by that peer.

The mentor should be a peer, a specialist, or even a manager. The mentor must know the company, not just the job, and needs the same human skills as the manager in the orientation process. The mentor's duties can be determined much the same way as you did for the work group's role in the orientation.

HOW TO USE TEACHING AND TRAINING TO GET RESULTS

Organizations that give high priority to training reap tangible results: competence, high performance, careful workmanship, responsible behavior, commitment, self-confidence, high self-esteem, positive attitudes, and cooperative behavior.

Training is the process of increasing one's skill and ability to perform specific tasks. *Development,* on the other hand, is a process of increasing one's capability to perform a range of tasks. Its objectives are usually broader. By contrast, *education* instills basic concepts, knowledge, and values. Much of the on-the-job instruction that you do is training rather than development or education.

The basic training process involves (1) identifying needed skills, (2) evaluating employees' skills in relation to those needs, and (3) choosing the approach and method for training. These are the three main considerations:

1. *Who?* Nearly all new employees need training, but some need more than others.

2. *What?* This depends on the job and the new employee's background and capability.

3. *How much?* Time needed depends on the desired level of proficiency as well as possible long-range development.

In nearly all organizations, the first-line manager has a significant role in training in tandem with other departments, such as Personnel. By and large, the most relevant training for you will be conducted as a shared responsibility among yourself, Personnel, the organization, and the employee. IMPORTANT: You have a major role in setting the climate, reinforcing the learning, and applying the training.

Whatever your responsibility, here are eight suggestions to help you identify and discharge your role more effectively:

1. What specific part of the training are you expected to handle: actual instruction, skills, information, evaluation?

2. Who will handle the other aspects? What will be your relationship with them?

3. How much of your time will it involve? Make a quantitative estimate. Examine your overall job demands and reshuffle schedules and priorities if necessary. Avoid the frustrations of trying

to squeeze training in with everything else. If possible, it's better to postpone (or delegate) your lower priority duties.

4. What training do *you* need in order to prepare for training the employee? There are workshops designed to train trainers, and they are widely available and potentially very helpful.

5. Provide the necessary support and follow-up. The surest way to make a program succeed is to reinforce the concepts and techniques taught.

6. Get familiar with the course and the program content through study, briefings, and discussions. Then actually try them out.

7. Talk to the trainee in advance, providing any material and other information that will help the trainee (new employee) get familiar with the training program. Discuss employee needs, interests, role while in training, expected performance while in training, "homework," and post-course follow-up.

8. Follow up. Get feedback from the trainee on his or her perception of the training period. What is needed that has not yet been developed? Plan for how trainees will use the training.

As a manager, the method of conducting and presenting the training should best stimulate the new employee's learning. Whether formal or informal, your approach can make a considerable difference.

> EXAMPLE: Imagine a program that teaches how-to-do-it techniques by lecture only. Boring? Unmotivating? Unproductive? You guessed it!

FUNDAMENTAL CONCEPTS OF LEARNING

- People learn fastest and best by doing. This especially applies in a practical job situation. It also applies in mental work, whether managerial or technical.

- Trainees need timely and frequent reinforcement. This is not a time to be stingy with recognition strokes. Rather than wait until the end of the week, reinforce performance and learning as close as possible to the time when the performance takes place.

- Provide for practice and repetition under a variety of conditions. Operations should become second nature to employees, and this is best developed through repeated trials. Variety prepares the employees for different situations.

- Make the material meaningful. This requires the use of familiar examples, while presenting the material in organized and manageable units.

- Facilitate the transfer by learning. This goes along with the learning-by-doing idea. If a trainee understands the general principles, he or she is more likely to adjust to the task.

- Use stimulating aids and a variety of presentation methods. A multimedia appeal to many of the senses will have greater impact on the individual.

- Finally, give feedback with no demeaning criticism.

THE INFORMAL PROCESS: HOW TRAINING AS YOU GO WORKS FOR MANAGERS

Informal training consists of all unprogrammed attempts to train and develop employees, whether as part of coaching, instruction, or counseling. Whether you plan it or not, informal training will occur.

Preparing for informal training requires the same skills as coaching, plus the technical knowledge that will enable you to instruct the workers. Here's what to do "as you go":

1. Use a self-improvement strategy, including such things as using time effectively, understanding yourself and how people react to you, effective communication, and goal directedness.

2. Use strategy and skills to increase your influence on the work group, such as knowing employee motives and needs, creating a positive work environment, giving feedback effectively, knowing when and what to delegate, and developing responsibility.

3. Use a system, such as PPRS (see Chapter 5), to integrate training with the employee's overall plan.

PROVEN TECHNIQUES FOR ESTABLISHING AN EFFECTIVE FORMAL TRAINING PROGRAM

There are two kinds of formal training: off the job and on the job (OJT). Of the two, you're most likely to be involved in OJT.

Here are the most common types of off-the-job training programs:

1. *Vestibule training.* This is useful for providing experience as close to the real situation as possible. CAUTION: Where expensive equipment is involved, this training can be very costly.

2. *Classroom instruction.* Here the employee learns concepts and techniques relative to the job. It's good for teaching basic ideas.

3. *Vocational training.* This is often done formally in schools and colleges. It broadly prepares the employee for various jobs within an occupation or profession, but it often lacks specific reference to the present job.

4. *Programmed instruction.* Here, the teaching is individualized. The material is presented in a sequential way, and the learning is reinforced as the trainee makes the correct responses. PI has great potential, especially with the advent of microcomputers.

OJT programs include these three types:

1. *Apprenticeship programs.* This consists of a formal program of study and work that the employees must complete in a certain time frame in order to qualify for full membership in the occupation or profession. Usually built into the program is an assurance of high standards of performance and a sense of pride in the work.

2. *Job rotation.* This program moves workers around to different jobs in order to gain wide experience and understanding. According to a predetermined plan, the new employee might work for a few weeks in shipping, then in the finishing department, then in assembly, and so on. The variety of experience prepares the employee for a permanent job.

3. *Coaching/mentor approach.* Coaching in relation to training is basically placing a new employee under a manager's wing for instruction and guidance. Mentoring involves the same process but includes employees along with the manager. These programs usually develop commitment and competency. They seem natural to undertake by managers at most levels.

So there you have it! There are many options and approaches for training the new employee. Which should you choose? Practically speaking, the decision is often made for you. However, if you have the choice, your decision will depend on your objectives, the type of work, the level of skills involved, and your philosophy about development. As an overall guideline, Figure 6.10 can be helpful in deciding on training programs or recommending an appropriate program to those who make the decision.

DECISION TABLE FOR TRAINING PROGRAMS

Rating Factors (1 = Very Favorable;
5 = Very Unfavorable)

Programs	Long-range Develop-ment	Short-range Develop-ment	Specific Job Profi-ciency	Concept and Knowledge Develop-ment	*Cost	**Manager's Time
Off-the-Job						
Vestibule	3	1	1	2	4	3
Classroom Instruction	1	3	4	1	3	1
Vocational Training	1	3	3	1	4	1
Programmed Instruction	4	1	2	2	2	2
On-the-Job						
Apprentice-ship	1	2	2	1	3	2
Job Rotation	2	2	2	3	2	3
Coaching	3	1	1	3	2	4
Mentor System	3	1	1	3	2	3

*Assumes the company subsidizes the training; this is cost to organization.
**Assumes the typical and appropriate role of the manager in the training.

FIGURE 6.10

MURPHY'S LAW OF TRAINING

Phil Murphy had built a reputation as an enterprising fore-man and one who would not let the opportunity go by to lend his name to a well-known buzzword such as "Murphy's Law" (whenever something can go wrong, it will). But Phil Murphy's law of training was something different. Phil describes his law of training in three basic principles:

1. Never assume people are trained for the job before they start it.
2. Never assume they'll train themselves.
3. Give 'em the knowledge when they need it, not when you want to give it to them.

WHY THE MANAGER MUST BE A HELPER

Twenty years ago—even ten—if the manager was told by the company that he was a helper, he would have thought management was going soft. Not anymore. Now the helping role is a regular dimension of the job, as demonstrated in companies such as Hughes Aircraft, TRW, Phillips Petroleum, Mead Corporation, and other corporations, large and small. It's not coincidental, either, that each of these companies is active in career development.

As a helper, you assist and encourage the employee in his or her development. In many companies, this is built into the evaluation system, where your effectiveness is determined largely by your supportive attitude and behavior. The supportive approach is not only more in tune with today's employee; it's also more productive in the long run.

Here's what to do as a helping manager:

1. Coach the new employee on a regular basis.

2. Discuss problems in the interest of helping the employee resolve them.

3. Anticipate problems and share experiences with employees.

4. Look for ways to encourage and help improve performance rather than to punish poor performance.

5. Invite employees to discuss problems with you.

6. Share information with employees when you think it will be of interest to them.

7. Encourage development and developmental opportunities.

8. Teach employees the job and the necessary skills, with emphasis on learning and taking responsibility on their own.

9. Treat employees as responsible people, capable of handling the job and contributing.

10. Invite contributions and encourage employees to share ideas and suggestions for improvement.

HOW TO TELL WHAT IS TYPICALLY ON THE NEW EMPLOYEE'S MIND

The new employee typically experiences three main types of problems: emotional, learning, and work problems. All three may appear together and are not easily separated. In addition, there are three different stages in which you can deal with the problem: prevention, intervention, and treatment. With the new employee, you can work to secure good solutions at each stage.

Common problems include adjusting to the new organization, to the procedures and policies, to the work, and, of course, to you. The new employee's biggest fear is being rejected. This can manifest itself in such things as asking too many and often irrelevant questions, overcautiousness, tagging along. While each can be normal and even healthy behaviors, they become a problem when they are excessive.

WHAT TO DO: Remember the barometers of a healthy relationship: being spontaneous, authentic, aware of what's going on, and experiencing growth. If you achieve these, you're also handling the new employee appropriately.

Other problems vexing to the new employee include work schedules, finding reliable transportation to and from work, and hazing from other workers. You may have no direct control over the situation, but you can counsel through active listening. By talking about his or her feelings, the new employee can often resolve the problems.

Adjustment and learning problems often relate to typical fears experienced by the employee. Adjustment problems are often caused by fear of being rejected; learning problems by fear of failure. You can best deal with this by taking a positive attitude and looking for the right solution.

When the new employee experiences such problems, here's what you can do:

1. Deal objectively with the problem. Separate the person from the behavior and focus on the behavior.

2. Use the managerial problem-solving process, along with your knowledge of employee motivation.

3. Convince yourself that there is a mutually beneficial solution.

4. Allow time for problems to be ironed out.

5. Enlist other employees to help the new employee learn and adjust.

Finally, recognize the positive things the new employee has done. Be supportive in a personal way, such as, "I like the way you handled that job." Positive reinforcement and stroking works with the new employee as well as the old employee, with minorities, men and women, disabled and able-bodied, old and young. Your patience and persistence will pay off many times over.

HOW TO HANDLE MINORITY AND DISABLED EMPLOYEES

Minority and disabled employees present extraordinary challenges for the manager. Often a different perception exists when dealing with the minority employee.

A CASE-IN-POINT: Consider the case of absenteeism with two new employees, one "majority" (white male) and the other "minority" (black male). Which is apt to get the most attention? Regrettably, it's often the minority employee. Most minorities do not want to be treated differently, yet there is a tendency to do so.

WHAT TO DO: You should apply all rules and policies without discrimination, and you should also be aware of other workers' perceptions. Nonminority workers are often quick to show resistance and negative attitudes. The new minority employee senses this and naturally distrusts the situation and, probably, you too.

Adrienne Geiger says you must handle the resistance and hostility of others, and this requires skill in interpersonal relations and communications.[1] WHAT TO DO: Coping with your own feelings is a good start. Some special training and concern should be directed toward understanding the minority employee's situation. This should result not in special treatment but in a more effective relationship with the minority employee.

Disabled persons present another special employment disability. One of the biggest problems is being too solicitous—doing too many things for them that they *can* and *want* to do for themselves. WHAT TO DO: Focus on the "can do's" rather than the "cannots." Try to balance your interest among co-workers and disabled workers.

Beware the tendency to treat disabled workers differently from normal learners.

> A CASE-IN-POINT: Bill is a disabled employee with a hearing impairment. So you find a task for him that is painfully noisy for most workers but not for Bill. You get lots of praise because of how you "handled the handicapped." Sounds OK? Everyone's happy, right? Wrong! The job assignment is fine, but the labeling that resulted is not. Whenever disabled or minority workers get labeled as a class (such as, "women are good at details" or "blacks are agile"), it promotes a stereotype that can be harmful to any individual subjected to it.

THE SEVEN SYNDROMES

Authors Robert B. Nathanson and Jeffrey Lambert describe seven syndromes that impair healthy development.[2] Do you recognize them?

- All that matters is your label.
- I feel sorry for you.
- Don't worry, I'll protect you.
- You present too many problems for us to handle.
- If I'm lucky, we won't see each other today (often expressed by co-workers who are repulsed by a particular appearance or condition).
- I'm amazed by your courage.
- Who is more anxious, you or I?

In this last case, responsibility rests with both you and the disabled employee to try to lighten up the situation.

[1] Adrienne Geiger, "Managing Effectively While Implementing EEO," *Training and Development Journal*, 35, no. 4 (May 1981).

[2] "Integrating Disabled Employees into the Workplace," *Personnel Journal*, 60, no. 2 (February 1981).

What can you do? Here are some guidelines to help you deal with the disabled or minority employee:

1. Focus on what the employee can do, not on what he or she cannot do.
2. Talk with co-workers—educate them. Discuss their concerns and give them any facts you may have.
3. Be understanding but treat everyone the same as far as expectations are concerned. Apply policies and rules to all alike.
4. Educate yourself about special employment situations.
5. Coordinate with personnel and other specialists on the subject.

REMEMBER THIS: Disabled people—as well as the elderly, minorities, and women—differ as much as anyone else in their individual abilities and attitudes. If you truly want to help them develop and adjust, your first rule should be to treat everyone as an individual, whether a minority or majority, disabled or unimpaired.

CHAPTER 7

How the Manager's Function as a Counselor Affects Performance

We can really respect a man only if he doesn't always look out for himself.

—GOETHE

IT has been estimated that one of every five interactions that managers have with employees is a potential or actual counseling situation. Because all industry needs better counseling from managers, Your training and development will stress this activity more and more. Your skill in handling counseling problems and administering emotional "first aid" can save your organization time, labor costs, and morale, and it can result in increased commitment and effort when employees feel management really cares about their problems. As a result, your organization has a vested interest in your ability to assume the role of counselor.

Many of the concepts introduced in Chapters 3 and 4 have practical application here. In the pages that follow, you are offered a wide range of tools, such as active listening and nonjudgmental feedback, that will equip you to handle employee counseling situations. Your goal and the goal of this chapter is to build the necessary skills to make counseling a worthwhile and rewarding part of first-line management.

HOW TO USE COUNSELING AS AN EFFECTIVE
MANAGEMENT TOOL

Counseling is concerned with solving problems that have an emotional basis. It involves revealing and discussing the issue and can only be done when the time is appropriate. Problems having little or no emotional involvement are usually resolved through advisement or coaching and require only simple interpersonal exchange. Counseling, on the other hand, is integrally bound to authentic interpersonal communication.

As a manager, your main concerns are (1) the balance between personal and organizational interests, (2) the attainment and application of necessary skills, and (3) the counseling boundaries you need to observe as one who is not a professional counselor.

AN IMPORTANT POINT: Your main responsibility is to the unit and its objectives. So why a counseling responsibility? Two reasons: (1) to help improve work performance, and (2) to help another person who needs and wants assistance in solving a problem.

Your personal responsibility is to treat the employee with dignity and respect. And, of course, you do not want to make a bad situation worse.

> EXAMPLE: Fred has a marital problem that results in a serious performance deficiency. He asks the manager if he should get a divorce. If the manager ignores the problem, Fred's work could deteriorate even more. But by taking an interest, the manager is able to get Fred to a trained professional who then helps get the matter resolved.

In the final analysis, only you can decide when and how to counsel. And this decision relates to the basic conditions and policies that govern your position.

> A CASE-IN-POINT: An employee reports to you that he cannot get the hydraulic system working. It appears, on the surface, like a technical problem. Then you learn that the worker has neglected maintenance, abused the equipment, and doesn't get along with the maintenance man. It's up to you whether to counsel, ignore the problem, refer it, or postpone discussion.

EMOTIONAL FIRST AID: USING YOUR EVOLVING COUNSELOR ROLE

Despite the professional counseling and psychological services available in many organizations, there is a growing need for on-the-spot counseling, and you are the logical person to administer it. The manager's counseling is like emotional first aid for the purpose of relieving the immediate crisis.

Your most important counseling and interviewing areas include:

1. Day-to-day counseling and coaching
2. Performance appraisal
3. Career and development counseling
4. Selection interviewing
5. Out-placement counseling (layoffs, dismissal)
6. Retirement counseling
7. Exit interviewing

Of these, career counseling and coaching have won the spotlight in today's modern organization.

To put it simply, your role in counseling calls for an objective, understanding response that helps the employee reach a solution to his or her problem. To do this, you must recognize the difference between counseling and such activities as conversation, instruction, and information. Counseling goes beyond these three and requires additional skills, a high esteem for others, and a helpful attitude.

YOUR FIRST-AID KIT FOR COUNSELING EMPLOYEES

As a counselor, you basically need two kinds of skills: communicating and influencing. Here are the tools you need in your first-aid kit:

1. *Presence.* Showing interest, concern, and respect; total concentration on the problem at hand.
2. *Active listening.* Relating to what the employee is feeling; giving a nonjudgmental summary of these feelings.

3. *Reflective listening.* Reflecting back to a person what he or she is saying and what it appears to mean.

4. *Supportive responses.* Letting the employee know that you support him or her.

5. *Interpreting.* Giving your own view about what you observe in the situation.

6. *Assertion.* Openly stating your own feelings about the situation.

7. *Information and referral.* Deciding when the employee needs professional counseling, as well as help in finding it.

8. *Asking questions.* Eliciting answers by letting people explain in their own words.

Developing interest and skill in the counseling role can bring you several benefits, such as:

1. Building trust and a more open work relationship.

2. Commitment.

3. A more emotionally healthy work force.

4. Developing managerial skills.

5. Solving work problems.

6. Developing your own self-esteem and sense of purpose.

Of course, there are costs involved, too. Counseling requires skills, and that means time and energy. In order to help others, you must solve your own personal problems, and this could mean getting counseling help yourself.

The benefits outweigh the disadvantages, though. The opportunities you create will make your task well worth the effort. WHAT YOU NEED TO DO: In a nutshell, show concern, assert your own feelings, and listen, listen, listen!

FOUR KEY PRINCIPLES OF GROWTH AND CHANGE

One of the major aims of counseling is change, be it change of behavior, attitude, skills, or thinking patterns. To consistently induce change in other people, you must be aware of these four principles that operate to make change happen:

1. Permanent change requires the psychological involvement of the individual. The person must want to change and must feel and believe that the change is in his or her best interests.

2. The change must be feasible. The person must be capable of follow-up.

3. The right conditions must be present for change. The person must be ready and the time appropriate. He or she must feel that the change is nonthreatening to the things that are believed to be important.

4. The Law of Effect. Behavior that is reinforced will continue and increase; and behavior that is not reinforced will diminish and eventually disappear. Thus, reinforcement is essential for bringing about a permanent change in behavior.

THE MANAGER'S GOLDEN RULE

Treat others as if you were going to have to live with the consequences.

The Manager's Golden Rule requires that you think about the result of what you're doing. Suppose, for example, you stimulate the employee to become a better contributor. Think about your own commitment. Once he or she contributes, are you ready to listen, follow through, support? If not, you might be better off by not trying to change the employee's behavior until *you* are ready.

THE FIVE CRITICAL STEPS IN THE COUNSELING PROCESS

The counseling process consists of the stages in a typical counseling session. Here are the five basic steps:

Step One: Determine the purpose. With a clearly defined sense of purpose, the counseling session will be more to the point.

Step Two: Identify the problem. Determine the nature of the problem, who owns it, and how it is work related. HINT: It's best not to accept the employee's assessment at first because of the tendency to identify symptoms and not the problem itself.

Step Three: Develop a clear picture of the employee's needs. Explore the employee's difficulty and listen with empathy. Feel *with* not *for* the employee. Use questions that give the employee latitude to express his or her concern or feeling.

Step Four: Seek a resolution. Real progess lies in successive accomplishments of goals that truly lead to a solution. Resolution includes discussion that clarifies the issues, airs feelings, identifies alternatives, and develops a background for better understanding of the problem.

Step Five: Determine a solution and follow up behavior. Weigh the alternatives and devise a solution that is satisfactory to both parties. The contract idea is important here. You must arrive at a clear understanding of what the employee will do and how you will know that it is being done.

KEEP THIS IN MIND: In all stages, listening skills are crucial, and responsibility must be established. Employees must be held responsible for their own problems and must be encouraged to solve them. But your support is essential throughout.

Counseling is a golden opportunity to reinforce behavior. This is done not only through recognition and reward but also by your ability to communicate your interest and commitment.

Of course, what you say greatly influences the employee. But nonverbal behavior says just as much, particularly through these four avenues: (1) attitude, (2) awareness and attention, (3) facial expressions, and (4) body talk. In short, you want to reinforce your concern for the employee by what your body says. If you are really listening, you will show it by a relaxed posture, an interested expression, direct eye contact, and a calm tone of voice.

COUNSELING PHILOSOPHY: WHERE IT'S COMING FROM

There are numerous philosophies that underlie a counselor's approach to his or her client. All are more academic and therapy oriented than what is required of you. Your basic understanding of some of the more important principles, however, can help you with your counseling activity. TWO THINGS TO REMEMBER: (1) No single philosophy has the answers to all counseling problems and (2) most philosophies were developed for extensive therapeutic purposes. In the work environment, all need to be modified to make them work well.

You can develop an overall picture of counseling philosophies by considering three perspectives:

1. Responsibility for the solution.

2. Depth of the analysis.

3. Time orientation; or a focus on present and past behavior as it relates to future consequences.

These are depicted in Figure 7.1.

WHO IS RESPONSIBLE FOR THE SOLUTION

Client   Counselor

A second dimension is depth. Some philosophies want to delve into every nook and cranny of our psyches; others look only at what is observed outwardly, describing it and not drawing any inferences.

DEPTH

Highly   Highly
Analytical   Descriptive

A third scale is time orientation. This is similar in some ways to depth. It is mainly a question of focus on past causes versus present results of future consequences.

TIME ORIENTATION

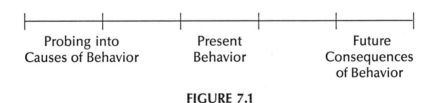

Probing into   Present   Future
Causes of Behavior   Behavior   Consequences
                                             of Behavior

FIGURE 7.1

Here is a brief description of various counseling psychologies currently in use:

1. *Psychoanalytic.* This view says that emotional problems are caused by forces deep inside a person, which are generally subconscious (outside one's awareness). Sigmund Freud, the founder

and best known practitioner of this system, identifies these forces as the *id* (our caldron of emotions), *ego* (rational justifier of one's self), and *superego* (the moral conscience). Each acts as a "check and balance" to the others, but problems arise when one dominates over the others.

Psychoanalysis seeks to educate and help the client (employee) achieve a sense of control that will bring the forces into balance and produce a healthy life. It is obviously an in-depth approach and focuses largely on the past.

2. *The Transactional Approach.* Dr. Eric Berne developed TA largely to help people evaluate and solve their own problems without the complexities of psychoanalysis. TA is described more comprehensively in Chapters 3 and 4 of this book.

TA places responsibility on the client from the beginning. It is highly analytical—mainly self-analytical—and focuses primarily on the present.

3. *The Self-Actualizing View.* This is called client-centered counseling by psychologist Carl Rogers, who pioneered this technique, and is concerned with personal development. Self-actualization says that we perceive the world according to self-concepts and then behave accordingly. When self-concept is not consistent with the real world, problems arise.

Therapy takes an understanding, empathetic approach. The counselor has high positive regard for the client and helps the client talk about his or her problems to resolve them. The responsibility is very definitely the client's. Depth is variable, depending on how far the client wants to take it. Time orientation is in the present.

4. *Behavioral Modification.* Behavior MOD, as it is known, aims to change behavior through the right stimulus and then reinforce the response. Given a certain stimulus (the promise of reward, punishment, and so on), the person will respond in the direction of the desired outcome. EXAMPLE: If you offer employees more pay, you will get greater effort according to this system.

Responsibility is shared between the counselor, who applies the techniques and reinforcers, and the client, who carries out the behavior response. Emphasis is on doing, so responsibility is not really a big issue. Depth is not a feature nor is concern with past behavior.

5. *Responsibility Psychology.* Also known as reality therapy, this philosophy assumes that people are able to take responsibility for their behavior, and that what we are and do is a product of our own decisions about ourselves and our lives.[1] The degree of emotional health is related to the extent to which a person acts responsibly in the decision-making process.

The counseling session will stress identifying the reality of a situation and how the client wants to solve the problem. Obviously, the responsibility lies with the client. It is present-day oriented and requires varying levels of depth.

Responsibility psychology is making its mark throughout the nation and the world in seminars, counseling sessions, books, journals, and in management practice. Assertiveness training and transactional analysis highlight responsibility psychology, as do "winning attitude," or "take charge of your life" types of programs. Certainly this philosophy will prove tangibly beneficial to you as you assume the role of counselor.

HOW TO CHOOSE THE BEST COUNSELING APPROACH FOR MOST MANAGEMENT SITUATIONS

In any counseling system, you have a choice of approaches, ranging from directive to nondirective. This refers, essentially, to who does the talking, who makes the decision, and whose objectives are going to be observed.

A *directive* approach puts you in the driver's seat. You do the talking, make the decisions, and set the objectives.

EXAMPLE: Sam tells his employee, "I think you should transfer to the loading dock."

The *nondirective* approach reflects what the employee is saying and feeling. You guide him or her by clarifying the decisions that must be made.

EXAMPLE: Sam asks his employee, "What do you want to do now?"

---

[1] Described by Dr. William Glaser in *Reality Therapy* (New York: Harper & Row, 1965).

In reality-based counseling, you need a combination of both approaches. The proportion will depend on the axis of responsibility. HOW TO DECIDE: Whose problem is it? If it's yours, use the directive approach. If it's the employee's, your role is to listen and encourage him or her to solve it. HINT: With personal problems, it's best to use a nondirective approach. Figure 7.2 shows the variety of responses you could make when taking these different approaches.

COUNSELING APPROACHES

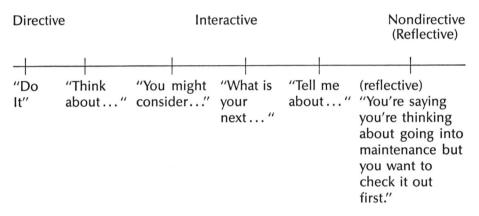

| Directive | | | Interactive | | | Nondirective (Reflective) |

"Do It"   "Think about..."   "You might consider..."   "What is your next..."   "Tell me about..."   (reflective) "You're saying you're thinking about going into maintenance but you want to check it out first."

FIGURE 7.2

What approach is best? It depends. You need to consider many factors that enter into the problem. In the final analysis, the best approach is a matter of judgment. Some useful guidelines for forming that judgment follow.

A CASE-IN-POINT: Suppose Sally says to Mary (manager), "I don't know what to do. Joe keeps bugging me about getting my work out. I try as hard as I can, but I haven't been here as long as he has." If Mary uses a directive approach, she could reply, "I want you to work at your pace and not worry about what Joe says." Or she could use a nondirective approach and say, "Sounds like you're really upset about this." Suppose further that Mary sees that Sally's problem is affecting her department's work. A useful strategy here would be to first deal with the emotional issue. Her best response would be, "You feel in a real bind because you can't seem to meet Joe's approval." This is an active listening response that not only reflects feelings but gets at the basic issue of Sally's need for approval from Joe. Once Sally expresses her feelings and becomes aware of the issue, then Mary could clarify her position with a directive, "You're accountable to me, not to Joe. I'll worry about Joe."

	Favors Directive	Favors Combination (interactive)	Favors Nondirective (reflective)
WHICH APPROACH TO USE?			
Manager's problem	X		
Employee's work-related problem			X
Mainly personal issue			X
Requires immediate solution	X		
Employee's spouse wants solution (now or later)			X
Employee problem but you want prompt solution		X	
Employee having difficulty expressing feelings			X
Employee expresses feelings freely but not willing to solve problems		X	

Employee sets goals in conflict with company		X	
Employee not willing to set goals	X		
Employee not getting along with other employees— affecting work		X	
Employee says she/he feels overworked			X
Employee is actually overloaded with work		X	
Employee wants you (manager) to decide what she/he should do		X	

PROVEN WAYS TO COMMUNICATE AS A COUNSELOR

When you counsel an employee, there are two ways to focus on the problem: cognition and catharsis. The first emphasizes thoughts and opinions. The latter means to bring out feelings. An emotional catharsis gets pent-up feelings off your chest; you end up feeling better and on the road to recovery.

When you decide to respond cognitively to what the employee is saying, you will be dealing with a subject chosen by him or her. You can either respond to it or change the topic as you see fit. WHAT'S BEST? Choose the subject that concerns the employee most.

You also have a choice of responses, including:

1. *Silence.* Useful when the employee is developing his or her thoughts.

2. *Brief verbal acknowledgment.* Similar in purpose to silence but adds a little support.

3. *Restatement.* Allows the employee to focus on what he or she is saying.

4. *Probing.* Helps you find something out—to get more information in order to solve a problem.

In most cases, feelings are part of the situation. Emotions are natural, and in a problem of any importance, it's normal to have feelings about it. So they need to be understood and addressed in order to solve a problem intelligently. For this, cathartic communication is more effective.

As a manager, your main responses to feelings should be reflective summary or active feedback. Cognitive responses are not appropriate here because they usually block rather than promote catharsis.

Reflective summary is actually a reflection of feelings or sometimes of feelings and thoughts combined. It tries to pull together the feelings and information into a meaningful pattern. When you mirror this back to the employee, it helps him or her to connect things. And it encourages further catharsis.

Active feedback uses the same concept but is not as passive. It's useful in problem solving because it guides the counseling session toward resolution.

A CASE-IN-POINT: Here's how the two approaches might be used.

| Employee: | *The last couple months have been hectic. I don't even want to talk about it, it's been so bad. First, there's Mike being transferred, then this speed-up on top of it. I've about had it.* |

Reflective Summary

| Manager: | *"Things have happened that made the last two months hectic and you've reached the point where you feel tired of it all."* |

Active Feedback

| Manager: | *"You really sound discouraged—to the point of wanting to throw in the towel. Do you feel discouraged that your extra effort is not recognized around here?"* |

The active listening response gives the situation more definition. It also allows some "reading between the lines."

Which should you use—cognitive or cathartic response? Generally, your choice depends on your goals, the employee's goals, and what's going on at the time. As a rule, try to respond to feelings early on, simply because it reduces tension. The exception: Some employees are uncomfortable about verbalizing feelings and might feel threatened.

You also have the option of simply giving advice. There are many instances when suggestions are needed, and you can appropriately provide them. CAUTION: The employee must be receptive and actually want the suggestion. Otherwise, it's best to respond in ways that promote employee responsibility.

WHAT TO REMEMBER AND WHAT TO AVOID IN COUNSELING SITUATIONS

Regardless of the counseling approach you choose, these principles will increase your effectiveness in any situation:

- Have empathy rather than sympathy.

- Be supportive.

- Be open with employees.

- Listen.

- Proceed with a valid set of assumptions, including people *can* change their behavior.

- Maintain your standards and objectives.

- Separate the behavior from the person.

And, of course, there are some "don'ts" to keep in mind:[2]

- Lack of clarity in your own responses and questions.

- Talking when silence is best.

- Interpreting when the employee starts to speak.

- Taking literally what a person is saying.

- Letting the session wander into trivial things.

---

[2] Walter Mahler, *How Effective Executives Interview* (Homewood, IL: Dow Jones Irwin, 1976).

- Leading the conversation and limiting the opportunity to answer.

- Describing the person rather than the behavior.

- Ignoring or overlooking nonverbal clues.

- Letting your emotions take over.

- Giving advice when the employee needs to discover his or her own solution.

HOW TO SPOT A COUNSELING PROBLEM QUICKLY

Counseling needs present themselves as one or more of these four types: (1) instruction, (2) reinforcement, (3) information, and (4) guidance. WHAT TO DO: Distinguish and keep them clear in your mind. Otherwise, you might get involved in the wrong need at the wrong time. Since needs are not always presented as they really are, it's important to recognize the real need.

> EXAMPLE: Your employee tells you that the equipment does not seem to be working right. You know the machinery has been checked, so there must be some other issue. After talking with the employee, it turns out that he really wanted reinforcement and appreciation for working overtime the night before.

How do you spot counseling problems? There's no easy formula, but the first thing you must do is to be alert to what you observe and to see how an employee presents himself or herself. Watch for mannerisms, unusual behavior, absenteeism, tardiness. Also, pay attention to talk among co-workers and/or other managers, reports from staff and/or personnel, and news from outside.

Recognizing counseling problems requires that you observe both verbal and nonverbal behavior. Remember that people cannot hide their feelings, even when they do not talk about them.

THE SORTING PROCESS: WHAT IS THE PROBLEM AND WHO OWNS IT?

As you become aware of a counseling need, you will eventually want to understand the problem. WHAT TO EXPECT: Most of the time, the real problem is not the one that surfaces first.

EXAMPLE: Unraveling the real problem is like diagnosing a knock in your car's engine. Maybe it's a problem with the fuel, but more likely something else is out of adjustment.

To counsel more effectively, you must first know what the problem is. WHAT TO DO: Talk about it with the employee. Try to get as much information as you can, and try to get the employee to talk about his or her feelings. As you continue to talk, the real problem will emerge.

Next, determine who owns the problem. This is one of the most critical decisions you must make. It determines the extent of your participation and approach. WHAT TO DO: Refer to Chapter 4 for guidelines on mutual problem solving.

When the employee owns the problem, your main role is to listen. With highly personal problems, passive listening is useful, if only to keep yourself from assuming some of the problem. Active listening, on the other hand, increases your involvement yet maintains objectivity and independence from the problem.

A CASE-IN-POINT: Here is how the two techniques might be used.

Employee: *I am hoping to get this custody thing settled before my son starts summer baseball.*

Passive Response

Manager: *Uh-huh.*

Active Response

Manager: *You seem concerned about this custody matter interfering with your son's baseball.*

You'll find that active listening helps you:

1. Learn to deal with strong feelings without fear of arousing them any further.
2. Sort out the employee's and your own responsibility in a problem situation.
3. Help the employee understand his or her feelings and to accept them as they are.
4. Form a more meaningful relationship with employees.
5. Promote better listening on the part of the employee.

When you own the problem, one of the most useful techniques is the "I" message.[3] This conveys what you, the manager, are feeling.

A CASE-IN-POINT: Martha is chronically late for work. Instead of saying, "Martha, you are thirty minutes late; you're messing up the schedule!" the manager says, "Martha, I have a problem when you come in late. I can't get the work out on schedule." This puts things in perspective. Martha feels less threatened and is more apt to take responsibility for being on time.

COUNSELING AND COACHING: HOW TO HANDLE THE DAY-TO-DAY SITUATIONS

Counseling goes as naturally with coaching as butter with bread. Counseling may be needed at any stage in the coaching process but particularly in instruction and evaluation. During the instructional stage, counseling is concerned with five types of learning problems:

1. *Poor listener.* If you find yourself repeating instructions too many times, chances are the employee is not actively listening. Urge him or her to respond verbally to your instructions.

2. *Mental or physical slowness.* If the person is obviously of limited intelligence, prepare yourself to be patient. You need to understand, use empathy, and give support.

3. *Low motivation.* Reasons for low motivation can be varied and complex. Your counseling need is to understand what makes the employee tick. Look for clues to attitudes and drives. Listen reflectively to verbal and nonverbal behaviors.

4. *Emotional problem.* Depending on the severity, prepare to refer this person for professional help. Don't play psychologist or try to do too much. Give even-handed treatment and assert your own needs. Be firm but supportive.

5. *Basket case.* These are people who simply will not respond to instruction for a variety of reasons—mostly emotional. The counseling need is extensive. Rather than frustrate yourself, you're better off consulting with the appropriate staff people—and your boss—about this individual.

---

[3] See Thomas Gordon, *Parent Effectiveness Training and Leadership Effectiveness Training* (New York: New American Library, 1975).

Counseling in the evaluation phase is one of your greatest challenges as a manager. Successful managers do certain things in common. You might not follow the exact procedure, but these steps should prove helpful:

1. *Do your spadework.* Get information you need and make accurate observations.
2. *State your objective and your concern.*
3. *Give specific feedback.* Address emotional and behavioral aspects; identify the exact behavior you want changed.
4. *Discuss improvement alternatives.*
5. *Encourage employee decision and commitment.*
6. *Work to develop a plan that resolves the problem.*

Part of the evaluation process involves assessing development needs of the employee. Some needs are simple, others not so obvious. Your best bet is to know your people individually, their capabilities, weaknesses, and needs. WHAT TO DO: Use listening and counseling skills to increase the employee's awareness of needs. By confronting what you see and feeding it back to the person, he or she becomes challenged to do something about it. The checklist following can help you.

CHECKLIST FOR ASSESSING DEVELOPMENT NEEDS

- Do you know the intellectual capabilities of your employees?
- Do you understand their emotional patterns and needs?
- Do you know their goals and aspirations?
- Do they have personality deficiencies, such as anger, shyness, defeatism, and so on?

PRACTICAL COUNSELING STRATEGIES AND TECHNIQUES YOU CAN USE

Here are the main strategies for structuring counseling (and coaching) sessions:

1. *Strike while the iron is hot.* Look for the right time and occasion to counsel—as close as possible to the event.

2. *Focus on results.* The employee sees his or her problem more clearly when observing the outcomes.

3. *Use case examples.* Employees can relate to specifics more so than to general feedback.

4. *Keep your own options open by giving the employee options.* Doing this develops the employee and invites him or her to join in the solution and to take responsibility.

5. *Try another viewpoint.* Use your creative ability and discuss it with people in another area who aren't as familiar with your operation.

6. *Engage the group.* If a problem involves more than one person, bring the resources of the group to bear on it.

Try these techniques for successful counseling:

1. *Role play.* Have the employee practice the behavior that causes the problem. If the employee made a mistake, give feedback and let the person see that he or she did wrong. CAUTION: This technique can backfire unless you get across the points necessary and refocus on the positive.

2. *Visualization.* Have the employee imagine an ideal solution. This approach can help him or her focus on goals and effective solutions.

3. *Role reversal.* Here you get the employee to reverse roles in his or her problem situation. This approach develops understanding and sensitivity to other's needs.

4. *Underlying thought.* Try to get to the underlying feelings by making the employee listen actively to himself.

5. *Self-concept confrontation.* Here you get the employee to look at his or her self-perception and straighten out the distortions.

6. *Vicarious modeling.* Have the employee identify someone who demonstrates a behavior that the employee would like to have. Then the employee acts "as if" he or she were that person. This reinforces desirable behavior and helps build confidence.

7. *Contracting.* This requires a specific understanding and a commitment to act in a certain way. In return, you agree to observe and respond in some way. This is an excellent way to build trust.

You've probably heard about *group counseling* and its pros and cons. Most group counseling takes place in a professional setting. However, should the need arise, it's a good idea to know something about it in order to make a better judgment when referring an employee.

In a group counseling session, the members discuss their problems under the guidance of a professional counselor. The group members share their experiences and give feedback to other members, thereby opening the possibility for several perspectives to a given problem. The group serves as a means of support and helps individuals build confidence.

> EXAMPLE: One successful counseling group is Alcoholics Anonymous.

On the other hand, group counseling precludes privacy and often limits the attention an individual would get from the counselor. The success of the group depends on the skills of the counselor and the willingness of the members to open up. All in all, the group format can be valuable and help increase human relations skills.

Once the problem is resolved through counseling and you've established a productive relationship, follow-up is necessary. And, this is an on-going process. REMEMBER: Today's solutions lead to tomorrow's problems.

HOW MANAGERS CAN SPOT AND DEAL WITH PERSONAL PROBLEMS AND UNUSUAL BEHAVIOR

As a manager, you must recognize that problem behavior is often related to emotional conflict and frustration. Basically, frustration is an observable by-product of one's inability to function or reach goals. Such inability may be due to real or imagined constraints.

Personal problems come in a wide assortment, ranging from work-related to external emotional problems. The following list gives a range of typical personal problems. Consider how they would affect worker performance or status:

1. Disturbance with fellow employees.
2. Worry about advancement or lack of career progress.
3. Dissatisfaction with present job or salary.

4. Financial problems.

5. Demotion, layoff, involuntary transfer.

6. Worry about job security.

7. Marital problems; conflicts in outside relationships.

8. Illness/personal health, job-related stress.

9. Problems with children.

10. Problems in relationship with immediate manager.

11. Voluntary transfer and/or promotion.

12. Problems related to age.

13. Problems related to discrimination.

14. Drugs and alcohol.

15. Emotional health; moods, depression, mental disorder.

The checklist following tells you how to recognize whether personal problems exist.

WHAT TO LOOK FOR TO SPOT SIGNS AND SYMPTOMS OF PERSONAL PROBLEMS

- Frequent or excessive absenteeism; patterns of absenteeism.

- Frequent tardiness and early departures.

- On-the-job accidents (especially unusual circumstances or negligent acts causing injury to self or other employees).

- Improper handling of materials or equipment (potentially resulting in breakage).

- Fluctuation in overall performance level; unsteady or unpredictable production rates.

- Poor judgment; change in working ability.

- Negative attitudes toward job assignments and responsibilities.

- Disrespect for authority.

- Increased outward expression of anger; improper or offensive language.

- Obvious deterioration in personal appearance and manner.

- Reports of involvement with the law.

- Wage attachments.

- Change in actions and communication patterns (especially those producing conflict).

- Any other change you perceive or observe compared with past behavior.

- Excess in habits such as smoking, eating, and drinking.

It's one thing to observe problem behavior but quite another to approach the troubled employee. An employee may or may not openly ask for assistance and usually does not want a direct response. WHAT TO DO: When an employee's behavior indicates an obvious personal problem and formal disciplinary procedures have not been implemented, these useful strategies can help you approach the employee:[4]

1. Establish levels of work performance you expect.
2. Be specific about supportive behavioral criteria; that is, absenteeism, poor job performance, and so on.
3. Be consistent.
4. Try not to analyze the problem yourself.
5. Restrict negative feedback to job performance.
6. Be firm.
7. Be prepared to cope with the employee's resistance, defensiveness, or hostility.
8. Get the employee to acknowledge the problem.
9. Show the employee he cannot play you against higher management and/or the union.
10. Give information on the availability of counseling sessions.
11. Discuss drinking only if it occurs on the job or if the employee is obviously under the influence.
12. Get a commitment from the employee to meet specific work criteria and monitor this plan for improvement, based on work performance.
13. Explain that the employee must decide whether or not to seek assistance.
14. Emphasize the confidentiality of the program.

---

[4] From Christine A. Filipowiez, "The Troubled Employee: Whose Responsibility?" *The Personnel Administrator* (June 1979).

All of these basic quidelines could not be complete without a list of specific "don'ts." So, do not:[5]

1. Play the role of psychologist.
2. Debate with employees about personal problems.
3. Terminate the discussion without considering available special services.
4. Protect the employee or cover up his or her problems.
5. Be misled by sympathy-involving tactics.

HOW TO KNOW WHEN AND HOW TO MAKE REFERRALS

You are in a key role for recognizing troubled employees and steering them toward proper assistance. From your day-to-day interaction, you know the employees and are aware of their normal behavior patterns. Your familiarity enables you to help employees establish a direct and appropriate solution or plan of action.

The best way to make referrals is to promote self-referral by the employee. Remain objective and remember your responsibilities to the organization when you decide about referring. WHEN TO DO IT: Look for the right time—usually when the employee asks, hints, or implies that he or she wants to do something about the problem.

When making a referral, your main responsibility is to communicate and provide information about personal assistance services. WHAT TO DO: Become well aware of available resources within the community, including health agency services, union-sponsored programs, and other mental health assistance.

WHAT'S AVAILABLE FROM INDUSTRY COUNSELING PROGRAMS

Informal and formal Employee Assistance Programs (EAP) are used throughout the business community. Informal programs are most closely associated with you, the manager, as the key agent responsible for verbalizing concerns relating to employee personal problems and their possible cures. Formal programs usually include company counselors, psychologists, physicians, and specific procedures for discussing problems and receiving help.

---

[5] Adapted from Hermine Zogat Levine, "Consensus: Employee Counseling Services," *Personnel* (March–April, 1981).

Employee assistance is commonly oriented toward intervention and prevention. Intervention is most common but not necessarily the most effective or easy to administer. Many companies have found informal programs helpful for preventing some personal problems.

Industry programs vary considerably in their comprehensiveness and emphasis. While this may be so, their basic theme is the same:

1. Emotional problems are costly, in terms of lost productivity, absenteeism, accidents, and interpersonal conflict.
2. Workers will often not seek help; they must be encouraged and stimulated to do so.
3. Treatment plans, to be most effective, must include significant others (SOTs) at home and work—perhaps not in the treatment itself but in the strategy and solution for improvement.
4. Improvement of mental and physical health in the job situation includes preventive measures, such as counseling programs, accident reduction, and quality of work life (QWL) programs.

Occupational health programs are concerned with both physical and psychological conditions. Studies have shown that many personal problems are attributable to unfavorable QWL in the form of alienation, meaningless work, loss of sense of importance, and stress-induced illness. Industrial QWL programs have shown tangible success in the form of reduced absenteeism, fewer grievances, and a lower accident rate.[6] Such programs can eliminate certain stress producers such as highly restrictive work rules.

CAREER COUNSELING: HOW TO BRING THE EMPLOYEE ALONG

Your role in employee career development goes hand in hand with the counseling/coaching relationship. Since you work closely with them on a daily basis, you provide a useful vantage point for career planning. You also are in a good position to collect information from the total work enviroment.

---

[6] Randall Schuler, "Occupational Health in Organizations: Strategies for Personal Effectiveness," *Personnel Administrator* (January 1982).

Ideally, responsibility for career development is shared equally among organization, employee, and the immediate superior. However, this model is not practical in most cases. The real responsibility lies with the employee. You can be helpful by performing a supportive role and nurturing the career development plan objectively and skillfully. THE KEY: You and the employee must establish a productive counseling relationship. To do this, you need empathy, positive regard, and continuity.

Employees need to begin their career planning by performing a self-analysis, identifying needs, wants, strengths, weaknesses, and perceived characteristics. You facilitate this evaluation by remaining objective and supportive and guiding the employee through a complete personal assessment.

As the employee embarks on a well-defined career plan, he or she requires continuous feedback. Even if negative, this feedback when provided objectively, can help to correct performance or modify action plans. REMEMBER THIS: Your feedback must be continuous. The yearly performance appraisal is not enough to satisfy employee needs for on-going guidance.

You can assess individual development needs in two ways: through the stage concept or by using the basic interest idea.

The stage concept is concerned with the different phases (or stops) in a career. A typical classification follows this four-phase model;[7]

1. Apprentice
2. Colleague
3. Mentor
4. Sponsor

This model suggests a skilled work setting reminiscent of the traditional crafts and trades. WHAT TO DO: You need to be aware of the employee's learning stage and relate it to his or her situation. Needs vary as the person progresses through the stages.

The second approach assures the employee's basic interests. One useful system identifies three orientations: data, people, and things. Virtually every job focuses on one or more of these areas. Figure 7.3 shows how skill orientations and jobs come together under this scheme.

---

[7] P.H. Thompson, G.W. Dalton, and R.L. Price, "The Four Stages of Professional Careers—A New Look at Performance by Professionals," *Organizational Dynamics* vol. 6, no. 1 (Summer 1977).

SKILL ORIENTATIONS AND SPECIFIC BEHAVIORS

Data	*People*	*Things*
Synthesizing	Coaching	Manipulating
Copying	Counseling	Transporting
Processing	Supervising	Fabricating
Compiling	Negotiating	Driving
Comparing	Instructing	Setting up
Analyzing	Persuading	Handling
Coordinating	Assisting	Feeding
	Treating	Tending

JOBS UNDER THE SKILL ORIENTATIONS

Data	*People*	*Things*
Typist	Personnel	Mechanic
Accountant	Manager	Farmer
Computer programmer	Teacher	Truck driver
Teller	Counselor	Painter
Air traffic controller	Clergy	Computer repairman
Systems analyst	Politician	Landscaper
Copyreader	Receptionist	Cook
Engineer	Entertainer	Machinist
Draftsman	Physician	Supply clerk
Artist	Waitress	

Based partly on the work of John L. Holland, in *Making Vocational Choices: A Theory of Careers* (Englewood Cliffs, NJ: Prentice-Hall, Inc. 1973). Also, see Richard N. Bolles, *Success Life/Work Planning Guide* (Chicago: Success Unlimited, Inc., 1982).

FIGURE 7.3

By recognizing these basic interests and skills in employees, you can be more effective when giving career guidance. Once you establish a basic interest, it's not likely to change. The employee may shift focus *within* the category, but the basic interest remains.

EXAMPLE: Sally may change her preference from operating a machine to doing a precision setup instead. But her basic skill still lies with things.

How do you know the employee's basic skill orientation? One can use direct observation, testing, and experiential evaluation. For you, direct observation is the best.

TESTED TECHNIQUES FOR EFFECTIVE CAREER COUNSELING

An effective *career discussion* is an active two-way exchange in which you and the employee are both giver and receiver. You are the catalyst who initiates discussions and clearly defines the organization's needs. The employee provides information while managing his or her own career plan.

Here are certain guidelines that will help you conduct the career discussion:

1. Zero in on career orientations; ask open-end questions such as "Tell me about . . . "

2. Listen actively; do not interrupt; restate what you think the employee is saying and feeling; ask for clarification if you need it.

3. Provide direct, honest feedback.

4. Follow the employee's thought pattern; do not jump to conclusions or impose your own judgment.

5. Point out options/alternatives; evaluate necessary skills.

6. Avoid distractions; discuss in a private place.

7. Recognize that an employee may be fearful of counseling.

8. Be aware of nonverbal cues.

Programmed counseling is based on statistical sampling and analysis to provide factual input. It provides another perspective from which to draw counseling ideas. Here's how it works: Statistical data from a variety of sources (employee records, national studies, work-force studies, and so on) are combined with a step-by-step procedure for identifying work elements and developing a career plan. It produces a picture of the present and anticipates future events based on observable trends.

> EXAMPLE: If you recognize a trend toward automating a welding operation, you would incorporate this information in your career discussions with a welder.

Visualization is a process in which a person conjures a mental picture of an event or situation. Using visualization as an approach for teaching employees to manage their career development will help increase awareness. Once employees become aware of their feelings, they can explore alternative career paths, envisioning responses and behaviors to different conditions. Then they can begin to decide on directions.

> A CASE-IN-POINT: An American soldier was imprisoned for three years during the Vietnam War. This soldier had played very little golf prior to entering the military and, of course, did not have the opportunity to play golf as a POW. Partly to occupy his mind, he began to visualize himself playing golf. He played the game over and over in his mind. When he finally went home, he went out to play golf with friends. Incredibly, he shot an 80 in 18 holes!

However, the employee must recognize and accept his or her responsibility for achieving luck and success. Your main task is to maximize the organizational opportunities and influence the employee's outlook while minimizing unrealistic expectations.

WARNING: Many an enthusiastic employee gets pumped up by a dynamic image only to find later that it's all hype. The employee turns sour and no longer trusts you or the organization. WHAT TO DO: Be realistic. If a job is a dead-end one, say so. At the same time, emphasize realistic opportunities that do exist.

PROFILE OF A CAREER DEVELOPER

Many people can remember someone who was particularly influential in their career. Here's one:

> When I first came to work with the company, I didn't know what I wanted to do. Then when I was assigned to Mr. Stover's section, I began to discover my real interests and eventually got into shipping, which is what I really love.

> It wasn't so much anything he did that influenced me—it was more how he approached things. He seemed to know exactly what to do. It was like he had a master plan in his own mind that was unraveling bit by bit every day, with every piece falling into place. This man didn't have to give me instructions more than once. You knew right away what he had in mind. He was a company man—no doubt about it—but when he talked to me about my interests, it was like he really cared about me. And it

was easy talking to him because I could trust him to keep things private.

One thing that puzzled me about him was why he didn't seem more concerned about moving up in the organization. If anyone would make a good upper-level manager, he would. I think he has higher things in mind but not positions as much as responsibilities. And maybe he's just so interested in people that he won't use them to get ahead. He taught me a big lesson here— one I'll always remember: Wherever my career takes me, whatever I do—even if I don't always like it—do my best; give 100 percent and your rewards will follow; it'll get you what you want.

HOW TO EASE THE PAIN THROUGH DEPARTURE COUNSELING

Departure counseling occurs when an employee leaves the organization, either voluntarily or otherwise. Its purpose is to assist the employee in phasing out old experiences and facing new ones and to get information and feedback helpful to you and the department.

When the departure is voluntary, the counseling should include an exit interview. Try to get information on the employee's perceptions of the department and the job, suggestions for improvements, and insights that will contribute to your unit's effectiveness.

WHAT TO DO: Use the basic interview process (from Chapter 6) for conducting an exit interview. Follow these steps:

1. *Prepare* for the interview by knowing your objectives, having a question list, and arranging a suitable place and time.

2. *Conduct* the interview by putting the employee at ease, using active listening without criticism, and sharing objectives, understanding, and confidences.

3. *Follow up* by reviewing notes, determining how you will use the information, and developing action plans for implementing suggestions.

REMEMBER: People might have some reservations about giving feedback unless they are sure the information will not hurt anyone. If the employee understands that you will use the information constructively, he or she will share it more freely.

When severance is involuntary, several problems may arise, including the emotional reaction. In general, the employee's reactions occur in these stages:

1. *Shock and denial.* The first response is often, "There must be some mistake. I can't believe it."

2. *Anger and rage.* This is often their way of striking back psychologically at the source of the information, usually you.

3. *Defense mechanisms.* These are ways to escape from the unpleasantness, including:

   a. *Avoidance/escape.* Casting it out of one's mind.

   b. *Denial.* Continuing to pretend it didn't happen.

   c. *Displacement/projection.* Scapegoating, taking out anger on other innocent targets.

   d. *Repression.* Submerging one's feelings rather than venting them.

   e. *Reaction formation.* Reacting oppositely to the real feelings.

4. *Despair, depression.* Developing a sense of futility or hopelessness.

5. *Reflective grief.* Beginning to reflect on the past and how he or she could have changed the course of events. This is the first sign of constructive behavior.

6. *Positive behavior.* Taking on the attitude that life must go on and initiating positive actions. At this point, you can assist by referring the person to other information and counseling sources.

The decision for removal must be made carefully, and generally not by you alone. You'll want to discuss the factors leading to the decision with your superiors or personnel officers.

WHAT TO DO: You must document legally and organizationally valid reasons for termination and provide that information to the employee. Be certain the employee receives all benefits and pay owed to him or her.

Termination, at best, is a stressful experience—for you as well as the employee. IMPORTANT: Do not feel guilty about firing the employee. The employee may try to pin the blame on you, but it's the employee's behavior that caused the dismissal, not *yours*. Try to benefit by learning from the experience. This positive attitude can help prevent possible recurrence.

CHAPTER 8

How Leadership Development Is Your Opportunity for Growth as a Manager

A man's reach should exceed his grasp, or what's a heaven for.

—ROBERT BROWNING

LEADERSHIP is one of the most critical and scarce resources in organizations today. Many talented people are choosing specialized staff positions rather than assuming positions of leadership partly because of the demands and stresses associated with it. This trend should and can be reversed. But here's the irony: Altering the situation requires effective leadership.

The old adage "leaders are born, not made" is more fiction than fact. Given native ability and an interest in the work, it's possible to develop leadership capability in most people. Every manager is a leader, but managers are very unequal in their leadership capabilities. True, not everyone is destined for greatness, but nearly everyone can be a better leader. This chapter will help you develop a realistic image of yourself as a leader, not by scrapping the ideals that are so important for your professional growth, but by understanding the subject in concrete and meaningful terms. You'll increase your awareness of the leadership role, improve your skills in leading others, establish your leadership ideal and the qualities necessary to achieve it, understand your own style as a leader, and increase your capacity for handling various situations. In so doing, you have an opportunity to grow beyond your expectations.

THE ART AND SCIENCE OF LEADERSHIP

Organizational leadership is defined as the process of prescribing, influencing, and facilitating the achievement of organizational objectives. Managerial leadership is that part of organizational leadership that facilitates and motivates employee performance and cooperation. IMPORTANT: Performance alone is not sufficient as an indicator of managerial leadership; you need cooperative effort from the group, too.

> EXAMPLE: The foreman who is able to motivate operators to meet or exceed standards is fulfilling part of the leadership role. If he or she obtains genuine cooperation in the process, the leadership role is complete.

Over many years of research, evidence shows that effective leaders possess two overall qualities: consideration and structure. The former incorporates the human qualities of empathy and ability to communicate. Structure includes the qualities of objectivity, judgment, and breadth. The ability to plan and organize, for example, is part of structure. The most effective leadership combination would be an almost equal blend of the two. However, the situations and environments of managers differ greatly, and this makes any set of guidelines for effective leadership difficult to prescribe.

The science of leadership is concerned with the study of leadership and its techniques. Its approach is as rational and uniform as possible in order to get predictable results every time.

Leadership is such that science can provide only a part of the answer, however. Leadership is both science and art—and the art prevails in any complicated and uncertain situation.

You can define the art of leading as the use of higher principles, vision, intuition, and judgment in leading others. In the true art of leadership, you do not *try* to lead—you simply do what you think has to be done. And the result is leadership.

Are leaders born or made? Generally speaking, here is our response: 80 percent made, 20 percent born. The 80 percent is known as "nurture," where leadership is made. It includes development of personal values such as moral integrity, courage, common sense, intellectual acumen, and social concern.

WHERE AND HOW TO GET POWER

Since leadership is an influencing process, the wellsprings of leadership are likewise found in sources of influence. And from these sources you derive power. There are four basic sources of influence:

1. *Situation Power.* This simply means being in the right place at the right time with sufficient resources and support. Put these together and you get *clout.*
2. *Authority.* This is the legitimate right to decide.
3. *Personal capability.* The most influential are competency and interpersonal skills.
4. *Personality (charisma).* Charismatic leaders take action, are willing to act, make decisions, and get things accomplished.

The *charismatic* leader possesses personal magnetism, emanating from his or her personality. A *functional* leader influences others by performing his or her tasks as designated within the position. Examples of settings in which charismatic and functional leaders operate most effectively are shown in Figure 8.1.

SETTING FAVORABLE TO CHARISTMATIC
AND FUNCTIONAL LEADERS

Charismatic	*Functional*
Sales training	Budgeting
Stimulating performance	Paperwork
Negotiation	Giving technical instruction
Counseling and coaching	
Providing good direction	Administering disciplinary measures
Clarifying values	Interpreting policy
Resolving conflict	Planning and scheduling
Creative decision making	Rational decision making

FIGURE 8.1

Formal leaders have positional authority; *informal* leaders do not. With formal leaders, authority itself is potential power; but without personal influence, the leader remains weak. The informal leader is accepted by the group and can become quite influential. THE BEST FORMULA:

Informal + Formal = Managerial leadership

To increase your personal clout, here is a process you might find useful:

Step One: Start with your own position. Analyze your authority, support, and other sources of organizational influence.

Step Two: Assess your strengths and abilities, focusing on what you can do, not on what you can't. Determine what new skills and knowledge you need to increase your effectiveness.

Step Three: Examine your goals and values, the kind of life you want to lead, the kind of person you want to become. Try to identify the factors that hinder your future development.

Step Four: Understand your followers. Recognize that they also have goals, as well as a stake in the success of your operation.

Step Five: Know your product or service—the end result of your effort. In the final analysis, the success of that is the reason you— and your department—are there.

Step Six: Cement your understanding with your own boss. Let him or her know your needs and plans. Find out what your boss expects of you.

Step Seven: Give direction, not directions. Help employees focus on the goal by keeping your own sights on it. Effective training means helping them learn rather than lecturing.

AN EFFECTIVE LEADER: WHAT THE LEADER DOES, FEELS, AND IS

Behavior:
What the Effective Leader Does

- Communicates goals and direction.

- Responds to followers' needs.

- Takes initiative.

- Thinks about consequences.

- Converts thoughts and plans into action.

- Approaches each situation on its own merits. Uses the style that works best.

- Inspires and stimulates others to achieve objectives.

- Gets others to reach further than they would without a leader.

- Charts his own path; takes necessary and reasonable risks—big risks when higher principles are at stake.

- Listens to others; empathizes.

- Helps followers develop themselves.

Attitudes:
How the Effective Leader Feels

- Concern for the best interests of people.

- Positive focus.

- Developmental; helpful.

- When necessary, tough-minded or gentle and understanding.

- Uncompromising dedication to worthwhile values and goals.

- Accepting of responsibility for own behavior.

- Open-minded—to different people, views, approaches.

Personal Attributes:
What the Effective Leader Is and Has

- Spontaneity.

- Enthusiasm.

- Perseverance.

- Integrity.

- Intelligence, at least commensurate with the group.

- Courage; willingness to take risks.

- Common sense.

- Health—sufficient to function energetically.

- Values; firm set of values—own, not someone else's.
- Ability to think both rationally and intuitively.

HOW TO DEVELOP YOUR OWN LEADERSHIP PHILOSOPHY

A philosophy is a system of thinking about the meaning of things and how one uses them in relation to others. You should form your own philosophy of leadership in order to develop healthy, clear thinking perspectives as you handle problems and challenges. Here are seven guidelines for developing your leadership philosophy:

1. Begin with your own purpose in life—your guiding principles for living.
2. Read about the subject. Good examples are *Pathfinders*[1] and *Managers for the Year 2000*.[2]
3. Develop a clear self-image—what you want to become and how you will achieve your purposes.
4. Put your job and your life in a perspective that is best for you. Make your priorities a conscious decision.
5. Know others; respect their purposes and the organization's as well.
6. Stick to the basics. Seek truths, not gimmicks and superficial explanations.
7. Make sure your actions reflect your principles.

Principles are the building blocks of any meaningful philosophy. They reflect your basic conclusions on cause and effect. Here are seven principles of effective leadership:

1. Every worthwhile endeavor requires leadership for its successful completion.
2. Leadershp by example is many times more effective than leadership by coercion and deception.
3. Leadership qualities can be developed, given a normal mental capacity.
4. Leadership is a positive force that stimulates goal-directed behavior in others.

---

[1] By Gail Sheehy (New York: William Morrow and Company, 1981).
[2] Edited by William H. Newman (Englewood Cliffs, NJ: Prentice-Hall, 1978).

5. Effective leadership develops self-leadership in others.

6. Leadership styles are secondary to leadership purposes.

7. Any leadership style is proper as long as it respects the best interests of followers, the leader, and the organization.

YOUR LEADERSHIP ROLE AND EC³

EC³—employee, company, customer, and community—each influence a leader's role and style. Employees look for certain things in their leader. Customers expect quality, service, and economy, which in turn define, indirectly, the leadership role. The community requires you to bring community values into your decision. And, of course, your organization sets the tone of your leadership opportunities. YOUR JOB: You must reconcile the different demands, make sense of them, and resolve contradictions among them.

The organizational setting includes the management structure, policies, system, company philosophy, position authority climate, management traditions, and the organization's overall plan or script. Each bears upon your leadership behavior and role, specifically:

1. *Structure.* Elaborate structure limits your discretion as a leader.

2. *Policies.* You take on the role of enforcer and implement policy; thus, your discretion is limited by it.

3. *Management system.* The flow of information and accountability limits your flexibility, authority, and decision-making ability.

4. *Company philosophy.*

5. *Position authority.* This includes how your position is defined and what you are authorized to do.

6. *The organization's traditions.* These are "the ropes" that you must know thoroughly.

7. *The organization's script.* Applied to the organization, it is the unwritten destiny that reflects the underlying success or failure of the organization.

Leadership is also shaped by a number of outside influences, among them:

1. *Culture.* The attitude, practices, traditions, and values in a group or in the society.
2. *Values and beliefs.* The ideals and beliefs that are deemed important.
3. *Traditions.* Long-standing practices that take on an air of reverence.
4. *Political climate.* The prevailing atmosphere—conservative or liberal, tense or relaxed, free of controlling.
5. *Technology.* The prevailing method approach to making the product or service.

All these factors on and off the organization converge on the leadership role and define it. In the last analysis, that definition is yours to make.

WHAT IS LEADERSHIP STYLE AND HOW IMPORTANT IS IT TO YOUR SUCCESS?

Leadership style is the approach you use to influence others to produce the desired outcomes. It's so crucial to the leader's job in an organization that the wrong style, or the right style at the wrong time, can send the entire organization into convulsions and even extinction.

A CASE-IN-POINT: A new manager arrived at a large truck manufacturing plant with a different from usual approach. He was more consultative than the former manager. He asked questions and sought advice from workers. At the end of the first week, the employees filed an avalanche of grievances. The new young manager was dumbfounded. He really thought he was being supportive and participative; this was how he preferred to deal with workers. What happened? The change in style upset the workers—it undermined their feeling of security, of knowing and predicting the boss's behavior.

Each of you has a style you most prefer regardless of the situation. This is your basic style that is rooted in your personality, experience, and home life. It is unlikely to change much. Situational style is the approach you select based on the circumstances confronting you. You can change it depending on what works best at the time.

Leadership qualities are revealed in particular styles. If a group of machinists describe their manager as "autocratic" or "directive," they are saying, in effect, that his or her orientation is toward structure. If they say he is "democratic" or "consultative," they are saying he is oriented toward consideration. The further a leader operates toward the consultative end of the scale, the more decision-making authority is delegated to employees. Conversely, the further the manager operates toward the directive end of the scale, the more authority he or she wants to retain. (See Figure 8.2.)

SCALE OF LEADERSHIP STYLE

Directive   Consultative

FIGURE 8.2

The directive approach is normally an efficient way to communicate information, goals, and expectations. It tends to minimize the number of loose ends concerning the work. Properly applied, this approach is particularly effective with new employees. On the negative side, the directive style can create a dependency situation and stifle your employee's development.

The prime value of the consultative style can be found in such words as attitude, acceptance, and commitment. This is the most effective method when attitude change or development are primary concerns. This approach is also very effective as a means of obtaining information. When problem solving is important, this style works well. HOW TO CHOOSE: Remember that your choice is not an ethical one but rather a practical matter—how to best get objectives (human and task) accomplished. Your own attitude will play a large role in your success. You must be willing to listen and possibly to change your views as a result.

Here are several important points to keep in mind:

1. There are varying degrees of directiveness and consultation. Most choices of style fall somewhere in between the two extremes.

2. Your own personal preference needs to be considered.

3. The appropriate style is suggested by the factors in combination rather than individually. However, any one single factor can change the situation toward the opposite style.

> EXAMPLE: Suppose all factors suggest a consultative approach, except that you have several new workers who need training. The training factor would argue for a more directive approach, at least until the employees become proficient in their jobs. At that point, a consultative approach would become appropriate.

HOW TO MAKE YOUR LEADERSHIP STYLE WORK FOR YOU

Your personal leadership style has an important bearing on the performance of employees. You need useful guidelines concerning *which* style is effective under *which* circumstances.

The key to developing your leadership style is flexibility. It's important to understand that no one style is suitable for all purposes. You should use one that is appropriate to the conditions at hand.

> EXAMPLE: In emergency situations, there is little time for discussion. The nursing supervisor tells others what to do. However, when this same nursing supervisor sits down with a nurse for performance review, the directive approach is inappropriate because the situation requires two-way communication to be meaningful.

In order to select the appropriate leadership style, you need to know what conditions favor one or the other style. The conditions can be described in three broad areas: organizational, individual, and situational. (See Figure 8.3.) The first two were discussed earlier in this chapter.

A situational view of leadership identifies systematically which leadership approach works best under a given condition. Figure 8.4 shows one way to analyze leadership situations. The model says that there are eight situational combinations of three

FACTORS THAT FAVOR A DIRECTIVE OR
A CONSULTATIVE STYLE

Favor a   Favor a
Directive Style ◄─────────────────► Consultative Style

Organization Factors

Favor a Directive Style	Favor a Consultative Style
Structured tasks	Unstructured tasks
Simple, unskilled work	Complex work
Programmed working relationships	Fluid working relationships
Very concrete objectives	Intangible objectives
Favorable or very unfavorable relationships with the group	Fairly good relationships with the group
High or low leader position authority	Moderate leader position authority

Individual and Group Factors

Favor a Directive Style	Favor a Consultative Style
Low job interest	High job interest
Limited education and training	Extensive education and training
High followership orientation	Low followership orientation
Group not mature	Mature group

Directive ◄──────── Leader's Own Basic ────► Consultative
                    Style Preferences

Situational Factors

Favor a Directive Style	Favor a Consultative Style
High urgency for action	Low urgency for action
Very high or very low risks	Moderate risks
Limited time	Ample time
Individual action involved	Team or group action involved
Decision acceptance not essential	Acceptance important
Leader has the information needed	Leader has incomplete information; needs group output

FIGURE 8.3

factors: position power of the leader, the task structure, and leader–member relations. For each, there is an appropriate leadership style. Overall, you might say that situations 1, 2, 3, and 8 call for a task-oriented leader. On the other hand, situations 4, 5, 6, and 7 call for an approach oriented toward human relations. What the model does, then, is increase your ability to predict outcomes that, in turn, put you in better control of the situation.

EIGHT SITUATIONS FOR LEADERSHIP EFFECTIVENESS*

	Situation							
	1	2	3	4	5	6	7	8
Position Power	Strong	Weak	Strong	Weak	Strong	Weak	Strong	Weak
Task Structure	High		Low		High		Low	
Leader– Member Relations	Good				Poor			

*Based on model developed by Fred E. Fiedler and M.M. Chemers, *Leadership and Effective Management* (Glenview, IL: Scott Foresman, 1974).

FIGURE 8.4

One of the most popular notions of leadership style is depicted by the Managerial Grid.[3] The grid expresses the most effective combination of people and task orientations within a given situation and has had a considerable impact among managers around the country. (See Figure 8.5.) You can use it to examine your own approaches. Ask yourself, "Am I overly task oriented?" or "Have I reached the 9.9 level of team management?" According to the grid, 9.9 expresses an ideal combination of people and task orientation.

By using the same people- and task-orientation axis, you can view the grid in terms of degrees of structure and consideration. CAUTION: The grid is built on attitudes, while structure/considera-

---

[3] Robert Blake and Jane S. Mouton, *The Managerial Grid* (1964).

tion is based on actual behavior. To find out which leadership orientation contributes most to your leadership effectiveness, it is almost always best to look at how people actually behave; in other words, at structure/consideration.

THE MANAGERIAL GRID

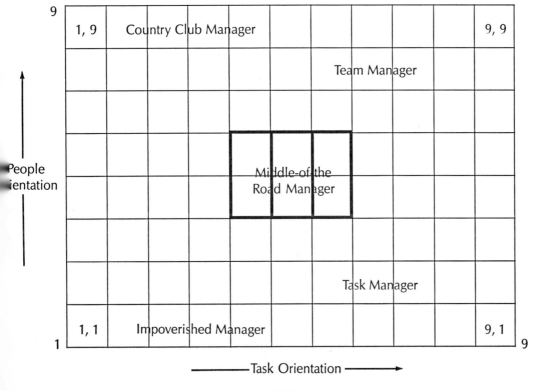

FIGURE 8.5

TESTED TECHNIQUES TO HELP YOU FIND AND USE YOUR FULL POTENTIAL

Realizing your full potential is directly related to your self-image, self-esteem, and self-motivation. Self-image (how you see yourself in terms of success/failure, capability, relations with others, personal influence, skill and role behavior) and self-esteem (how you feel about yourself) form a mental picture or view about yourself. A high self-image is essential for superior leadership. A low self-image will naturally produce opposite results.

Different self-images reflect important aspects of yourself. Among them are

1. *Leadership.* If high, you will accept challenges, take risks. If low, you rely more on position, rules, and so on.

2. *Physical.* A positive physical self-image produces awareness of and caring for your body.

3. *Social.* Confidence in social situations affects how well you work with a group and how you interact with others.

4. *Intellectual.* This affects your ability to learn and to handle the mental part of your job.

5. *Psychological.* What you are as a person, your own growth potentials, flexibility in responding to the needs of a situation, your ability to change—all are part of and determined by this self-concept.

People are known to work day and night to achieve a goal that actualizes their self-image. What's important is that behavior be consistent with the self-image and that the image itself be realistic. The healthy self-image is anchored in reality and experience, and when positive can produce remarkable accomplishments, advancing the frontiers of your potential and achievements.

HOW TO RAISE YOUR SELF-ESTEEM

1. Decide what you want to accomplish, the new behavior you want. Visualize yourself in action, getting the results you want.

2. Examine your beliefs and develop new ones that support your new behavior.

3. Scrutinize your thought process; determine how you can replace unproductive ways with more positive ones.

4. Give positive recognition—to yourself and others.

The basis for motivating yourself is most often rooted in three areas: achievement, power, and affiliation. Here are some thoughts and guidelines about this:

1. Whatever your motivating force, the important thing is to be aware of it and recognize it in others.
2. In order to influence others effectively, you need to give them appropriate recognition.
3. People will perform their jobs as expected if you provide the appropriate recognition.
4. Motivational styles develop from early life and are not changed overnight. Permanent change requires consistent recognition and reinforcement.
5. Since many employees are affiliation motivated, and most leaders just the opposite, the biggest challenge to a manager/leader is to understand this and work with people accordingly.

Regardless of your motivational level, you must recognize certain constraints. Leadership substitutes replace, supplement, or neutralize the need for leadership, and they generally are found in four places:

1. *The subordinate.* Employee characteristics such as education, work experience, skill, and attitude are potential substitutes for leadership. EXAMPLE: A highly skilled and experienced worker requires little task-oriented leadership.

2. *The task.* Typically, tasks that are routine, long term, and provide immediate performance feedback are less likely to require direction.

3. *The organization.* Potential substitutes include formal rules, procedures or policies, specialized and active staff functions, cohesive work groups, organizational rewards, physical distance.

4. *Self-management.* Persons motivated by promise of individual reward usually become autonomous to direction.

REMEMBER THIS: Leadership substitutes are aids, not just constraints, to your leadership job. They can help you as much as hurt. WHAT TO DO: It's best to concentrate on what you *can* do; that way, you'll end up having more influence on the worker *and* the system.

HOW TO BE A PERSON-TO-PERSON LEADER

Interpersonal leadership is the face-to-face influence and direction you supply to people in accomplishing your unit's and group's effectiveness. The qualities that distinguish the interpersonally effective leader are basically those of an effective person, as described in Chapter 4.

As a manager, you spend most of your leadership time in person-to-person engagements (sometimes combat). Your job holds many frustrations, and among the hardest to handle are those involving personal styles. Just as leaders have their preferred style, people typically have a dominant orientation. By understanding it, you can usually pinpoint reasons for conflict. As your skills increase in this area, you'll become a better leader.

There are five major interpersonal tasks, each of which has been covered in previous chapters: (1) delegating, (2) coaching, (3) counseling, (4) communicating, and (5) performance appraisal. In each case, leadership goes a step beyond the task because it requires a more active involvement with the employee. It is the *action* orientation that distinguishes the leader from just a performance appraiser, coach, communicator, delegator, or counselor.

> EXAMPLE: When the employee says, "I see now what went wrong there—I'll have to work on improving that," the leader says more than "OK." He or she says, "Good. What will you do to bring that about?" REMEMBER: The effective leader looks not at the effort to be spent but rather at the value of the goal to be achieved.

The Path–Goal idea of leadership serves as a useful framework for actively helping your subordinate cope. (See Figure 8.6.) You set a path toward achievement of a goal by breaking down their emotional barriers and redirecting their efforts. The leadership style you choose (directive, supportive, and so on) should respond to the situation at hand.

> A CASE-IN-POINT: Jones assigns a job to an employee, Smith, who agrees to perform it. Jones instructs Smith in the task, and she appears to understand. Now the due date is approaching, and Jones notices that the work is only half completed. Jones discusses it with Smith, who tells him that the work is too boring. What's happening? Smith's goal path is not as clear and direct as Jones originally thought. Smith is feeling dissatisfied and unchallenged by the job. Jones can reverse the situation by using a supportive style and redefining the job and its importance. It may turn out that the job can be streamlined, or that Smith can be given more and better resources to finish.

PATH–GOAL APPROACH

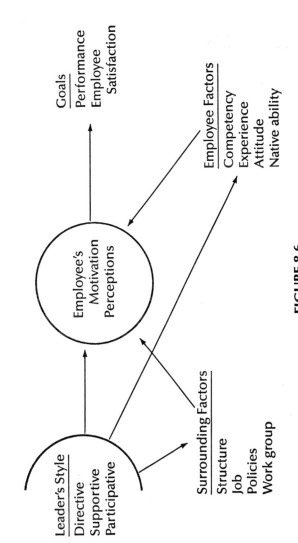

FIGURE 8.6

DON'T MOTIVATE—LEAD!

Remember the question, "How do you motivate?" And remember the answer, "You don't!" Motivation is an internal force that either exists or doesn't. All you can do is arrange the conditions that stimulate and direct an employee's motivation.

An interpersonally effective leader responds to employees' motivational needs by helping them become more productive and satisfied. Given a trusted and reasonable manager, employees will usually ask openly for help. After all, you are the most direct contact they have in the organization.

As a manager, you have two leadership functions: facilitating performance and facilitating cooperation. To accomplish this, two facets of leadership come into play: assuming responsibility and taking initiative.

The aspect of responsibility most closely related to leadership is that of personal commitment. This suggests accepting responsibility for your own behavior and for the results produced by your unit. NOTICE THIS: Once you assume responsibility for yourself and make clear what you perceive as your own responsibility, employees are apt to assume their responsibility.

> A CASE-IN-POINT: A manager who continually passes the buck by claiming that personnel is responsible for employee morale and maintenance is responsible for the sorry conditions of the facilities and so forth, is encouraging employees to do the same. And guess who they're going to use as a scapegoat? If you said the manager, you're absolutely correct.

Initiative means following up on your observations based on your perceived needs of the situation. There is much to be said about "striking while the iron is hot," as soon as you have an accurate perception of the problem *and* your own responsibility in it. CAUTION: There are risks involved, no safe risk-free options.

HOW MANAGEMENT LEADERS HANDLE CONFLICT

Conflict and pressure can interfere with group and individual performance whenever a difference exists between what workers expect and how they are treated. It's your responsibility to keep a realistic, well-defined focus for everyone. Each employee, through your leadership, must have an accurate perception of what is needed and expected. WHAT TO DO: Employ the basic principles for group membership and behavior when dealing with role conflict and pressure. These are discussed in Chapter 4.

Be aware that role conflict and peer pressure might arise within yourself, too. They may develop as organizational or departmental changes create new roles and expectations. These changes can range from operating procedures, as a new job order never before handled, to more structural changes, such as job-sharing, flex time, and so on.

Restoring morale needs solid leadership, action, and tough mental fiber. Your role is to aid the employee when he or she signals a need for leadership and to support the belief in the value of work performance. The need for leadership is clear and direct. WHAT TO LOOK FOR: The signals are usually readily evident. Listen for comments such as, "This place is so depressing..." or "I don't care anymore."

Be aware of various situations that may cause morale to collapse. Any change or event that affects work goals or group membership is tied to morale. People are extremely sensitive to the "how to" and "with what" of performing their jobs. Fear and apprehension about the current and future work situation can also affect morale. WHAT TO DO: Look ahead, plan, and prepare employees for potential obstacles.

Employees are very sensitive to their status and their role. You need to be aware of these barriers in order to deal with them. For example, if you know about an electrician's reluctance to dismantle a carpenter's work to get at a trouble spot, you might begin by acknowledging his personal dilemma. FOOD FOR THOUGHT: Status is, after all, tied in with recognition. It's not the status or role people desire and adhere to—it's the recognition that comes with it.

HOW TO CREATE THE CLIMATE FOR INNOVATION

Did you realize that you are probably trained and educated to use only 50 percent of your brain? Or that a part of your personality that you developed in early childhood has been left untapped, like an undeveloped resource, and might deteriorate so much that you can no longer use it when you need it? In order to use the other 50 percent of your ability in solving a problem, certain conditions are necessary. Some apply to individual activity and others to group activity.

There are no deep, dark secrets to learning how to get into a creative frame of mind. You must do a few rather simple things:

1. Have a sincere desire to solve the problem.
2. Believe in your ability to decide the matter on your own initiative.
3. Quiet yourself and your surroundings. If necessary, go to a location where there are few distractions.
4. Detach yourself from immediate pressures and preoccupations.
5. Visualize a scene, such as a landscape or mountain stream, and hold it for a few minutes. This will help unlock your imagination and let you shift to your creative side.
6. Read for further ideas.

KEEP THIS IN MIND: Ideas always favor the prepared mind. There is no substitute for knowledge.

Brainstorming is a technique whose main purpose is to solve problems creatively. What you want to do is to invite ideas—the more the merrier. Encourage hitchhiking; do not make idea ownership an issue; identify the origins later if you need to.

HOW TO DO IT: First, make it a voluntary activity. Encourage people to think of all kinds of possibilities; even a visual image of something totally unrelated, like an ice cream cone. This will help remove the blinders and get them out of the rut of exact thinking. You must think in approximate terms in order to generate really new ideas. Here are some zany thoughts of the type that could produce truly remarkable ideas and solutions:

1. A computer is like an egg.
2. An umbrella—how is the company like an umbrella?
3. A turtle—how does my unit resemble a turtle?
4. My mother-in-law—how does she resemble my current problem?

Wishes are important in this first phase. This is one time when wishful thinking is needed. Why? Because it opens the realm of possibilities and expands one's reach. Wishes also reflect needs (I wish we could go for a week with no down-time; no rejects), and this stimulates aspirations and goal-setting.

In stage two, the yellow caution light is on. Use your mediating self to process the information; combine ideas into a manageable list; ask for clarification (but no criticism!) so that everyone understands the ideas. The major objective here is to tranform the original list into one that captures and summarizes the main ideas.

In stage three—red-lighting—critics who have been chomping at the bit can have their heyday. Here, you turn to your safekeeping self and make judgments about the ideas—how workable, how important, which one(s) to recommend and which not.

The process should operate in the sequence described. The leader—whether you or someone else—must understand clearly the purpose and tasks in each state and make sure the atmosphere is relaxed and open. Concerning the timing, it is best to have a clean break between stages: for example, an hour of Stage 1, then coffee or lunch break; return for Stage 2, then break again before Stage 3. Why? Because shifting mental gears is best done by actual physical movement.

WHY A LEADER MUST SOMETIMES BE A FOLLOWER

Most supervisory and management writings say very little about followership. Yet, followership is requisite to leadership. Every leader is also a follower, from the Chairman of the Board to the first-line foreman. Regardless of the role you take, there is an accountability, and this involves followership.

The skills and qualities needed for effective followership are three-fold: listening and learning, self-discipline, and persistence. It's worth noting that out of total managerial communication time, studies show that about 45 percent is spent in listening, in contrast to 30 percent talking, 16 percent reading, and about 9 percent writing.

A useful starting point in learning to listen is to become aware of your own listening habits. Ask yourself:

1. Do I listen actively?
2. Am I aware of what the other person is really saying, in addition to or instead of the words I want to hear?
3. Does my mind wander to something else when another person speaks?
4. Am I constructing defenses of my own to screen out things I may not want to hear?

5. Do I see listening as part of my job or as something I must stop and do out of courtesy, before getting back to my work?

Listening and learning go together, but learning also goes a step further. Essentially, *learning* means being receptive to new ideas and willing to change if the change will improve your situation or solve a problem. Let's first cast aside certain myths about learning:

Myth #1: I'm too old to learn. There's not a shred of scientific evidence to support this myth. Plenty of people today in their fifties, sixties, and seventies embark on new careers and learning experiences of all sorts.

Myth #2: You've got to go to school to learn, and I can't do that at this point in my life. The second part may be true, but the first is totally false. Most learning takes place outside of school, not in it.

Myth #3: The best learning takes place in the school of hard knocks. If you've learned everything through hard knocks, they sometimes leave such lasting impressions it's hard to envision any other perspective. In reality, it's possible to learn in many different ways.

The second skill needed for effective followership is *self-discipline.* Self-discipline is a combination of personal autonomy and control. Fundamentally, self-discipline is a matter of directing your actions in order to meet objectives. If those objectives are compatible with the organization's, then the self-discipline is desirable to the company. As a self-disciplined manager, and a follower, you are a tremendous asset to the organization. From the boss's standpoint, you can be trusted to carry out responsibility, to meet deadlines consistently, to take initiative in getting your work accomplished. Your reporting (accountability) to the boss will focus on important results, which many higher level managers prefer over voluminous, detailed reports that obscure the main points and waste their time. WHAT TO DO: If things do not get accomplished as expected, don't present alibis but rather give suggestions and plans for preventing a recurrence. In a word, be your own person—poised, goal oriented, reality oriented, and determined.

Persistence is actually a part of self-discipline. It refers to the determined and consistent effort to obtain or accomplish something. The key ingredient is a goal that you value highly and are willing to expend energy to achieve. Usually when there is lack of persistence, you also find a lack of commitment to the goal. This means that the goal itself must be worthwhile, genuine, and important.

> EXAMPLE: The persistent manager who is strongly convinced that the pay system is obsolete will work to improve the system. Even though he does not control the system, he will make his concerns known to those who do and will pursue the matter to its conclusion. This manager will be respected by his boss, his peers, and subordinates as a person who follows his convictions. He will be trusted to see things through to completion, and even though his requests place demands on managers and staff people, they will perceive him as more effective and valuable than the less active manager.

HOW TO DEAL WITH STRESS EFFECTIVELY

Probably the greatest personal difficulty you experience on the job is stress. What's dangerous is not the stress itself but how it's handled. The more stressful the situation, the more your body and nervous system experience harmful, even fatal, symptoms like gastric secretions, perspiration, enlargement of the adrenal glands, and elevated blood pressure.

According to the National Institute for Occupational Safety and Health, the ten most stressful jobs include foreman (6th), unskilled laborer (1st), secretary (2nd), assembly-line worker (3rd), and factory machine operator (9th). Not only holding one of these jobs yourself, but having the others in your environment—perhaps reporting to you—makes it especially important for you to develop a strategy for dealing with stress.

Personal life factors can impact greatly on managerial performance. Figure 8.7 shows 25 selected items from the Social Readjustment Scale developed by Drs. Thomas Holmes and Richard Rake. These events were found to frequently coincide with the onset of illnesses and are therefore linked to certain diseases and ailments. At what point is illness probable given the recurrence of certain life events? According to Holmes and Rake, if you total 150 points on the scale within a two-year period, the probability jumps to 66 percent, and at 450 points it leaps to 90 percent or near certainty. RATE YOURSELF: Multiply the number of points per event by the number of times it occurred over a two-year period.

Here are 25 selected items from the *Social Readjustment Scale* and their assigned values, from 100 = most conducive to illness, to 0 = least conducive.

EVENT	VALUE
Death of a spouse	100
Divorce	73
Jail term	63
Personal injury or illness	53
Marriage	50
Fired at work	47
Retirement	45
Pregnancy	40
New family addition	39
Change in financial state (either direction)	38
Death of close friend	37
Change to different line of work	36
Foreclosure of mortgage or loan	30
Change in responsibilities at work	29
Trouble with in-laws	29
Revision of personal habits	24
Trouble with boss	23
Change in residence	20
Change in social activites	18
Mortgage or loan less than $10,000	17
Change in sleeping habits	17
Change in eating habits	15
Vacation	13
Christmas	12
Minor violation of the law	11

FIGURE 8.7

Researchers have shown that stress itself is not so damaging as how it's handled. If you are in the 300-point category, by understanding the changes and preparing yourself to cope with them, you could very well land in the 34 percent who do not suffer physical and mental illnesses as a result of stress.

THE KEY: Strategy. As you develop your strategy for handling stress, here are some helpful guidelines:

1. *Get control of your work situation.* First, sort out the factors you can influence and concentrate on those. Don't fret about the things you cannot control.

2. *Keep your work and private lives separate.* Your vacations and weekends wil be more restful and your work life more productive by concentrating on each as an endeavor in itself.

3. *Build a satisfying family life.* The family serves as a buffer for stress problems at work. And a satisfying home life can affect an unsatisfying work situation.

4. Whatever you do to manage these, *do what you enjoy and enjoy what you do.* Each person should select the form of diversion best for them.

5. *Develop a sense of quiet and engineer your environment accordingly.* Noise is stressful, and your body responds to it. SUGGESTION: Find a place where you can be quiet without interruptions.

6. *Anticipate stress and plan your response to it.* By not letting stress take you by surprise, you can prepare your body and mind to respond appropriately. If there is any one antidote for stress, it's the sense of mastery—the feeling of being on top of the situation.

7. *Look at the expectations others have of you and your own expectations.* Do they match? If not, how can you realistically bring them closer together? The distance between or the unmet need is an indicator of the amount of stress you are experiencing. Map out clear-cut, specific paths to close the gap of the unmet needs.

8. *Manage your time.* More on this later.

9. *Work on changing the stressful aspects of your situation.*

10. *Exercise and moderate your habits.* Practically anything excessive—drinking, smoking, eating—can reduce the body's efficiency. Moderation and exercise help both your physical and mental conditioning.

KEY QUALITIES THAT PRODUCE THE ORGANIZATIONALLY EFFECTIVE LEADER

A lot of what you hear about leadership ignores the most important aspect of all—the system in which you operate. You can talk about the personal and interpersonal aspects and get way off base unless you bring in the organization and the system. For example, what do you do when you need to consult more with your employees but your boss does not believe in employee participation because it gives away management prerogatives? It's not a simple question of either obeying or disobeying the boss. It's more a matter of how to do it while preserving unity of purpose within the system.

The part of the overall system that affects your leadership most is the management system. This means the framework and procedures for managerial decision making. There are four basic types of management systems:

1. *Management by Rules and Regulations (MBRR)*. In this system, the leadership role is to enforce and implement policies, rules, and methods. You and your employees have very little decision-making latitude, and you are evaluated on how well you follow the present decision guidelines.

2. *Management by Results (MBR)*. You are evaluated mainly on the basis of outcomes and achievements. Quantitative standards are typically used in this system, such as 500 units per week with no more than 5 percent rejects.

3. *Management by Objective (MBO)*. This widely publicized system evaluates decisions and behavior on the basis of predetermined objectives. MBO is a planning system as well as an evaluation system. The main difference between MBO and MBR is that MBO stresses objective setting on the part of the managers and employees, whereas the standards and objectives are taken as given in MBR.

4. *Management by Initiative and Self-control (MBISC)*. This system grew out of the job enrichment movement. It stresses teamwork and decision making by line employees and has been used in companies such as TRW, Motorola, Volvo, SAAB, Volkswagen, and Ralston Purina. Managers become mainly facilitators and coordinators. Workers are the decision makers and rely mainly on their own initiative and self-coordination.

Figure 8.8 shows the factors that favor each of the management systems mentioned. It's useful for evaluating systems, and even though managers usually do not decide which systems to use, it will help you to understand why your system works the way it does.

Task structure refers to the degree of controls and predetermined methods in a job. If high, MBRR is naturally the system of choice, because it is a highly structured system. Reading across the table, it says that when task structure is high, MBRR and MBR are most appropriate; when moderate, MBR; and when low, MBISC is the system of choice.

ORGANIZATIONAL FACTORS AND MANAGEMENT SYSTEMS

Organizational Factors	MBRR	MBR	MBO	MBISC
Task structure	High	High	Moderate	Low
Nature of objectives	Qualitative General Hard to Measure	Quantitative Specific Measurable	Quantitative Specific Measurable	Either Either Either
Leadership style	Directive and Bureaucratic	Directive	Consultative	Consultative
How much risk in achieving objectives	Very high/ Very low	Moderate	Moderate	Moderate/ High

FIGURE 8.8

Note that all these organizational factors taken together determine which management system is best. The appropriate system depends on all factors combined, so you would need to examine the work relations, nature of objectives, and so on before deciding which is best.

Leadership style is one of the factors in determining the system, although style must also adapt to the system that exists. So it works both ways. WHAT TO DO: Choose a style consistent with the system, and the style you select will influence the choice of the system itself.

HOW TO LEARN TO WORK WITH YOUR BOSS'S STYLE

Working with the boss's style is important to you for various reasons, including keeping your job. It's simpler than some think and not as simple as others believe. Your leadership style determines how your employees will react—cooperatively, grudgingly, or outright defiantly. Managers respond in the same ways to *their* bosses.

Managers tend to be less vocal because they do not have a union or a cohesive peer group to turn to as do their employees. So when the boss shows no respect, managers often swallow their resentments and turn to other ways of venting their feelings—such as drinking, eating, exercise, sports, families, and other outlets, including employees who will listen or tolerate it. Being in harmony with the boss's style is not just an ideal state; it's a healthy, productive one. Just as children feel more secure when parents are in accord, employees feel more secure about where they stand when management is united.

Does this mean you should adjust your style to the boss's? If it involves compromising personal integrity, no. Otherwise, yes, to the degree necessary to show a consistent attitude toward employees and avoid destructive conflict with your boss. WHAT TO DO: Do not seek complete harmony by mimicking the boss's style. Rather, understand the boss's style, where he or she is coming from, and how it affects you. If the boss gives you orders, does not seek your opinion, and only asks: "Any questions?", you might ask yourself if this is the way you should carry out orders with your own employees. If no, determine what approach you can use that will be acceptable to the boss and still meet your needs. This does not mean sneaking in a consultative style, but it may be possible to present the directive as an order, give reasons for it, and ask employees about their reactions to it. IMPORTANT: *Do not* mention the boss or that this is the boss's command.

HOW TO MANAGE YOUR TIME

Since you do not have at your disposal all the time-management tools that higher level managers enjoy, we need to do a little "chewing-gum-and-baling-wire" treatment of the subject. The time-efficient manager is not so much the one who sits down, plans out the day or week, then writes out a blow-by-blow schedule of priorities for accomplishing all the important things. This is more a pipe dream than a reality, much like the foreman who prides himself in his time management only to find his employee relations deteriorating so much that he is about to be demoted.

If you are like many managers, you have already been exposed to many of the typical time-wasters and time-savers that are promoted in seminars, articles, the company newsletter, and this book as well. This is good because it makes you time-conscious, and then you are likely to be more careful in using time.

> EXAMPLE: Managers consider the top time-wasters to be telephone interruptions, drop-in visitors, meetings, crises, lack of clear objectives and priorities, and personal disorganization. By knowing this, you then know the things on which you want to concentrate as you try to become the master of your time.[4]

You may also find help in many of the time-management suggestions from authorities on the subject, such as those presented by Paul Preston and Thomas Zimmerer in their book *Management for Supervisors.*[5] Here is a sample of their suggestions:

1. *Get started right away on important things,* which are often things you do not want to do.

2. *Use a tickler system—* a handy reminder system to keep you on schedule.

3. *Work at work.* Avoid excessive homework. Try to complete your tasks while on the job.

---

[4] Alan Lakein, *How to Get Control of Your Time and Your Life.* (New York: Signet, 1973).
[5] Paul Preston and Thomas Zimmerer, *Management for Supervisors* (Englewood Cliffs, NJ: Prentice-Hall, 1978).

4. *Have a "self" time.* Set aside free, uninterrupted time for you to reflect and plan.

5. *Run tight, efficient meetings.* Set strict time limits for meetings and stick with them.

6. *Answer your own phone and mail*—on a random sampling basis. This keeps you in touch with the important things.

7. *Combine and conquer.* Combine similar tasks and activities. It saves overall time.

8. *K.I.S.S.* Keep it short and simple. Get to the point.

9. *Expect the unexpected*—and allow time for it.

10. *Gang up on visitors.* Plan to involve others and have prearranged signals for concluding the visit.

11. *Avoid temptation.* Stay away from persons and situations that often waste time.

12. *Tighten your schedule.* Use odd times for appointments. Account for your time more closely by keeping track of your schedule. Schedule appointments at times such as 10:40, rather than regular hour or half-hour intervals. This will change your perception about using time and make others more time-conscious, too.

In addition, try some more of Dr. Lakein's key suggestions:

1. Have a light lunch to avoid getting drowsy.

2. Focus your attention on one thing at a time.

3. Save up trivial matters for a once-a-month three-hour session.

4. Reward yourself when you accomplish important tasks.

5. Handle each piece of paperwork only once.

6. Reflect at least once a month on your lifetime goals and how you can accomplish them in your activities.

7. Start with the most profitable parts of big projects.

8. Remind yourself that there is always enough time for the important things.

These ideas are proven time-savers and can help you make the most of your day. However, they produce better *time management*, not necessarily greater *time competence*. The difference is that time competence means making each moment worthwhile to *you*, in *your* job; while time management is basically arranging your time to accomplish a set of objectives. A good time manager, for example, might be so efficient that he or she is able to take on an additional workload. However, is that a worthwhile goal to *you?*

Most time-management programs do not address the issues of time competence. Nor do they discuss the most insidious time-waster of all—psychological games. It is estimated that within organizations, 50 percent to 70 percent of the time is spent playing games—psychological games that pay off in bad feelings and resentments. Unless you deal with the games themselves, you can try the time-saving ideas only to find they don't work. Why? Because the payoffs of the game are more attractive than the rewards of managing time.

Games are not the only way you can waste time at work.

A CASE-IN-POINT: Jim had his day planned out; he was going to take care of an important problem. By lunch time, he managed fifteen minutes on that problem because of phone or face-to-face conversations about various other things. Over lunch he talked with some other managers about the baseball scores, softball team, the union, the latest thing in the newsletter, the company's expansion plans. Before he knew it, what was to be a quick lunch took the entire hour and then some because he walked back with one of the mangers to see something in his area that interested him. To make a long story short, he spent most of his time interacting with others. Some of it was past-timing—talking about things of general interest; and some was work activity. But the main thing is that he did not accomplish what he set out to—and he probably felt frustrated about it.

Is Jim a good time manager? By the standards of most time-management experts, no. Is he time-competent? Yes, provided Jim's activities were important to him and his work. They certainly appeared important, and very possibly his high-priority problem was not really as critical to him as he thought. He managed his time poorly with respect to his stated goal for the day, but he was accomplishing something else—a personal and professional need for interaction. That satisfied a fundamental social need for affiliation among those who must also work together—*and from that standpoint he was time-competent.*

Like Jim, you must genuinely reconcile your professional needs to those of your unit. HERE'S WHAT TO DO: Follow the time-management suggestions but first decide on your basic purpose and values. Visualize how these relate to your goals at work.

EXAMPLE: You might procrastinate in doing a report because you do not see any value in it. The key here is not in learning how to discipline yourself to do the report on time but in understanding the meaning of the chore to your overall job. While you might not like doing the report, if you like your job and see the report as part of that job, you can more easily manage your time and complete the report. In this case, you will be time-competent and an organizationally effective leader as well.

CHAPTER 9

Why Knowledge of Business Concepts and Practices Is a Necessary Management Tool

"The optimist proclaims that we live in the best of all possible worlds, and the pessimist fears this may be true."

—JAMES BRANCH CABELL

LIKE it or not, you operate not in a vacuum but in an organization, a department, an industry, in an intricate network of economic and government policies. In a real sense, you're *part* of the nation's economic system. It functions with you, around you, and because of you.

The "hands on" daily applications of your job may not require an intricate understanding of business principles and economics. However, you know by now that being a manager involves much more than just technical knowledge. By understanding the nature of your business and how information flows through it, you increase your effectiveness as a manager in a very practical way. By being more "complete" in your understanding of the systems comprising your business world, you are in a much better position to comprehend and handle issues that arise among various parties you deal with. In short, by being better informed, you're likely to be a better manager.

WHY YOU MUST UNDERSTAND YOUR ECONOMIC SYSTEM

The American economy is in one sense very young and in another, very old. Young because it represents the most successful recent experiment in the world of economics; old because it represents more than three hundred years of growth and prosperity that rival anything since ancient Roman times. Some people think the economy works well; others don't agree. Mostly, it depends on where you sit politically and how prosperous you are. One thing is for sure: No other economic system in recorded history has consistently produced so much for so many.

An economic system refers to the mechanism a country uses to distribute its resources in order to produce and market the goods and services its people need. There are three basic kinds of economic systems:

1. *Capitalism.* The means of production (land, machinery, business enterprises) are owned by individuals.
2. *Communism.* The means of production are owned collectively through the mechanism of the state.
3. *Socialism.* The major industries are owned by the state.

The significance of the systems goes beyond the definitions. They are a way of life. They govern people and determine how much freedom you have for decision and action.

Any economic system must decide as its goals:

1. What products and services to produce and distribute.
2. How much to produce.
3. Who is going to produce them.
4. How they will be produced.
5. How they will be distributed.
6. Who may consume them.

Figure 9.1 shows how these six decisions are made and implemented in an economic system. It begins with the consumer, who buys goods and services in exchange for something else, usually money. Businesses use their income from sales to buy materials and services. The income over and above their expenses is called *profit*.

Under capitalism, the decisions are made primarily by individuals exercising free choice. Producers compete for sales to consum-

BASIC FACTORS IN THE ECONOMIC SYSTEM

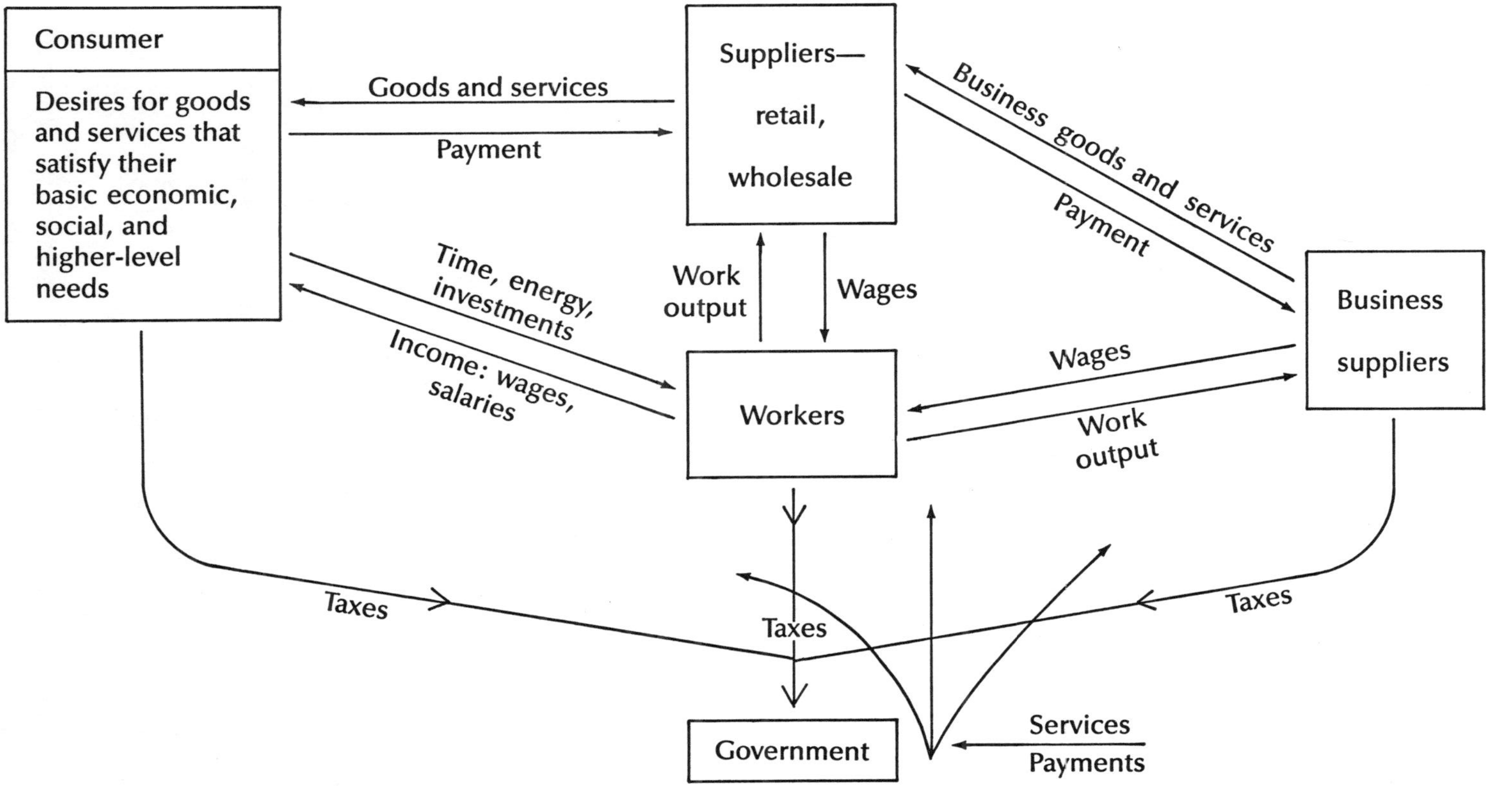

FIGURE 9.1

ers through the market system—supply and demand, and this becomes the nation's mechanism for allocating resources.

In communist and socialist countries, major economic decisions are made by the state. The result is an economic system in which every major facet is controlled by and administered by a bureaucracy. Rather than a profit incentive, these systems use other rewards such as status, special favors, recognition and so on. Private enterprise is permitted only on a very limited basis, mainly in agricultural production.

HOW GOVERNMENT'S ROLE IN THE ECONOMY AFFECTS YOUR ROLE AS A MANAGER

In the modern economy, the government (local, state, and federal) might take any of these roles:

1. *Protector.* Safeguard of its people through national defense and various laws that ensure individual liberty.
2. *Policeman.* A keeper of law and order; the enforcer of equality and economic order.
3. *Partner.* When people and government come together to provide a needed product or service. EXAMPLE: Public education is one of the biggest partnerships between government and people.
4. *Competitor.* Governments can compete with businesses at all levels. EXAMPLES: Public broadcasting, state-owned liquor stores, local mental health agencies.
5. *Customer.* Nearly all materials, machines, and other "hard goods" used by the government are purchased from private businesses.

Government is not there just to regulate business but also to preserve the economic system. A proper balance is needed—one that will encourage those who want to use their talents to succeed and one to discourage those who would violate others' rights to pursue their own destiny.

HOW THE TYPE OF BUSINESS YOU ARE IN AFFECTS YOUR MANAGEMENT

A business, as the main unit of the economy, has a special role and responsibility to provide goods and services to people. From this standpoint, profit is as *return*, or *reward*, for performing this role. When you view business in this way, you go beyond the owner's perspective and see the larger role of business as a provider of the things that are important in our lives.

Defining your business helps to underscore the importance of your job and your organization. To determine what business you are in, look at your main product and what consumer needs it satisfies. If you work in a shoe factory, your business is not just making shoes but supplying the footwear needs of people at X level of quality and X price, which brings X return to the firm.

Whatever your business, chances are it's in one of the key industries in the economy. These are identified by the U.S. Department of Labor, as shown in Figure 9.2. You might note that manufacturing is still the dominant industry in the U.S. economy. This, along with retail trade, health and medical care, and construction comprise the majority of the U.S. work force; hence, any changes in those industries can greatly affect the economy.

Every organization exists for a purpose. This reason for being, or *mission*, is to produce products or services that will be useful to customers and benefit the people in the organization. If an organization accomplishes its mission effectively, everyone is better off— the customers, the owners and employees, and society as a whole. The mission spawns many supporting objectives that must be attained for its accomplishment. EXAMPLE: The mission of Joe's Pizzeria is "to make the best pizza in town." To do that, Joe sets the following objectives:

1. Find out what pizza lovers like best about pizza.

2. To increase sales by 15 percent next year.

3. To deliver hot pizzas to the door within thirty minutes after the order is placed.

4. To make a return on investment of 20 percent before taxes next year.

5. To keep employee turnover under 10 percent per year.

6. To open two new "Joe's Pizzeria" restaurants in the next two years.

7. To raise $1 million next year to finance the expansion program.

The people who invest their money in a business and share the profits (or losses) are *owners*, of which there are three basic types:

1. *Sole proprietorship.* One person owns the business and is totally responsible for its success or failure.

2. *Partnerships.* Associations of two or more persons who operate a business as co-owners by voluntary legal agreement. *General partnerships* are those where all partners share equally in the business. *Limited partnerships* occur when one or more partner makes limited or specified contributions and has limited liability. *Joint ventures* are tem-

MAJOR INDUSTRIES AND EMPLOYMENT

	Employment (100's)
Retail Trade (All retail stores, eating and drinking places)	14,111
Manufacturing (Durable goods)	11,590
Manufacturing (Nondurable goods)	8,015
Public Utilities	748
Communications	1,183
Insurance	1,543
Education and Training	1,350
Construction	3,526
Transportation	3,024
Banking, Financial, Real Estate	2,400
Wholesale Trade	4,454
Research and Development Programs	170
Service Industry (except health care)	2,521
Medical/Health Care	4,886
Raw Materials Mining and Farming	700

Source: U.S. Department of Labor, Bureau of Statistics, *Employment and Earnings*, Vol. 25, No. 3, March 1978, Summarized from Table B-2, pp. 62–69.

FIGURE 9.2

porary partnerships in which two or more people undertake a business project for a limited time.

3. *Corporations.* Legal entities, created by charter that can carry on commerce as authorized in their charters. Owners are not liable for their debts except for the amounts invested into the corporation. Usually, shares of stock are for sale on the open market.

Which is best? Each has pros and cons that must be weighed according to the situation. Figure 9.3 provides some food for thought.

FROM BUSINESS TO ORGANIZATION: HOW THE SYSTEMS CONCEPT WORKS

A *system* is a collection of components whose purpose is to do the job for which it is designed.

> EXAMPLE: An electric power company is a system that generates and distributes electricity to its customers. A maintenance system keeps equipment running and productive. A foreman and crew, along with their equipment, constitute a system to make a product or render a service. Each of these systems has a specific mission that it accomplishes through the cooperation and interaction of its parts.

You can think of an organization as a system; that is, a set of interacting elements that work together to do a job. Managers and their subordinates form the work units that get the job done. NOTE: The most important element in any organizational system is the human element.

Systems that are components of larger systems are called subsystems. Thus, each person in a system can be considered a subsystem, as can each machine. The manager's job is to coordinate and control the subsystems to meet the organizational objectives.

The larger or environmental system in turn is called a suprasystem. Monetary, economic, legal, social, political, technological, demographic, labor, and life-style suprasystems affect an organization's ability to function. That's why changes in environmental systems must be forecasted, if possible, in order to assess possible future impact on the organization.

PROS AND CONS OF BUSINESS OWNERSHIP

Sole Proprietorship

Pros

1. It is relatively easy to start.
2. It is very flexible since only one person is making key decisions.
3. It can quickly respond to changing conditions because the owner can make adjustments without consultation with others.
4. The owner receives all the profits.
5. The proprietor pays only personal income taxes, not corporate taxes. All business expenses are tax deductible.
6. All business assets are considered personal assets.
7. The owner can protect technical secrets.
8. There is a great deal of pride in ownership. The owner is his/her own boss.

Cons

1. There is unlimited financial liability. Since there is no distinction under the law between the business and the owner, the proprietor takes all the risk. Even personal property must be sold, if necessary, to pay off business debt.
2. The business is limited by the amount of capital the owner can personally supply or borrow.
3. There may be deficiencies in management because the owner cannot be equally proficient in every business function.
4. When the proprietor retires or dies, the business ceases to exist.

Partnership

Pros

1. They are relatively easy to form.
2. They provide more financial support than usually is available in a sole proprietorship.
3. They include the expertise, capabilities, and efforts of more than one person. The skills of one person may complement the skills of others.
4. They permit individuals to specialize rather than having to do everything. This promotes efficiency.
5. They allow joint decisions that take advantage of the judgment and insights of more than one person.
6. Partners share all profits, as agreed in the partnership agreement.

Cons

1. Like sole proprietors, partners are individually (and jointly) liable for all business debts. Their personal property is in jeopardy.
2. Partnerships are more susceptible to interpersonal conflicts. There could be serious disagreement about contributions to the business and distribution of profits.
3. The business is disrupted when a partner cannot or will not continue. The agreement is terminated and a settlement must be made.
4. Partnerships are more difficult to terminate than proprietorships because more than one person is involved.

FIGURE 9.3

Corporation

Pros

1. Owners have limited personal liability.
2. Financial resources are much more diversified, allowing the corporation to issue more stock and borrow money for expansion.
3. Ownership and management can be easily divided. The corporation can hire management specialists to run the business effectively.
4. Corporations can grow large enough to employ technical specialists and consolidate operations to take advantage of economies of scale in manufacturing, marketing, financing, and purchasing.
5. Shares can usually be bought and sold, making investment attractive to a wide variety of investors.
6. Corporate life continues even when owners retire or die.

Cons

1. They are more difficult to get started.
2. They are more difficult to terminate.
3. Corporate taxes are imposed, taxes that proprietorships and partnerships do not have to pay.
4. Corporation are subject to more government regulations than other forms of businesses. There are many legal restrictions.
5. Although corporations are considered "persons" under the law, they are not perceived as persons by employees or the public. They often engender resentment because of their impersonal approach to people. *Note:* Good management can prevent much of this feeling among employees. Good public relations and social responsibility can help prevent it in the general public.

FIGURE 9.3 (continued)

EXAMPLE: An electric power company is itself a component of several suprasystems: the economic system, the industrial system, the local community system, the regional networks of electric power systems, and so on.

SIX CRITICAL INGREDIENTS TO MAKING A SYSTEM WORK

An organizational system has six basic components: (1) input, (2) conversion process, (3) output, (4) feedback, (5) decision, and (6) corrective action (Figure 9.4). A manager's role is to plan, organize, direct, and control the system's components so they operate synergistically to maximize productivity. Now let's take a closer look:

SYSTEM MODEL

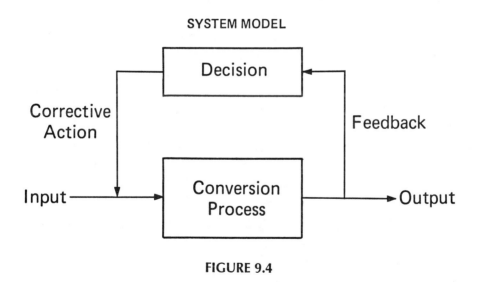

FIGURE 9.4

1. *Input.* These are the resources needed to accomplish a mission.

2. *Conversion process.* This part of the system, sometimes called operations or production, converts materials into finished goods. Resources are used to accomplish the mission.

3. *Output.* The end result, or the product or service for which the system exists and therefore all-important in evaluating the effectiveness of the organizational system. Every element of the system must contribute to this purpose. No matter how efficient a system may be, it's a failure if it does not accomplish its mission.

4. *Feedback.* An organizational system is not likely to function properly if managers do not know what is going on. You cannot detect and correct problems without feedback from inside and outside the system.

5. *Decision.* Basically, managers exist to make sure the system achieves its objectives. After analyzing feedback from the operation of the system along with data from the outside, you decide what changes are necessary. Incomplete information, faulty analysis, or poor judgment could cause you to make poor decisions, and the results could be disastrous. Good managers stay informed and use the best available decision tools and methods to make sound decisions.

6. *Corrective action.* Decisions, even good ones, are ineffective unless put into action. By corrective action, you keep the organizational system progressing toward its objectives.

A CASE–IN–POINT: Here's how an electric power company works as a system: Inputs consist of skilled manpower to perform the tasks and manage the process of electricity generation and distribution. Equipment needs include machinery to pump fuel, transport, repair machinery, lift heavy loads, and so on. Materials needed include fuel, water, wire, poles, and so on. Facilities, money, and time are other inputs that need careful management. By managing the resources, the power company generates and distributes electricity to its customers. But unless it delivers an uninterrupted flow of electricity, even the most modern power plant is a failure. To prevent this, managers work to measure quality, observe progress, talk to customers, and assess the overall effectiveness of the system. If the manager learns that a large generator is malfunctioning, his or her analysis will bring a recommendation whether to repair or replace the machinery. Suppose the manager decides to replace it. Before doing so, many steps must be worked out, including specifications, financing, scheduling, manpower procurement. Then the manager closes the loop and keeps the organizational system successful.

An *organization* is more complex than most other systems. It is made up of people and the subsystems that contribute to the organization—themselves complex systems. Each person is unique, with his or her own hopes, feelings, aspirations, values, and motives. This conglomeration of unique and complex human beings makes an organization difficult to manage.

Within an organizational system there are three primary functional subsystems: marketing, operations, and finance. *Marketing* determines the nature of the product or service to be created. *Operations* determine how to do it. *Finance* determines how to pay for it and handles the revenues. Supporting functions include personnel, accounting, engineering, research, quality assurance, and materials management. The latter includes purchasing, inventory control, shipping and receiving, warehousing, traffic, transportation, and materials handling. Each of these is a subsystem of the organization. Each is comprised of inputs, processes, outputs, feedback, and corrective action. And each has a manager who is responsible for its activities and accountable for its success.

NOTICE: Objectives among subsystems often conflict and must be resolved by the manager.

> EXAMPLE: Marketing needs large inventories to assure fast delivery to customers. However, this ties up money that finance would like to invest. Operations would like plenty of raw materials to keep production rolling, but inventory control strives for lower stocks and faster turnover. Production tries to increase production speed, but quality control must have time for inspections. WHAT TO DO: The manager must coordinate the efforts of all the people and functions to ensure that *organizational* objectives are met.

The organizational system includes many other subsystems in addition to marketing, operations, and finance. These are the essential supporting functions because the three primary functions could not be performed without them. The number and configuration of supporting functions will vary with the needs of the business.

Figure 9.5 shows the relationship of the primary and supporting functions.

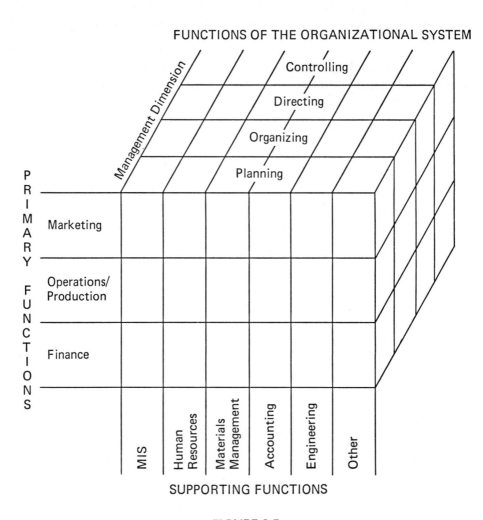

FIGURE 9.5

Here's what the esssential supporting services most often include:

1. *Human resources.* Conducts and administers the personnel program. Among its activities are recruiting, testing, clarifying,

evaluating, labor relations, benefits administration, and regulatory compliance.

2. *Materials management.* Responsible for procuring and managing the flow of materials until they are consumed or made a part of the products.

3. *Accounting.* Collects, stores, analyzes, and presents financial information to managers to help them control scarce resources. It is part of the Management Information System (MIS).

Every function must be managed. That is, they must be planned, organized, directed, and controlled. These are the functions of management and the subject of Chapter 2. REMEMBER THIS: Organizations are made up of people, and so you must be skillful at working with and managing them. If you do not know your people, you do not know your business.

HOW TO ORGANIZE DEPARTMENTS EFFICIENTLY

The basic unit of any work organization is the task—the operation or set of operations performed by a person or a team. Most taks are individual, such as wiring a headset. Others are team tasks, such as joining and fastening a steel beam in a construction project. Whether individual or collective, tasks are the focal point of any operation, and in order to be done effectively, they must be properly identified, described, and correlated with other tasks.

Various tasks, in turn, are grouped together into what are normally called sections or departments.

EXAMPLE: If you are the manager of the packing department, you will have people and/or teams performing different tasks, all related in some way to achieving the packing objective of your department. The grouping is made according to a certain logic, the underlying management principle called functional homogeneity.

There are five ways that departments can be organized; according to (1) function, (2) product, (3) geography, (4) customer, or (5) process. (See Figure 9.6.) The main reason for the particular choice is to achieve the most effective grouping in light of objectives.

Departmentation by *function* is the arrangement found most frequently.

GROUPING BY FUNCTION

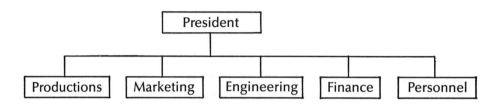

ORGANIZING BY LOCATION

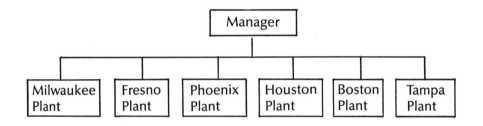

ORGANIZING BY PRODUCT

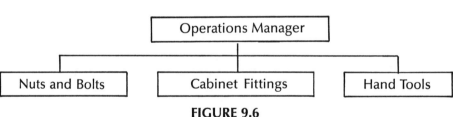

FIGURE 9.6

EXAMPLE: Within production there may be other departments, such as finishing, shipping, production control, quality control, maintenance, and assembly.

Another basis for forming departments, and similar to the functional breakdown, is departmentation by *process*. Here the dominant feature is not so much what the workers do but rather the process in which they are involved.

EXAMPLE: A printing operation is distinguished by different processes such as offset, lithograph, engraving, and so on.

Product is becoming a widely used basis for departmentation. Here the emphasis is on the goods or services produced. Major companies, notably Procter and Gamble and others in its industry, have organized along product line, primarily to provide accountability for the profit contribution of each product.

The other two bases for departmentation—*location* and *customer*—are used primarily for specific purposes related to sales or costs. Locating sales offices in various regions is a typical example of geographical departmentation. The National Management Association is organized on this basis in order to better serve the members in each region. In banking, branch banks are usually established on a geographical basis.

Departmentation by *customer* follows a similar logic, in that it fosters customer service and, of course, sales. It works best when there are distinct types of customers to be served, such as retail and wholesale, men or women, children or adults.

Which type of departmentation is best? This is a question that can only be answered according to the situation of your organization. Most first-line managers operate within a framework at some combination of functional, product, and process departmentation.

HOW TO WORK EFFECTIVELY WITH THE OTHER PARTS OF YOUR ORGANIZATION

At one time or another, you must work with various kinds of specialists and managers from other areas: engineers, accountants, union representatives, and so on. Within your organization, you'll find two types of horizontal or *cross-functional* relationships: *lateral*, when both positions are on the same level, and *diagonal*, between manager and specialists or managers at other levels. The types of tasks you'll encounter will be either *procedural* or workflow relationships, or *coordinative* which implies synchronizing your work with other managers and departments. (See Figure 9.7.) Such horizontal relationships can pose a special set of problems for you. THE KEY: In such relationships, communication is an essential element.

Another division of labor puts functions according to how closely they relate to the primary objectives of the organization. So-called *line* functions have the authority to make operating decisions; while staff functions are limited to giving advice, performing

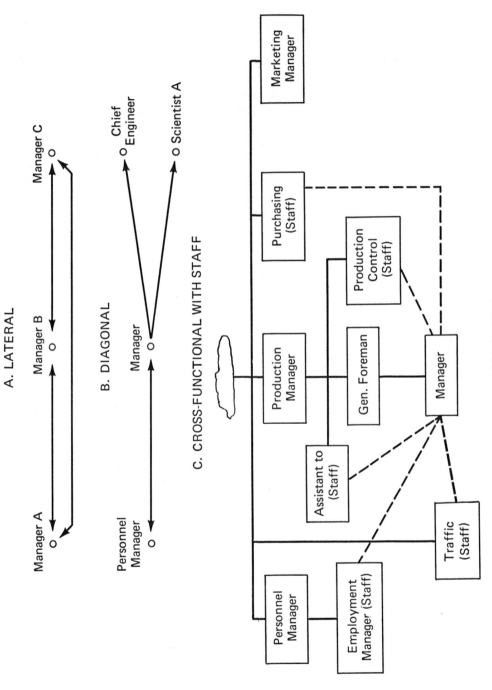

RELATIONSHIPS ACROSS THE ORGANIZATION

A. LATERAL

Manager A   Manager B   Manager C

B. DIAGONAL

                              Chief
                              Engineer

Personnel
Manager   Manager

                              Scientist A

C. CROSS-FUNCTIONAL WITH STAFF

Production Manager — Purchasing (Staff) — Marketing Manager

Production Control (Staff)

Gen. Foreman

Manager

Assistant to (Staff)

Personnel Manager

Employment Manager (Staff)

Traffic (Staff)

FIGURE 9.7

a service, or making decisions in a very specific area of specialization.

In business organizations, production, marketing, and finance are usually designated as line functions because of their direct relationship to business goals. However, this distinction blurs considerably in activities such as government, where traditional staff functions such as personnel are closely related to an organizational goal.

This difference can be quite dramatic for the first-line manager. Your authority is determined by the extent of the line–staff designation of the departments and specialities with which you work, as well as your own department. TO CLARIFY: You—even in a staff department—have line authority within your own department. However, in the organization, your authority might be only advisory.

Line versus staff conflicts stem from several sources, including (1) different viewpoints, (2) competition over authority, (3) reduced domain, (4) staff justifying their position, (5) status needs. WHAT TO DO: You can handle conflicts by coordinating and integrating your work with staff. You must each have mutual respect for the different roles and see your problem in the context of the larger system.

ARE YOU BEING DUMPED ON?

Some bizarre actions have been associated with problems of line–staff authority. In one case, a manager was discovered to have sneaked back into the plant at night, carried out scrap in a barrel, and dumped it in a river. It turned out that one of the machines was out of adjustment. The manager had asked maintenance to repair the machine but couldn't order them to do so; yet he was held accountable for the unit's scrap rate—machine or no machine. Had line–staff authority been clearer, this manager would not have experienced the frustration of not having authority to do the job.

While line versus staff is the basic division according to authority, another designation, called *prescriptive authority*, helps to clarify the in-between situation when staff people may have strong influence on decisions, if not the decision authority itself. Prescriptive is stronger than advisory authority but not as strong as command or line authority. A good example of prescriptive authority is the role of purchasing in some organizations. Here, the purchasing specialist recommends a certain vendor to the manager, who is then free to choose another vendor. However, if the manager rejects their judgment, he or she may lose any further support.

Here are two important principles to keep in mind:

1. *The "Principle of Compulsory Staff Advice."* Before managers make important decisions, they should seek the advice of staff people whose expertise can contribute to the decision. The manager is free to accept, reject, or modify the advice but at least must give the expert a fair hearing.

2. *The "Principle of Staff Independence."* Staff should be free to give frank advice without jeopardizing their positions. Obviously, the application of this principle would be beneficial to many an executive, including presidents of the country.

COMING TOGETHER FOR A COMMON GOAL

To better understand how others view things, first examine the perspectives of different areas of your organization:

1. *Production.* Their typical concern is to maintain the flow of work in order to remain as efficient and productive as possible. A short-range outlook prevails because it is here-and-now, hands-on type of work.

2. *Marketing.* Their perspective tends to be middle range. Marketing managers are mostly concerned with sales and market share. They are usually concerned with such things as merchandising, promotion, advertising, transportation, selling, and market research. Without marketing, your organization would likely go out of business.

3. *Personnel.* Their perspective is usually middle range. Mainly, they are concerned with harmonious relationships and making sure that enployees' needs are maintained for development and security.

4. *Engineering.* These logical thinkers prefer objectives longer in range than a few days but shorter than a year. Their work contributes immensely to the product, the organization, and its future success. Engineers consider themselves professionals and like to be dealt with in that way.

5. *Production Control.* Their basic job is to monitor operations and make sure they are proceeding effectively and proficiently. Their horizon is short range and tends to be reactive rather than proactive. Their job can best be done with your cooperation.

6. *Accounting.* Their perspective is short range and they are reactive in their behavior. They are concerned about tangible matters—in data and the bottom line. Accounting procedures can sometimes be a sore point with managers, but these procedures are some of the most rigorous and difficult to change.

7. *Finance.* The financial officers' perspective is middle to long range. They like to minimize risks and tend to deal impersonally with people. They have a great deal to say about expenditures, investments, and capital. HINT: don't try to out-fox the financial people. You'll find them more flexible to work with if you are up-front with them.

8. *Purchasing.* They tend to operate in the middle range. Their interest is in cost efficiency and they tend to be procedure oriented. YOUR BEST BET: Deal in tangibles and observe their policies and procedures.

By understanding these perspectives, you can better relate with people across departments. The main goal is an organizational one; thus, you will have to go a step beyond your immediate objectives in dealing with them and achieving win/win solutions.

Many of the departments and people mentioned here are part of your work flow. When they are, it means that not only do you relate to them as peers, but also you need them in order to get the work accomplished. WHAT TO DO: It is important that you understand the work flow. By being aware of it and how your role fits in, you'll show consideration for others, earn their trust, and build productive relationships.

> A CASE-IN-POINT: One assembly plant, at the time, had one of the longest monorails in the world. Many managers were not consciously aware of their effects on other departments perhaps a half-mile down the monorail. As a result, there were conflicts and resentments that were never resolved. A management consultant suggested that the various managers be educated about the flow of work to and from the departments. When they learned about others' perspectives, the managers developed a trust and cooperative attitude that helped to resolve many production problems.

WHY YOU MUST UNDERSTAND YOUR INFORMATION SYSTEM

Managers must have good information to do their jobs well. The way it is collected, stored, processed, and displayed is the function of the Management Information System (MIS). Its purpose is to provide you, the manager, with the facts you need to make the right decisions for your organization.

The MIS is a system that exists as a subsystem of the organization. It gathers and transmits data (input); it combines and files data (conversion); and it retrieves, formats, and displays information (output). In addition, MISs have managers who monitor progress and take corrective action to solve problems and keep the system going.

A few definitions: *Data* are raw facts about the organization and its environment. When relevant data are screened, processed, and combined in such a way that you can use them to make decisions, they become *information*. MIS involves processing of data and includes preparation of reports by summarizing, combining, displaying, and formatting. Then managers can quickly comprehend the meaning of the data and use them for decisions.

In order to accomplish its purpose, a MIS must furnish information that is accurate, complete, relevant, timely, and understandable. Nothing is more disastrous or frustrating than a judgment based on bad information.

THE COMPUTER AND MIS—AND THEIR IMPACT ON MANAGEMENT

In today's world, there is a computer for everyone. Almost any organization can afford the cost. In fact, computers are so versatile and inexpensive that an organization can hardly afford to be without one.

The purpose of the computer is to mechanize many of the data-processing functions associated with the MIS. By combining modules of hardware and software, you can tailor a computer to fit your needs. It can be programmed to stimulate organizational activities and do complex computations. It can make decisions based on rules incorporated into its program. It's a powerful and versatile tool that can expand your mental powers. CAUTION: Computers do not have the feelings, perceptions, or flexibility of the human mind. Your "human" input has no substitute.

A digital computer system consists of two components: hardware and software. Here is a brief description of its basic structural parts.

Hardware are the components designed to handle inputs, outputs, computations, and logical operations accurately and consistently. (See Figure 9.8.) They include:

1. *CPU (Central Processing Unit)*. The control unit that directs the sequence and flow of instructions and data through the arithmetic and logical unit and internal memory.

2. *Input devices*. Machines used for feeding data to the CPU. These include cards, magnetic tapes, disks, cassettes, optical scanners, keyboards, light pens, and so on.

3. *Output devices*. Machines used for retrieving data. These include many of the items listed as input devices plus printers, plotters, microfilm, and CRTs (cathode ray tubes).

4. *Storage devices*, commonly called *external memory*. These hold large data files and make them available to the CPU when required. They include magnetic cards, magnetic tape cassettes, magnetic disks drives, floppy disks, and fiber optics.

Software adapts the hardware to specific applications tailored for a particular user. It includes two categories of programs:

1. *Operating System (OS) programs*. These interface with the hardware and instruct it to do what the user wishes to be done. OS software includes *control* programs that supervise and schedule the CPU and *processing* programs that perform sorting, merging, and assembling, compiling, and interpreting applications.

2. *Applications* programs. They are the programs designed specifically to do the jobs assigned to the computer. There are programs for accounting, inventory control, purchasing, finance, and many other organizational functions.

Information processing, also called teleprocessing, *telecommunications*, or data communications, include the transmission and processing of raw data. Sending terminals accept the message from a human and change it so it can be transmitted via electrical impulse, microwave circuits, or fiber optics. Receiving terminals convert the data and make them understandable to humans. The transmission itself flows from telecommunication channels that may be simplex (one way only), half duplex (either way), or duplex

COMPUTER HARDWARE SYSTEM

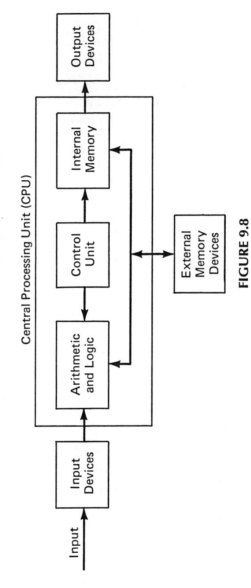

FIGURE 9.8

(both ways simultaneously). *Modems* convert a specific type of signals (digital) to another (analog) and then back, in order to send data over phone lines. Security measures, such as packeting and multirouting, protect data in transmit.

HOW TO GET THE MOST FROM YOUR MIS

Computers can relieve you of much spade work and repetitive activities. They allow better control because they provide quicker, more accurate, and more thorough reports. They help you see the "big picture" and integrate your efforts. This allows more time for planning and preaction control.

TEN DO'S AND DON'TS OF USING A COMPUTER-BASED MIS

- *Do* remember that the MIS is a subsystem of the organization that should service and support all other subsystems.

- *Do* consider the MIS as a tool to serve your needs, not as a tyrant that demands valuable resources without sufficient performance.

- *Do* learn as much as you can about the computer. There are no mysteries, just a different language and technological concepts.

- *Do* keep the mission of the organization and its strategic objectives in focus as you operate the MIS. The purpose for it sometimes gets lost in the doing of it.

- *Do* make people your first concern. The MIS should conform to human needs.

- *Do* remember that the computer is an aid for decision making, not merely a tool for record keeping.

- *Do* carefully consider security requirements. It's just as important to "lock" your data file as it is to lock your filing cabinet.

- *Don't* expect the computer to give you all the information you need.

- *Don't* underestimate the complexity and cost of developing and operating a computer-based MIS.

- *Don't* permit the MIS to produce massive volumes of data rather than summary reports.

Principles of quality control apply to data systems as well as to production systems. You need checkpoints, inspections, and audits to keep data as accurate as possible. When inputs are faulty, the computer has a fantastic capacity for compounding errors and repeating mistakes.

A CASE-IN-POINT: One company installed a new high-speed printer. A programmer intended to instruct the computer to index to a new page, then print a report. He omitted a comma, and the computer understood only the indexing instruction. The printer proceeded to almost fill the room with blank paper before the operator could react and stop the machine.

Frequent human mistakes include using wrong procedures or codes, incorrect data recording, omitting or adding data, lost data, recording in the wrong place, and using damaged input media. The causes: carelessness, poor procedures, inaccurate manuals, poor directions, and so on.

How can you prevent errors? You can use preventive measures such as better training, redundancy checks, verification, clear procedures, and better forms. Additionally, you can program the computer to make parity checks, edit, format checks, and other kinds of quality control checks. HOW TO DO IT: A good manual on data base management will give detailed instructions about these techniques.

The MIS poses difficult security problems, but you can protect against fraud and theft by limiting access to the terminal and computer. WHAT TO DO: Use identification codes and keep track of who uses the system and when.

To protect against disasters, you should have emergency procedures and drills. Use heat and smoke alarms, fire extinguishers, and panic switches. Periodically prepare duplicate master records (backups) and keep them in special vaults or at a remote site. DON'T FORGET to lock your electronic filing cabinet!

GETTING TO KNOW YOUR FINANCIAL MANAGEMENT SYSTEM

Financial management is concerned with preparing a financial plan, organizing and operating financial activities, and controlling financial operations. Figure 9.9 illustrates the responsibilities of the financial manager.

RESPONSIBILITIES OF THE FINANCIAL MANAGER

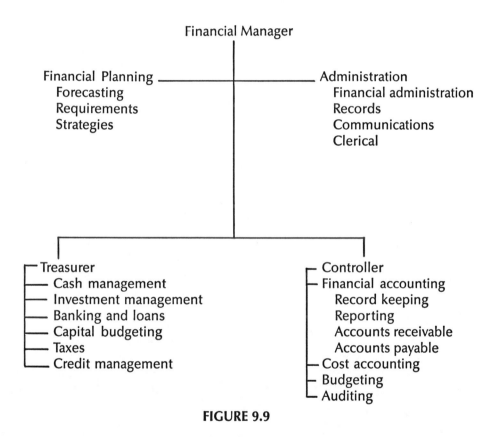

FIGURE 9.9

Two of the financial manager's primary responsibilities are to see that funds are available when needed and to assure that they are spent wisely. They are long-term (one year or more) and short-term needs (less than one year), which can be met by borrowing (debt), using retained earnings, or issuing stock (equity). The Checklist for Raising Funds provides a summary of the financial manager's options.

CHECKLIST FOR RAISING FUNDS

A. Debt funding
   1. Long term
      a. *Long term loans* may be negotiated with banks, insurance companies, retirements funds, and sometimes the government.
      b. *Bonds* may be issued under rules established by the state. Mortgage bonds are backed by real estate. Collateral bonds are backed by the firm's assets. Debenture bonds are not backed by collateral. Convertible bonds can be exchanged for shares of stock.
   2. Short term
      a. *Unsecured short-term loans* of a *line of credit* may be negotiated with a commercial bank. This can also be in the form of a revolving credit agreement similar to a personal MASTERCARD or VISA account.
      b. Secured loans require collateral, usually inventories or other semi-liquid assets.
      c. Collections of *accounts receivable* provide funds. When the firm does not wish to do the billing and collecting, it can sell the receivables at a discount. This is called *factoring*.
      d. *Floor planning* provides dealers with short-term loans from finance companies who take title to the inventories until they are sold.
      e. Sometimes a solid company with a high credit rating can sell *commercial paper*—unsecured notes of $25,000 or more that usually are redeemed in six to nine months.
      f. *Trade credit* is sometimes offered by vendors to attract business. This allows the firm to delay paying its bills for a few weeks. Sometimes vendors will offer cash discounts for prompt payment to encourage their customers to pay promptly rather than use trade credit.
B. Equity funding
   1. Long term
      a. Selling shares of *common stock* is a primary source of long-term financing for many firms.

Shareholders are part owners of the firm and have a right to vote at stockholders' meetings.

b. The company may issue *preferred stock*. The purchasers do not have voting rights but have a prior lien (after creditors) on the company assets.

2. Short term

a. *Retained earnings* are funds available after paying all expenses, claims, dividends, and taxes. When a firm is profitable, retained earnings are an important source of funding.

Basically, the financial manager has two possible strategies for raising money: debt or equity. Both have advantages and disadvantages, which may change as interest rates rise and fall and money market conditions vary. The financial manager's job is to select the best strategy for the situation at hand. (See Figure 9.10.)

Funds are used for either long-term or short-term purposes. Long-term investments are called *fixed assets* and include real es-

DEBT FUNDING VERSUS EQUITY FUNDING

Debt (Loans and Bonds)	*Equity (Common Stock)*
1. Purchasers have no ownership rights.	1. Purchasers become owners and can vote on corporate matters.
2. Interest must be paid regardless of profitability.	2. Dividends are paid at the discretion of the firm.
3. Purchasers have a prior claim (before owners) on the assets of the firm.	3. Stockholders have a claim against corporate assets after creditors are paid.
4. Interest paid is tax deductible.	4. Dividends are paid after taxes, then taxed again as shareholder's income.
5. Has a maturity date for repayment.	5. Has no maturity date and does not have to be repaid.
6. Risky because purchasers have a prior claim on corporate assets if default occurs.	6. Relatively little risk to issuing company.

FIGURE 9.10

tate, buildings, machinery, and equipment. These assets have a profound effect on the operation and financial welfare of the company. Short-term uses of funds include *cash* and *current assets* that are normally converted in less than a year. The flow of current assets (or working capital) is illustrated in Figure 9.11.

Financial accounting systems generate information for both internal and external use. Accounting reports include balance sheets, income statements, and special regulatory reports. They provide information for:

1. Strategic decisions and long-range planning.
2. Problem solving and one-time decisions.
3. Planning and scheduling current operations.
4. Monitoring and controlling operations.

HOW TO PLAN BY THE NUMBERS THROUGH SMART BUDGETING

Budgets are financial plans expressed in numbers. Budgets have been used for many years to control organizational activities. Various types of budgets include expense, cash, and capital budgets and proforma balance sheets and income statements.

Expense budgets establish spending limits for a planning period. By comparing actual expenses with the budget, you can

WORKING CAPITAL CYCLE

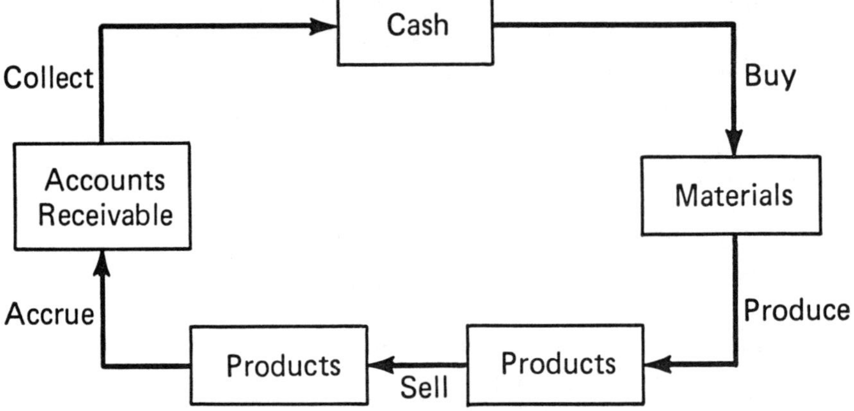

FIGURE 9.11

adjust the rate of spending to stay within the financial plan. Figure 9.12 illustrates how this works. The control chart shows that total expenditures through June are about 15 percent higher than the planned rate of spending. It is obvious that control action is necessary to reduce spending or to adjust the budget upward.

Cash budgets help an organization stay solvent. By making a schedule of expected receipts and expenditures, you can predict cash shortages and overages then plan to raise money or invest it, depending on the cash flow.

> A CASE-IN-POINT: A church recently saved several thousand dollars in interest by carefully preparing a cash budget for a new building. The contract cost was $510,000. By charting cash flows over the two-year construction period, the finance committee discovered that they needed to borrow only $405,000 over the period to make progress payments and pay off the contractor. They saved interest on the unneeded $105,000.

Capital budgets display proposed projects in such a way that estimated costs and dollar return may be compared. Since there are invariably more projects than there is money, you can identify the ones with the highest payoff and thereby invest available capital wisely.

Proforma financial statements are really forecasts of the organization's financial position at particular times in the future. They are useful for setting objectives as well as for controlling.

Zero-based budgeting is a technique for evaluating the worth of programs according to priorities. Before each budget period, all costs for each program are calculated anew (from base zero). This prevents the common practice of starting with the current budget and making only necessary changes to prepare next year's budget. Zero-based budgeting forces managers to evaluate every program, new or old, and justify its cost again. It's designed to provide funds for new productive programs and eliminate those that are no longer contributing their share to organizational objectives.

HOW TO KEEP TRACK OF THE MONEY THROUGH COST ACCOUNTING

Cost accounting keeps track of all the costs in the cost-volume-profit equation:

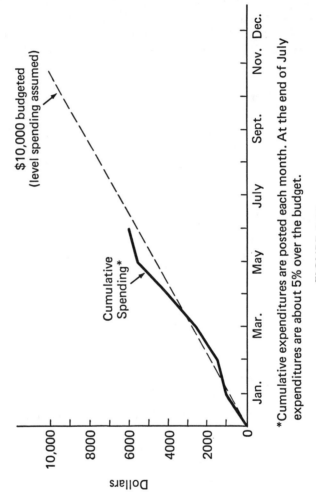

BUDGET CONTROL CHART
($10,000 is budgeted for the year)

$10,000 budgeted
(level spending assumed)

Cumulative
Spending*

Jan.   Mar.   May   July   Sept.   Nov.   Dec.

Dollars

10,000

8000

6000

4000

2000

0

*Cumulative expenditures are posted each month. At the end of July
expenditures are about 5% over the budget.

FIGURE 9.12

Sales Revenue = Variable Costs + Fixed Costs + Profit

or

$$R = VC + FC + P$$

where

Revenue = Amount of money generated by sales in a period of time

Variable Costs = Expenses for materials and services that are needed for manufacture of the product

Fixed Costs = Selling, administrative, and overhead expenses

Profit = Positive or negative result of revenue less costs

EXAMPLE: Here is an application of the cost-volume-profit equation:

Sales last quarter:	30,000 units
Selling price:	$10.00/unit
Variable costs	
Direct labor:	$4.50/unit
Direct material:	$2.00/unit
Variable overhead:	$0.50/unit
TOTAL	$7.00/unit
Fixed costs:	$100,000.00

How much profit or loss did you have last month?

$$R = VC + FC + P$$
$$\text{or } P = R - (VC + FC)$$
$$\text{so } P = 30{,}000 \times \$10 - (30{,}000 \times \$7 + \$100{,}000)$$
$$\text{or } P = \$300{,}000 - (\$210{,}000 + \$100{,}000)$$
$$\text{and } P = \$300{,}000 - \$310{,}000$$
$$\text{therefore } P = -\$10{,}000 \text{ (loss)}$$

Suppose your cost accounting system shows that direct cost for one unit of your product has increased by 4.7 percent. You need to know if the increase is due to labor, materials, or variable overhead. *Variance analysis* can tell you the answer. (See Figure 9.13.) An increase in labor productivity saves ten percent per unit and purchasing saves one cent per unit against standard costs. However, the output takes five more units of raw materials than budgeted. An investigation will reveal the reason for increased material usage. Once the reason is pinpointed, you can take proper corrective action.

EXAMPLE OF VARIANCE ANALYSIS

	Standard Cost/Unit	Actual Cost/Unit	Variance
Direct Labor	.56 hrs. at $10.00 per hr. $ 5.60	.55 hrs. at $10.00 per hr. $ 5.50	($ − .10)
Direct Materials	21 units at 20¢ per unit 4.20	26 units at 19¢ per unit 4.94	+ .74
Variable Overhead	3.80	3.80	.00
Total Directed Cost	$13.60	$14.24	+$ .64 (4.7% increase)

FIGURE 9.13

Nonfinancial items can also be analyzed with similar techniques. Consider the previous example. For each unit, the standard is .56 labor hours and 21 units of raw material. You determine that labor hours are within the standard but raw material usage is unusually high (Figure 9.14).

Time is budgeted by estimating how long it will take to complete required tasks. This may be plotted on a task and milestone chart, commonly called a Gantt Chart (after Henry Gantt, a pioneer in researching management principles).

Breakeven analysis demonstrates the usefulness of financial information in evaluating cost-volume-profit relationships. There are two types of breakeven analysis: aggregate and unit. Figure 9.15 shows an aggregate breakeven chart. In this example, you must sell 7000 units to cover all costs. Every unit over 7000 will add some profit.

The unit breakeven chart shows the cost and revenue from each item. Figure 9.16 shows an example. Note that variable costs per unit remain the same as quantity increases, while fixed costs decrease. The chart shows how much each unit contributes to fixed costs and profits as sales and production volume increase.

The unit breakeven chart is very useful to marketing and purchasing managers. For marketing, it shows the impact of sales volume on profits and helps to plan and control market penetration

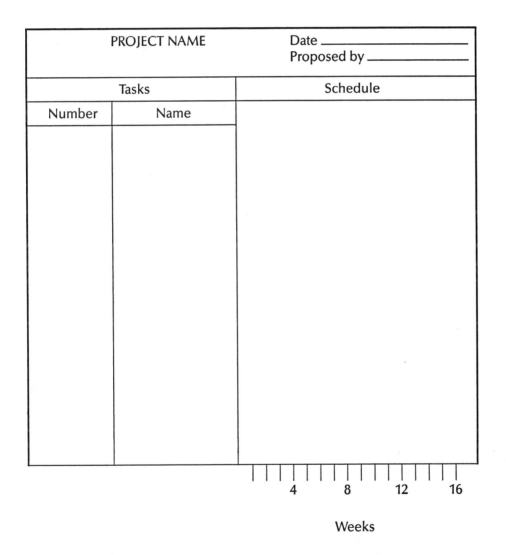

GANTT CHART
(Tasks and Milestones)

FIGURE 9.14

efforts. For buyers, it shows approximate costs and profits that vendors incur at various levels of production and illustrates why large-quantity purchases should produce lower price quotations.

Ratio analysis is a tool that measures the relationship between two quantities and expresses it as a percentage or a rate. Example:

$$\text{Net Return on Sales} = \frac{\text{Net Profit}}{\text{Revenue from Sales}}$$

AGGREGATE BREAK-EVEN ANALYSIS

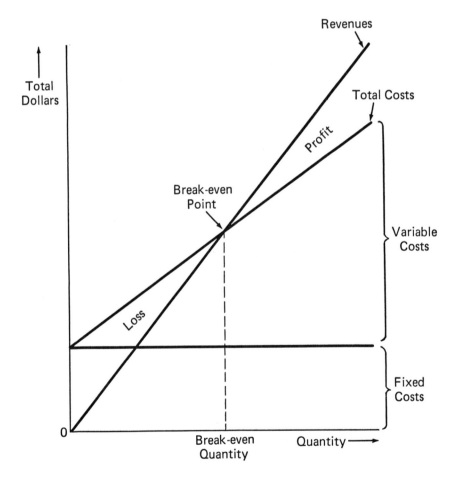

FIGURE 9.15

By comparing ratios with previous periods, you can tell if your company is progressing according to plan.

There are four categories of ratios:

1. *Liquidity ratios* measure your company's ability to meet its short-term financial obligations.

2. *Activity ratios* measure how well your company is managing its resources.

UNIT BREAK-EVEN ANALYSIS

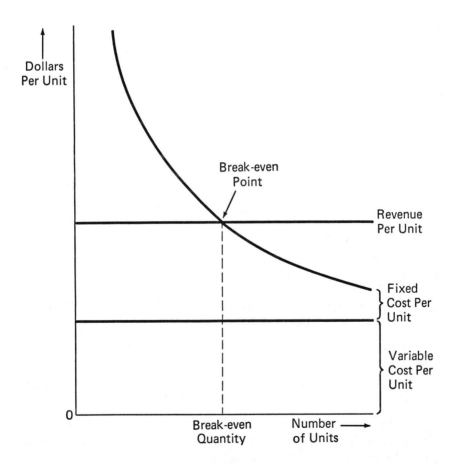

FIGURE 9.16

3. *Leverage ratios* measure solvency, or the firm's ability to pay both current and long-term debts.

4. *Profitability ratios* provide insight into the amount of return on investment or the proportion of sales that goes to profit.

Figure 9.17 lists many ratios currently used by financial analysts. CAUTION: A financial analysis looks at one point in time. To properly appraise the company, you should also examine past performance and assess the outlook for the future.

WHAT QUALITY AND PRODUCTIVITY MEAN TO YOU AS A MANAGER

Productivity is the force that expends the nation's economy. It increases wealth and improves your standard of living. By increasing productivity, you can:

1. Generate more real personal income.
2. Keep inflation down.
3. Increase profits.
4. Increase wages.
5. Favorably affect the nation's world trade balance.
6. Enhance personal prestige and self-image.

What factors affect productivity? Many, some of which are uncontrollable, can promote or inhibit productivity. These include:

1. *Production processes.* Improvements in layout, automation, or process flow can increase productivity.

2. *Product design.* A good design can avoid expensive materials, very close tolerances, or intricate shapes.

3. *Materials management.* Efficient techniques can save many dollars.

4. *Human resources.* People are the heart and brains of the organization. Their potential for improvement lies in power to reason, learn, adapt, innovate, set goals, and attain them.

5. *Time.* This is a resource and must be managed like any other.

A CATALOGUE OF RATIO ANALYSES

Liquidity Ratios:

Current ratio
$$= \frac{\text{Current assets}}{\text{Current liabilities}}$$

Quick ratio
(Acid test ratio)
$$= \frac{\text{Current assets} - \text{Average inventory}}{\text{Current liabilities}}$$

Cash velocity
$$= \frac{\text{Sales (\$)}}{\text{Current assets} - \text{Average inventory}}$$

Inventory to net
working capital
$$= \frac{\text{Inventory (\$)}}{\text{Current assets} - \text{Current liabilities}}$$

Activity Ratios:

Inventory turnover
$$= \frac{\text{Cost of goods sold}}{\text{Average inventory (\$)}}$$

Capital turnover
$$= \frac{\text{Sales (\$)}}{\text{Total assets}}$$

Fixed assets turnover
$$= \frac{\text{Sales (\$)}}{\text{Fixed assets}}$$

Working capital
turnover
$$= \frac{\text{Sales (\$)}}{\text{Net working capital}}$$

Collection period
$$= \frac{\text{Average accounts receivable}}{\text{Average sales per period (\$)}}$$
(usually in days)

Debt to equity ratio
$$= \frac{\text{Total debt}}{\text{Shareholders' investment}}$$

Fixed assets to net
$$= \frac{\text{Fixed assets}}{\text{Net worth}}$$

Current liabilities
to net worth
$$= \frac{\text{Current liabilities}}{\text{Net worth}}$$

Profitability Ratios:

Net return on sales
$$= \frac{\text{Net profit}}{\text{Net sales (\$)}}$$

Return on assets
$$= \frac{\text{Net profit}}{\text{Total assets (investment)}}$$

Return on equity
$$= \frac{\text{Net profit}}{\text{Shareholders' investment}}$$

Net profit on
working capital
$$= \frac{\text{Net profit}}{\text{Working capital}}$$

FIGURE 9.17

6. *Financial management, marketing, administration, engineering* and other internal functions contribute to productivity.

7. *External factors* can constrain or enhance productivity. These include government regulations, competition, labor unions, market prices, resource availability, tax policies.

Productivity is increased when the elements of an organization work together synergistically to produce goods and services that are worth more than the cost of resources plus the cost of conversion. It is measured by a ratio, computed as follows:

$$\text{Productivity} = \frac{\text{Value of Outputs}}{\text{Cost of Inputs and Conversion}}$$

The cost of inputs represents the total dollars paid for resources (materials, manpower, machines, money, facilities). The cost of conversion includes all operating and overhead expenses of the organization.

You may find it useful to split productivity into its major parts: capital, labor, and material productivity. This allows you to identify problem areas more easily.

Quality is related to the price and suitability of the product or service and the user's needs. There are three considerations in determining the right quality for your use:

1. *Suitability.* This is ultimately determined by the customers.

2. *Overall cost.* This includes the initial purchase price plus the cost of maintenance and the cost of doing without the product should it break down.

3. *Availability of suitable materials* to make the product. It can affect price, performance, and acceptance of the product or service.

Quality control means adherence to specifications. Once the final design is determined, the manufacture is accomplished via carefully worked out specifications. The quality control manager inspects raw materials, in-process items, and finished products to assure conformance to the specifications. Marketing sells, distributes them, and follows up with customers to make sure they perform satisfactorily.

HOW TO ASSURE THE RIGHT QUALITY AND PRODUCTIVITY

Manufacturers assure the right quality by (1) thorough planning, (2) careful purchasing, (3) good production methods, and (4) quality control inspections.

In-process inspections should be made at strategic points in production, such as:

1. Before an expensive process.
2. Before a lengthy process during which inspection is impossible.
3. Before covering important parts where defects could be hidden.
4. When responsibility is transferred from one foreman or department to another.
5. When items are placed in stock.
6. Before products are delivered to customers (finished goods inspection).

Inspection is expensive because it takes time, equipment, and trained personnel. WHAT TO DO: Plan your inspections carefully. The optimal number of inspections equals the point at which the cost of inspection plus the cost of defectives is at its lowest level.

Statistical quality control techniques determine mathematically the sample sizes and sampling frequency to assure acceptable quality of the entire batch of products. Of course, two types of errors are possible when samples are inspected:

1. *Producers' risk.* A good batch might be rejected.
2. *Consumers' risk.* A bad batch might be accepted because of sampling error.

Statistical methods are used to tell you the probabilities of these risks. Then acceptable quality levels (AQL) are determined and control charts prepared.

Your company probably measures productivity by the amount of profit it makes. If you can produce more or better products within your budget, you are increasing productivity. WHAT TO DO: Set objectives for higher output, lower cost, and better quality. Here are four rules:

1. If output is constant but costs decrease, productivity increases.
2. If output is constant but costs increase, productivity decreases.
3. If output increases but costs are level, productivity increases.

4. If output decreases but costs are level, productivity decreases.

Remember, poor quality adds to cost and decreases productivity. In measuring output, only good-quality products should be counted.

Do productivity and quality considerations apply only to manufacturing processes? Emphatically, *no!* Clerical, administrative, marketing, accounting, and all other processes are subject to productivity and quality considerations, too.

Here are six ways you can cut costs and still improve quality:

1. Look first at the high-cost areas.
2. Identify controllable costs.
3. Keep a positive attitude.
4. Carefully plan your actions.
5. Keep good records.
6. Anticipate and overcome employee resistance.

LIVING IN A CHANGING WORLD: KEY ISSUES FOR SOCIAL RESPONSIBILITY AND MANAGEMENT

Today, you see people who are depressed, economically disadvantaged, unemployed, exploited, crowded in declining neighborhoods, and living in conflict with spouses, families, neighbors, and the law. What has this to do with managing people at work? In a word, everything.

People bring their problems to work, where you must deal with them. More than ever before, your business is asked to take some of the responsibility to change social conditions.

> EXAMPLE: Yours is a rare company if it is not called upon to support United Way or similar civic causes. Corporate citizenship today implies support for higher principles such as equality, opportunity, and individual growth.

Basically, a social problem is any difficulty or conflict among people, in a group or society context, that impairs productive relationships. These include unemployment, failure to observe contractual obligation, prejudicial attitudes, unequal opportunity, destructive and unhealthy psychological behavior. From a historical standpoint, our society has gone through four phases in the development of these social problems:

1. *The decline of self-employment (1900–1930).* Workers become employees rather than tradesmen. Much of the shift took place in the early 1900s, with the advent and growth of large factories.

2. *The Economic Depression (1930–1940).* The Great Depression saw unemployment at unprecedented rates of 20 percent and over. With government's intervention, the New Deal, people developed a new dependency on government. While alleviating many existing social problems, the government grew in size, power, and expenditures.

3. *The Great Uprooting (1940–1950).* As a result of World War II, people became extremely mobile and better educated. Social problems took a back seat to post-war progress. However, out of all the new mobility and economic activity, the seeds were planted for future social problems, such as environment, equality, product safety, and a new generation of people dependent on government welfare.

4. *The New Social Consciousness (1960 to present).* Along with the new prosperity of the 1950s came new problems and attitudes. If you managed in the 1960s, you probably found nonconforming attitudes about establishment and authority. The main social problems were environmental and consumer oriented. Treatment of minorities and women and the increasingly visible poor people gained the national attention along with the increasing crime rate, drug problems, and health care needs.

Many of the social problems have always been with us and will probably continue, in spite of efforts to reduce them. What's changed are the solutions in varying levels of success.

Recall from Chapter 1 the EC³ idea—that you must be concerned with your employee, customer, community, and company. EC³ might have seemed idealistic at one time but in relation to social responsibilities, it is a stark reality. People *expect* business to take a significant role in alleviating social problems. Why? For one reason, business has the surplus money to do it.

Corporate social responsibility is widespread today, with more than 80 percent of major companies giving aid in such problem areas as environment, minority hiring and training, rebuilding central cities, education, consumer protection, and crime. Businesses *are* people, and they will behave no differently from people in general. Some may show little conscience at all, but most try to reconcile their business interests with the social good.

How do you respond to social problems? When your employees want to solicit funds on department time for Charlie's leukemia-stricken daughter, how do you respond? Or when you are aware that chemical waste from one of your operations is damaging your neighbor's favorite fishing stream, what do you do about it? There's no room for armchair speculation here. Rather than suggesting a right or wrong position on social issues, it's more useful to offer certain guidelines that can help you decide on your best course of action:

1. *Keep in touch with your main purpose and goal.* You are responsible first of all for the *work* of your unit.

2. *Examine your company's policies and practices.* If they are not consistent with your own conscience, then talk with your boss about it.

3. *Understand your organization's purpose and limitations.* Perhaps this is best stated this way, "Business is not suited to the tasks demanded in solving outside social problems anymore than churches are effective instruments of social reform. In other words, those who want business to solve all social problems are flogging a dead horse."[1]

4. *Be aware that people do not oppose change only the undesirable effects of change.* Focus on benefits of change rather than the problems, and look at problems as opportunities.

5. *Approach "isms" and radical ideas rationally.* Be wary of any person who believes social concern was invented by the present generation.

6. As you find yourself confronted with new demands, *maintain your own balance and strategies* for handling stress.

7. *Look for the payoff* as you consider socially responsible alternatives.

> EXAMPLE: There are certain profits to be gained in recycling or selling certain by-products that would otherwise be discarded as waste.

---

[1] Dr. Nicholas Glaskowsky, in Steinhoff, *The World of Business*, (New York: McGraw-Hill Book Co., 1979).

8. Know your contractual obligations, including any vain contract.

HOW THE INTERNATIONAL DIMENSION AFFECTS YOUR ROLE AS MANAGER

There are important reasons for trading with other nations. Most basic is that resources are distributed unequally in the world. The United States has abundant resources but little or no rubber, tin, zinc, bananas, coffee, to name a few. Some nations, such as England, must import nearly all the materials needed to support a modern economy.

Another important reason for international trade is the principle of comparative advantage. This means that one country might be able to produce something more economically than another because of favorable labor, climate, technology, and so on. EXAMPLE: Japan can produce automobiles more efficiently than, say, Saudi Arabia; and Saudi Arabia can produce oil more cheaply than Japan.

International transactions usually do not relate to your day-to-day business. However, consider your own organization and how you would be (or are) affected if it deals in international trade. Here are some:

1. *Product standards.* You might need to meet different standards for international markets.

2. *Measurements.* You might be required to use metric and imperial systems.

3. *Language.* You may need to attach instructions in a foreign language.

4. *Fluctuating demand and changing schedules.* Foreign sales are less predictable, and this could cause peaks and valleys in your work schedule.

5. *Cosmopolitan attitude.* This usually produces open-mindedness toward different nationalities and cultures.

6. *Decision making.* Decisions become more complicated when the international dimension enters the picture.

7. *Greater awareness of competition and politics.* These are two of the biggest issues in the auto industry today.

In summary, doing business with other countries affects your products, job requirements, decisions, and attitudes. Increasing your awareness of the process and the problems of international operations can help equip you to deal with them in your unit.

CHAPTER 10

Law for the Manager

A wise man once said "Person who have judgment he cannot collect, have nothing."

—Anonymous

LEGAL encounters are part of your everyday experience. As a manager, you'll be required to manage these situations appropriately. To do so, you need to fully comprehend the law and the legal process. This chapter is designed to provide you with the tools to do this.

Your private and workplace concerns have great common basis in the law. Understanding the law at a basic level will help develop your legal savvy in every aspect of your life. Thus, we ask you to step back a few paces from your immediate work situation and don your "citizen" hat along with your managerial one.

You will find the organization of this chapter somewhat different from the others in this book. Each section is set out in question-and-answer format, as an easy and convenient way to present this difficult subject to you. Admittedly, this chapter can honestly only "touch the tip of the iceberg." The total body of law is truly overwhelming and complex. Further, it changes daily. Even so, your basic understanding of the information presented here will improve your ability to perform your daily functions as a manager.

WHY MANAGERS MUST UNDERSTAND THE BASICS OF THE LAW

What Is the Law?

Law is a compilation of rules and regulations that in their totality provide guidelines for establishing standards of conduct. The purpose of the law is to:

1. Keep the peace by deterring unacceptable behavior.
2. Establish dispute-settling procedures.
3. Promote society's well being and generate desirable change.

How Did Law Develop?

A significant percentage of U.S. law was brought from England by our ancestors. Today, our laws have become a hybrid of the laws of many nations.

The laws of England have provided us with a strong foundation. The Common Law, England's law that has existed since the Middle Ages, is substantial and well reasoned. It rarely changes because it is fair, just, and hence readily accepted by judges in courts of law.

What Is the Law of the United States?

A great deal of what makes up United States law is English common law. Literally, it is located in volumes of case decisions that judges have rendered. The remainder of U.S. law consists of *statutes* enacted by our legislators on both the federal and state levels. All law is in written form.

The statutes, after judicial review, are then catalogued and indexed for easy reference. Today, certain statutes have been enacted mainly to clarify the common law. As a result, statutory law has become more significant than common law in many areas.

An area of the common law that has been replaced by statutory law concerns the rights of the consumer to recover from an unfair merchant. In order to handle complaints quickly and satisfactorily, many of these laws provide the consumer with specific procedures to follow and the authorities to contact.

> A CASE-IN-POINT: A door-to-door salesman oversells his wares to an unwary housewife. Upon reflection, she realizes that she did not want the product. Under many circumstances, she may cancel the deal and recover her down payment.

What Laws May We Frequently Encounter?

Certainly, common and statutory laws are among those with which you have to deal from time to time, but substantial areas called *administrative law* and *regulation* frequently affect your life.

Its authority is based upon statutes, themselves often meager in length and detail, frequently stating nothing more than a purpose and then the directing of a department, agency, or bureau of government to establish regulations to implement the legislative desires. These government organizations are normally labeled *administrative agencies.*

NOTE: Although they are often lower echelon people, frequently referred to as bureaucrats, their application of statutes, even interpretations of their own regulations, are very critical to the average person. You will find administrative agencies, even at the lowest levels of government, having increased control over what you do, whether it be for business or personal purposes.

> A CASE-IN-POINT: The new equipment your unit has been expecting and desperately needs cannot be installed until OSHA makes its ruling on the tolerable exhaust levels for that apparatus. Until then, you must continue using the old, less efficient equipment.

Improvements in transportation and communication have "shrunk" our business world. This has created a demand for reform and uniformity in many of our business laws and has resulted, after much trial and error, in the creation of the *Uniform Commercial Code (UCC)*. This law governs most business transactions.[1] The subject areas covered by the UCC include sales contracts, negotiable instruments, bulk sales, warehouse receipts, documents of title, and secured transactions.

> A CASE-IN-POINT: Does the unusual sale of a large percentage of the company inventory demand any special legal considerations? This question is raised by a manager who wonders if any notifications or approvals are needed, particularly since the company has outstanding a large accounts payable. Both the UCC's bulk sales provisions and secured transactions section should be referred to for the answers. In this case, legal assistance is clearly a necessity.

HOW MANAGERS ADMINISTER THE LAW

Who Applies the Law?

Formal law is applied through the federal and state court systems. Less formal administrative proceedings are contained

---

[1] Actually, the UCC is part of statutory law since it has been enacted by all states except Louisiana.

somewhat loosely in that system, as well as in a self-designed system of its own.

Federal. The primary and most important formal legal system is the federal judicial system. The Constitution of the United States established the Supreme Court, the highest court in the land. Its pronouncements affect everyone from both a business and personal standpoint.

The Federal Court of Appeals is next in line of authority. Its function is to review the decisions of lower courts. If requested, a Supreme Court judge may choose to have the court review the entire lower courts' decision.

There are other quasi-judicial organizations on the "appeals" level. They include: National Labor Relations Board, Consumer Products Safety Commission, Administrator of Environmental Protection Agency, Federal Mine Safety and Health Commission, Secretary of Army, and so on. These organizations are executive branches of the government that, from time to time, serve a judicial function.

There are other courts or agencies in the federal system but none with more practical importance than the Federal District Court. One district court covers each geographical area of the United States. It has original (first) jurisdiction over federal questions in which the amount exceeds $10,000 and in situations affecting citizens of different federal areas. Federal crimes, maritime law, and review of administrative agency decisions are included in its area of responsibility.

State. The organizational makeup of the state courts generally follows the federal sequence of a lower court, an appeals court, and a supreme court. (See Figure 10.1.) There may be variations. Note that many states have an additional level of lower courts to handle lesser matters. Such "local courts" provide this capacity.

The Common Pleas Courts typically handle probate matters, that is, processing deceaseds' estates, supervising trusts, guardianships, mental illness matters, and adoptions. This level of court also handles domestic relations matters, including custody and child support, higher dollar value civil cases between private parties, and serious criminal matters.

A CASE-IN-POINT: A dispute exists because the local government refuses to authorize your employer to start a plant expansion project. The court on the Common Pleas level, with original jurisdiction, will determine whether the local government is

A TYPICAL STATE COURT SYSTEM

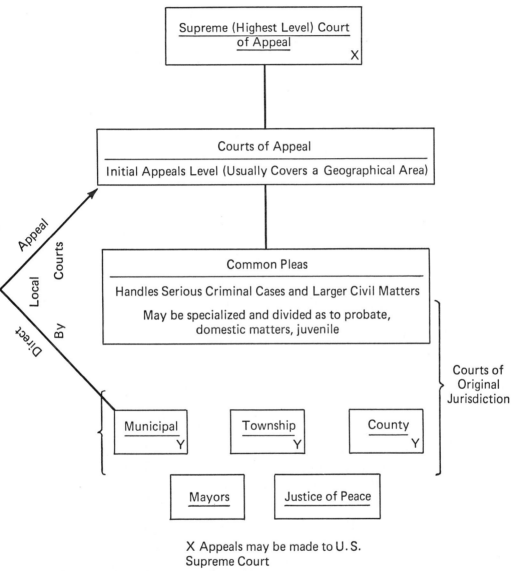

X Appeals may be made to U. S.
Supreme Court

Y Frequently handle small claims suits

FIGURE 10.1

within its powers to refuse the permit or if they will be directed to honor the request.

Administrative Agencies. These organizations, which prolife-rate on both the federal and state levels, have broad and numerous powers. They frequently touch our lives and that of our employees far more frequently than that of the court system itself.

A CASE-IN-POINT: The IRS disallows a deduction on a tax return based upon their own rulings. If you object to the ruling, you'll likely be surprised at their extensive appeals procedure, which may be required before you can go to the tax court or federal district court.

THE LEGAL PROCESS: ORDERLY MOVEMENT OF A COMPLEX SYSTEM

What Is Legal Procedure?

Legal procedure is the process by which disputes are *adjudi-cated.* The United States works under what is called the *adversary* system. A judge presides over the system.

In a civil action, the aggrieved party, or *plaintiff,* claims injury by the defending party, the *defendant.* The general procedure fol-lowed is outlined in Figure 10.2.

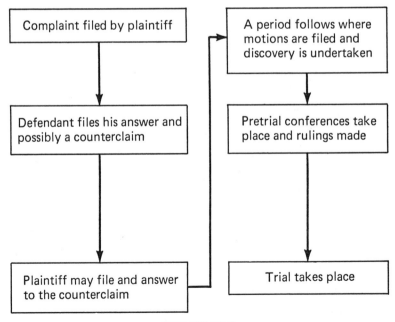

FIGURE 10.2

In a criminal action, the plaintiff is always a political entity.

EXAMPLE: *State vs. Jackson; City vs. Coal Company.* The defendant is a person or company charged with violating the criminal law.

Figure 10.3 gives an outline of the procedure followed if the defendant is charged with a serious crime.

Less serious crimes may be handled in the local court merely by paying the prescribed fine or posting bond.

SUGGESTION: If the offense is serious with possible jail time as a penalty, then it's good advice to obtain a lawyer. The expense will be well worth it. This advice applies whether you think you are guilty or not. In every case, you must be proven guilty beyond a reasonable doubt.

CRIMES AND TORTS: WHAT THEY MEAN AND HOW THEY DIFFER

What Are Crimes and Torts?

Crimes are violations of one's obligation to the whole community. Intent to commit a crime is normally required in order to establish guilt. *Torts* are wrongs committed against a person and/or property. Torts are not the result of any established contract between the parties but rather a duty based on an implied obligation.

A CASE-IN-POINT: Jones, on his way home from work, is distracted and runs his vehicle into a parked car. His action is breach of a public duty (a crime). He has also legally wronged the owner of the parked car (a tort).

Statutes set forth the crimes and their elements and establish the punishment for those charged and convicted. Within the scope of tort law, the injured party usually receives compensation for the wrong done to him or her.

A CASE-IN-POINT: In a criminal action, Jones is found guilty of reckless driving. He is fined and pays court costs. This type of offense normally does not warrant incarceration (jail). In the civil action, Jones is required to pay the car owner his damages, that being the cost of repairing his car.

How Are Specific Crimes Classified?

Crimes are categorized as follows:

1. Crimes against the state and public order.
2. Felonies against the individual or property.
3. Misdemeanors and local violations.

What Are Crimes Against the State and Public Order?

These include treason, espionage, and bribery of a government official. *Treason* is the betrayal of one's country, frequently by spying upon the nation's military. Government secrets that protect the country are revealed through *espionage*. Both activities are believed to be inherently bad.

Bribery involves the offering to take or give a bribe (money or something of value) in order to influence a person in his or her official capacity. Whether the bribe is small or large, or the party aware or not, he or she is still guilty of the crime.

> A CASE-IN-POINT: An inspector looks the other way to violations of the health code and does not require a restaurant to meet standards of cleanliness designed to protect the public

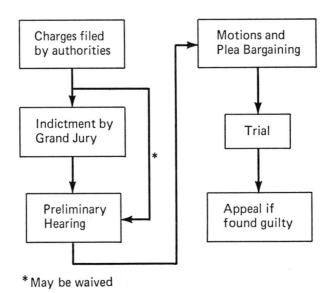

*May be waived

FIGURE 10.3

from potentially inedible products. The inspector receives free meals for himself and his family. He is guilty of bribery, as is the restaurant owner.

What Are Felonies Against the Individual or of Property?

Generally, a *felony* is a serious crime normally requiring a year or more of imprisonment as punishment. The possibility of a substantial fine exists as well.

Murder is the unlawful killing of a human being with malice, express or implied. *Manslaughter* is a lesser offense, usually because the act was unintended or committed in the heat of passion.

Theft statutes include *robbery,* the involuntary taking of a personal property in the owner's presence, usually by force or fear; *burglary,* the breaking into a home or building; and *larceny,* the taking of another's property without permission.

Obtaining property by false pretense or *fraud* is similar to theft. The criminal, frequently called a "con man," normally will make untrue claims in order to defraud the owner of his or her property.

There are, of course, numerous other revolting crimes such as arson, kidnapping, and sex-related offenses. Victims of such crimes should seek assistance of the local police.

What Are Lesser Crimes?

Some of the crimes previously described may be considered less serious if the amount involved does not exceed a large sum. EXAMPLE: "Petty" larceny in some localities may pertain to theft under $100 or $200. These crimes are called *misdemeanors.* Included in this category are such offenses as public drunkenness, disorderly conduct, trespass, most traffic offenses, and various types of personal altercations.

> A CASE-IN-POINT: Susan takes a piece of costume jewelry valued at $5.00 from the local department store. When stopped at the exit, she is charged with shoplifting (petty larceny or petty theft).

NEGLIGENCE AND LIABILITY: HOW TO HANDLE THE BREACH OF OBLIGATION

What Are the Essential Elements of a Tort?

As mentioned before, a tort occurs when someone fails to live up to the legal obligations owed to fellow citizens. *Negligence* involves the breach of that basic duty; the reason why, or the cause of the injury; and damages sustained. When all three elements are established, the responsible party will then be held liable.

> A CASE-IN-POINT: Gable keeps some combustible substances in his garage., While leaving the garage, he trips over the substances and a fire is started. Gable's neighbor sustains damages of $10,000. Gable is liable for the loss since it was his obligation not to cause harm to his neighbor's property. His conduct was a breach of duty and the cause of the fire and damages.

Generally, a person's actions are compared with the conduct that a reasonable man would display in the same set of circumstances. Failure to measure up to the "reasonable man" standard suggests lack of due care, or negligence.

NOTE: There are certain individuals or organizations who cannot be sued. Among them are certain close relatives, who may be in collusion with the claimant. Federal and state governments also may avoid suit simply because they provide themselves with sovereign immunity.

What Happens When Several Parties Contribute to the Occurrence of an Accident?

Not all situations are necessarily caused by the actions of one individual. It may in fact be true that a number of people by their independent activities are responsible for an accident. This type of circumstance may be treated differently, depending on the laws of the state in which you reside.

A small number of states subscribe to the doctrine of *contributory negligence*. This provides that the party bringing the action must be totally free of negligence himself. Otherwise, he or she will be unable to recover damage, even if the relative proportion of negligence of the defendant far exceeds that of the plaintiff (even 90 percent to 10 percent). The justification for this approach is that degrees of negligence just cannot be compared, and since responsibility does exist on both sides, all parties are left to lick their own wounds.

> A CASE-IN-POINT: Harriet was hit by a lift truck at work. The incident occurred in an aisle that was well marked with signs "caution, moving vehicles." Harriet claims the lift truck operator was negligent because he was speeding and was not alert to

her presence. Under contributory negligence, Harriet was found to share some of the blame. By stepping into the aisle, she contributed to the accident. Her suit was therefore dismissed.

Comparative negligence has become very popular these last few years, and now more than two thirds of our states have adopted it. It provides for an apportioning of the negligence to the various parties to the accident. Damages are awarded based on an application of the percentage of liability to the injuries sustained.

> A CASE-IN-POINT: A and B are involved in an accident in California. A's damages are $100,000 and B's damages are $25,000. An investigation reveals that B's actions placed A in a very dangerous situation, but if A were a bit more alert, he may have avoided the accident or reduced its severity. The jury finds A 20 percent responsible for the events so he will be able to recover 80 percent of his damages from B.

What Are Variations of Basic Negligence Situations?

Assumption of risk and the intervention of forces are frequently raised by defense counsel to excuse or mitigate the actions of their clients.

In a situation involving risk assumption, it must be shown that the plaintiff voluntarily entered into a risky situation. If this is proven, he or she will not recover for injuries.

> A CASE-IN-POINT: Zero, while aware of the risk, agrees to attempt a balloon assent over a hazardous area. The trip is affected by bad weather, and he suffers frostbite and other injuries. He cannot recover for his injuries.

How Is Liability Established in Intentional Tort Situations?

The courts and legislatures require that specific elements be proven in order to establish guilt or *liability*.

Malpractice. Suits of this type are typically brought against professionals such as doctors, lawyers, and architects. Today, corporate executives, public officials, and teachers have been required to defend malpractice actions. In general, the conduct of the person (organization) must have deviated from the normal standard of conduct or level of proficiency found in that community. Also, a direct causal relationship between the deviation and the injury sustained must be established.

A CASE-IN-POINT: Iverson went to her physician for treatment of a lump on her breast. The doctor admitted her to the hospital, where tests were made in order to determine if the lump was malignant. Before the tests came back indicating the tumor was benign, the doctor removed the breast. The doctor had malpracticed.

Assault and Battery. *Assault* involves threatening harm to another person. There must be some evidence of an ability to do harm and an awareness of the situation by the innocent party. *Battery* is the unlawful application of force to the person, including touching another. Obviously, battery will be excused if done in self-defense. There may be criminal as well as civil charges brought as a resuls of assault and battery.

A CASE-IN-POINT: Nelson, a telephone company employee, is attempting to repair a pay phone. A customer, irritated by the delay in service pushes and then strikes Nelson. He defends himself, only provoking the customer further, who then breaks Nelson's nose. In the criminal matter, the customer pleads guilty to assault and battery; Nelson brings a civil suit for his injuries.

False Arrest and False Imprisonment. When a person is deprived of his or her freedom without just cause, those responsible are guilty of false imprisonment. This would include any form of detention that denies a person liberty to go as he or she pleases.

Character Statements. In this category fall libel, slander, and defamation. They may all deal with the "publishing" of untruthful statements about another person. *Libel* is normally an untrue statement pertaining to a particular person. Commonly, these statements made in newspapers are caused by untimely deadlines. *Slander* is a spoken untruth that damages the character and/or reputation of a person. Generally, some financial loss needs to be shown by the injured party in order to prevail in court.

A CASE-IN-POINT: Manager Morton does not want employee Jenkins to transfer to another department, so Morton tells the other manager that Jenkins has been absent ten of the last thirty workdays with an incurable illness. The absence information is true, but it is not true that Jenkins' illness is incurable—that is mere speculation, at best. Morton may be found guilty of slander.

A communication that speaks evil of another's reputation or a company's products is *defamation* if untrue.

A CASE-IN-POINT: Orville was unhappy because Duke was getting all the choice business at his restaurant. Orville made it
known among certain food suppliers that Duke was having financial trouble. He also had his employees suggest to customers
that Duke's restaurant was having troubles with the Board of
Health. After suffering an unexplained loss of business, Duke
traced down the source of the rumors and sued Orville
for slander and defamation. He should receive substantial
damages.

Trespass.   Going back throughout recorded history, a person
has the right to enjoy the use of his or her real estate without
interference. Intrusions such as "taking shortcuts," uninvited solic-
itors merchandising their wares, stray animals, and errant vehicles
are considered *trespass.*

The interference with one's free and uncontrolled use of his
goods and property is a trespass to personal property. A frequent
situation under this area of the law is *conversion* and occurs when
one takes another's property without permission.

A CASE-IN-POINT: You give Smith Watch Repair Co. your
watch for repair. Through a mixup your watch is sold to a
completely unaware customer. The watch repair company will
bear the responsibility.

To What Extent May We Defend Our Property?

You may protect and defend your property as long as you do
not use excess force. The force you may use must be consistent with
the extent to which the intruder is doing wrong.

What Are Considered Business Torts?

One business tort already mentioned was defamation, the dis-
paraging of the goods of a competitor. Making use of a trademark,
service mark, patent, copyright, or company name belonging to
another are all business torts.

WHAT YOU NEED TO KNOW ABOUT CONTRACT LAW

How Are Contracts Classified?

Formal contracts are expressed in writing and require a seal or
other formalities. EXAMPLES: Commercial paper and letters of

credit. The remainder are classified as *informal* contracts, whether in writing or not. All verbal contracts are considered informal.

Executory contracts are those that have been entered into but have not as yet been performed by either party. When all the parties to a contract have completed the legal obligations required by the contract, it is said to be executed.

When only one party makes a contractual promise, this is a *unilateral* contract. EXAMPLE: A contract to pay a reward. In the *bilateral* contract, both contracting parties make a promise. EXAMPLE: The willingness of your neighbor's son to cut your grass for a specified sum.

An *express* contract is one in which the promise is stated in specific direct terms. An *implied* contract is based upon implications or conclusions that evolve from the circumstances. EXAMPLE: If you go to a person who performs a service without concluding on a price in advance, you would be expected by implication to pay his or her standard fee for the services.

A *valid* contract is one that has all the elements necessary to the ordinary enforcement of the contract. A *void* contract is not a contract at all since it does not have the necessary elements. An *unenforceable* contract is one that meets the basic requirements of a contract but that the courts, for some reason, will not enforce.

> A CASE-IN-POINT: There is a statute in the state of Utopia that declares: If a person who has purchased goods on credit does not pay within six years and suit by the creditor has not been commenced in that six-year period, the contract is unenforceable. Plainly, the money is still owed, but there is no way to collect it through the courts.

What Are Contract Elements?

Contract elements are those items required by law that must be a part of an understanding between contracting parties or the understanding will be held void. They are most commonly identified as follows:

1. Agreement (offer and acceptance).
2. Genuine assent of both parties.
3. Consideration.
4. Competency.
5. A lawful objective.

6. In the form required by law, if any.

AGREEMENT, OFFER, AND ACCEPTANCE: HOW TO BEGIN THE CONTRACT PROCESS

How Do We Enter into Agreements?

Many agreements are entered into after varying degrees of negotiation, bickering, or horse trading. Depending on all sorts of variables, including time available, importance of the deal, the personalities of the parties and other factors, a contract may evolve with ease or with some difficulty. Occasionally, a contract may be generated by a simple forthright action which, by itself, may signify the desire to contract. The person to whom the offer is made is called the *offeree*. The *offeror* makes the offer.

What Are Critical Factors in Considering if an Offer Has Been Made?

Depending on the circumstances, you should be able to answer yes to these questions:

1. Has a firm offer been communicated?
2. Is the offer clear and definite?
3. Was an offer intended?

On many occasions, inquiries resemble offers. Frequently, salesmen's activities may be looked upon as offers when the purported offer is really a "wouldjatake." The courts would call it an "invitation to trade," or an "invitation to do business." Among those activities that fall into this category are newspaper advertisements, billboards, TV and radio commercials, mail order solicitations, and the chant of the auctioneer.

As far as the typical consumer transaction is concerned, a true offer occurs only after the consumer has responded to the invitation.

> A CASE-IN-POINT: Andrew places an ad in the local newspaper announcing that he has a famous brand of washing machine for sale at 20 percent off. He may even "offer" them to the public by using the word "offer" in his ad. Blue shows up at the store and accepts the invitation by stating, "I'll take one of those." At this point, Andrew may or may not sell.

What Actually Is an Offer?

An *offer* is a relatively complete and definite statement to the offeree that manifests an intent to contract. Terms need not be absolutely certain, but they must be sufficient enough to enable the court to determine the parties' intent.

> A CASE-IN-POINT: Burns says to Carter "I will provide you with all the skilled labor and equipment necessary to erect a two-hundred-foot tower for four thousand dollars." Carter agrees. Later, Carter tries to get out of the deal by arguing that it lacked certain specific terms. The court will hold the contract void since important provisions, which might be critical, are not included and not yet agreed upon.

How Long Is an Offer Effective?

The duration of an offer is frequently determined by specific statements in the offer itself. If no provision is made for time of acceptance, the offer will lapse after a reasonable period of time. Offers will also be terminated if rejected, withdrawn by the offeror, or by the death of a party.

> A CASE-IN-POINT: Charlie offers Durwood his car for $1,000. Durwood responds with, "I'll pay you nine hundred dollars." What Durwood did was make a counteroffer, which made Charlie's offer void. Unless Charlie accepts Durwood's counteroffer or they compromise in some way, Durwood is out of luck.

What Constitutes an Acceptance?

The underlying basis of a contract is mutual consent of the parties. Therefore, it follows that an acceptance must be some form of affirmation that the offeree agrees to the offeror's terms and conditions. This may be accomplished in a variety of ways.

In a verbal offer, with direct communication between the parties, an immediate yes or no or perhaps a nod of the head will signify acceptance. There are other actions that constitute acceptance, such as the bang of the auctioneer's hammer or even silence when the parties have done business that way in the past. EXAMPLE: "Call me if you don't want the product we discussed."

Courts look upon the offeror of the contract as having "control" of the contract situation since his or her terms and conditions are the basis for contract rights and obligations. The offeror then is presumed to be able to protect himself from risks.

TWO AREAS MANAGERS MUST CONSIDER: CONSIDERATION AND CAPACITY

What Is Consideration?

The formal definition of consideration is the waiving of or the promise to waive a legal right at the request of another. Informally, it's "what you give for what you get." Both parties must give consideration for a contract to be enforceable.

> A CASE-IN-POINT: Miller offers to paint Nevin's car for $100. The consideration of Miller is the carrying out of the task of painting Nevin's car. In turn, Nevin's consideration is the payment of the $100. If one party fails to perform, the injured party may sue for damages.

What Isn't Consideration?

Consideration is considered by many a difficult area of contract law. There are occasions when it may seem that there is consideration but, in fact, there isn't. Hence, no contract can exist.

A *preexisting obligation* occurs when a party already owes the other party. If the condition is made a provision of the contract and there is no other consideration required of that party, he or she has no ability to enforce the contract.

> A CASE-IN-POINT: Reilly, the cop, arrests a criminal who is attempting to break into your company factory. Your company had announced a reward for information leading to the arrest and conviction of anyone attempting to steal any company property. Reilly will be unable to receive the reward since he is already receiving consideration (pay) for performing the service.

Past consideration refers to situations where the parties attempt to support a present promise by making it a part of some prior contract or obligation.

> A CASE-IN-POINT: Sorey purchased an appliance from a retail dealer. The warranty was provided by the manufacturer. The dealer installed the appliance, which worked properly. Sorey came to the appliance store to pay for his purchase. While there he negotiated with the dealer for an extended warranty on the

appliance, which the dealer would provide himself. Sorey paid nothing extra for the additional warranty coverage. He could not enforce this addition to the contract if he needed it since he gave nothing in consideration in return for the dealer's additional promise. The consideration Sorey gave was in the past.

What Is an Unliquidated Debt?

This is a debt that is uncertain as to amount because there is a legitimate dispute as to what sum is actually owed. Upon the settlement of the dispute, the debt is said to be liquidated and the amount payable.

> A CASE-IN-POINT: Uris disputes the amount owed to Vance for carpeting installed in his office. He feels the workmanship does not measure up to other carpet installation work in the building. Vance agrees the work is not up to snuff. When the parties settle on a lesser amount, which Uris will then owe, they will have liquidated the debt. Uris will be liable for that sum, not the greater amount.

When Is Consideration Unnecessary?

Seldom is consideration unnecessary, but there are a few situations where the need for it is overlooked for one reason or another:

1. *Charitable Subscriptions.* If you promise to give a gift to some recognized charity and they rely on your promise, your promise will be enforced.

2. *Barred Obligations.* There are situations in which a person is unable to recover a debt because the time for recovery has passed in which to bring suit (statute of limitations) or his debtor has been discharged in bankruptcy. The person may recover the sum owed when the creditor is able to convince the debtor to pay the debt anyway at some later date, despite the lack of liability.

3. *Promissory Estoppel.* This occurs when you induce a person to do something by promising that if they do the requested act you will do something for them. The courts will enforce your promise without any consideration.

Who Has Capacity to Contract?

Capacity to contract identifies those who have the ability to enter valid contracts, incur obligations, and acquire rights. The largest group who do not have full capacity are minors.

Minors are those who are underage, usually under eighteen years of age. Until that time, the law views such persons as having less than equal bargaining power with adults. The "Shield of Minority" is given them for their protection. The result is that the minor may void most contracts he or she enters into.

There are some exceptions. Minors who contract for necessaries are liable for their fair value. Necessaries are those things a minor needs to reasonably provide for his welfare. Conversely, a minor who is already provided with necessaries by his parents will not be obligated to a third party who furnishes them, too.

NOTE: Parents are legally liable for the support of their children; that is, they must pay for the reasonable value, based on their standard of living, for necessaries furnished by others when the parent has neglected to furnish the necessaries themselves. Of course, it should not be overlooked that parents are entitled to the earnings of their children while they have the duty to support them.

Do Others Lack Capacity to Contract?

To a limited extent, intoxicated persons lack capacity to contract. If their reasoning abilities and judgment are sufficiently impaired, they would have the same option to disaffirm the contract as anyone under a disability.

Insane persons are protected in many jurisdictions by a variety of legislation. Here, as far as lack of capacity is concerned, some jurisdictions will hold the incompetent to his contracts, but he or she may void them by relying upon other legal protections, including undue influence, duress, and unconscionability.

HOW TO PROTECT YOURSELF FROM IMPROPER AGREEMENTS

What Happens When the True Facts of the Situation Differ from the Purported Facts?

There are occasions when an agreement is not intended even though the parties have entered into a contract. This occurs when there has been some impropriety on the part of the parties. Examples of this are fraud, misrepresentation, duress, and undue influence. In such cases, the innocent party is allowed to void the contract.

What Is Fraud and What Is Misrepresentation?

Fraud is generally defined as an intentional misrepresentation of a material fact specifically meant to induce another to take inappropriate action. The innocent party usually incurs resulting damages. The method of accomplishing the fraud is irrelevant; only the "negative" result is important.

> A CASE-IN-POINT: Helms applies for a job. On his application, he indicates that he has a certificate of proficiency in certain laboratory testing procedures. In fact, Helms prepared the certificate with the help of a printer friend. After a period on the job, his certification claim was checked out and found false. Helms may be fired and sued for any damages he caused.

Misrepresentation is generally construed as somewhat less onerous than fraud. It is the misleading of a person by placing in that person's mind an impression that does not agree with the true facts of the situation. Again, loss or damage must result.

> A CASE-IN-POINT: Igor operated an investment company. He contacted Jenks to tell him that he understood that a mineral discovery was being concealed by a certain corporation. His purpose was to get Jenks to buy stock in the corporation in order to get a commission. In truth, Igor had heard only vague rumors that a discovery had been made. He jumped to conclusions and stated facts that were not really accurate. If Jenks buys stock in the corporation and loses money, he will be able to recover from Igor. The damages will not likely be any more than his actual loss.

What Is Duress and What Is Undue Influence?

Duress is an unlawful constraint upon a person to contract when he or she would not otherwise have done so. The constraint is either physical or the threat of it or by imprisonment. *Undue influence* is looked upon as a form of coercion or deception used most frequently when aged or mentally weak people are involved. The courts must establish that the parties have unequal bargaining power or are influenced by a person considered to be a fiduciary (a person in the position of having the other person's trust and confidence).

> A CASE-IN-POINT: Maud, who is aged and lacks business knowledge and experience, is convinced that a contract whereby

Nance manages her affairs is in her best interest. Nance, an "Investment Advisor," has her sign such a contract by working on her fears and concerns. Then through a variety of devices, she bilks Maud out of her funds. Such an arrangement clearly suggests improper use of a fiduciary relationship. Maud will herself, or perhaps through a court-appointed guardian, seek to recover her losses.

How May a Mistake Cause an Agreement to Be Adjusted?

Certain contracts, which may generally fall into a certain category called *mistakes,* are subject to being modified or set aside. Clearly, a legal mistake should not be confused with bad judgment, carelessness, or ignorance. In such situations, claims of mistake will not be found sufficient to void the contract.

Mistakes most frequently found actionable are:

1. Mutual mistakes in which the parties held a mistaken belief concerning a material fact.

2. Mistakes resulting from errors in writing the contract instrument or honest errors in the interpretation of contract terminology.

A CASE-IN-POINT: Olson examines cloth under artifical light and finds it to be the color he wants to match with his living room carpeting. He signs a contract for drapes of that color but discovers a few hours later that in daylight the colors do not match. Since the salesman had also held the same belief as Olson, the contract will be set aside on the grounds of mutual mistake.

What Is Unconscionability?

Unconscionability is a contract in which the terms are clearly unreasonable and adverse to the interests of one contracting party. The Uniform Commercial Code is the first widely accepted law that used the term. The intent of the UCC is to prevent the gross injustice that may result from unequal bargaining positions of the parties. The unconscionability concept prevents this type of arrangement from existing without remedy.

What Contracts Are Not Legal?

There are certain kinds of contracts that cannot be entered into because they are not permitted by law.

1. *Crime and Tort Bargains.* We hear more and more today that there is "A contract out on that guy." The meaning is clear—someone is seeking revenge and is willing to pay to get even. Deals of this nature are plainly against law and order and are illegal.

Violation of federal anti-trust laws and certain state laws amount to entering into an illegal contract. This type of arrangement is grouped under the category "Restraint of Trade."

2. *Bargains in Violation of Statute.* Included in this category are gambling, certain unregulated stock market dealings, charging excessive interest on loans, and certain licensing laws.

Usury is the charging of a rate of interest above that permitted by law. The variations permitted and forbidden are too numerous to consider here. A few general statements, however, might prevent your inadvertent entry into this illegal area:

1. As a private individual, don't expect to be able to loan money to another person at high rates; in most states only licensed lenders may charge higher rates.

2. If a loan is made to anyone, be sure you know how to compute interest rates based on the statutory formulas. You are not permitted to "ball-park" or estimate an interest rate and have it on the high side.

3. Do not assume that money may be loaned to a corporation at an unrestricted rate. Many states do limit the interest rate on corporate loans. Check your state laws.

NOTE: The Truth-in-Lending Law, also known as Regulation Z, is a federal law pertaining to a requirement that the lender reveal to the borrower the actual rate of interest (the Annual Percentage Rate, or APR) he or she is charging. This law does not establish usury nor relate directly to it. Its purpose is only one of informing the borrower as to the rates of interest he or she will pay for his consumer purchase, or loan.

Licensing laws are a convenient way of generating revenue for the various governmental units. However, failure to obtain a revenue-producing type of license does not mean the contract with the person failing to obtain the license is invalid. The contract is good whether the license is obtained or not.

Failure to obtain another type of license, one required in order to establish minimum standards of professional competency, can render a contract illegal. No damages are recoverable for nonpayment to an unlicensed person claiming professional status.

What Are the Effects of Illegal Contracts?

Generally, courts will leave the parties where it finds them in certain classes of illegal contracts; that is, wagering, crime and tort contracts, restraint of trade arrangements, and noncompliance to licensing requirements where professional standards must be met. In usury situations, the remedy depends upon the particular state law, with judgments varying from repayment of excess interest to forfeiting the entire amount owed.

In situations in which the illegal action is one-sided (as in a confidence game or a fraudulent contract) the injured party will at least be awarded his lost monies, if not additional punitive damages.

Finally, many business organizations place limitations on their employees, which some believe to be improper. These are normally found in employment contracts, frequently those that are entered into at the time of first employment. In a vast majority of cases, these agreements are held to be legal.

Contracts whereby a person agrees not to compete with the employer in a certain geographical area and for a specific period of time have also been held to be legal. These contracts are known as "convenants not to compete" and are allowed as long as the public is not being placed at an improper disadvantage and the employee is not being restricted excessively.

In What Situations Must Contracts Be in Writing?

In many situations, contracts need not be in writing at all. However, old English statutes still require a few executory agreements be in writing:

1. Where a person agrees to pay off another's loan or contract obligation, the contract must be in writing.

2. Promises to buy or sell interests in land, that includes not just the real estate but what's on and under it, such as mineral rights, must be in writing.

3. Agreements that cannot be performed within one year from the date the contract was entered into must be in writing. This includes employment contracts.

A CASE-IN-POINT: Alice, the manager, tells Ted, the new employee, that his job will be secure for one and one-half to two years. After Ted's first year on the job, the job is eliminated, and Ted is laid off. Ted complains that Alice reneged and he should be paid at least another half year's salary. Since the contract was not in writing, the courts will probably not find it enforceable, and Ted will not collect.

SUGGESTION: Any important contract should be put in writing, simply because its importance justifies extra care. None of us is immune from forgetting what was agreed to and what the terms and conditions were. If you have not dealt with the situation or the subject matter before, it would be wise to have legal assistance.

AGENCIES AND THEIR CHARACTERISTICS THAT MANAGERS SHOULD KNOW ABOUT

What Is an Agency?

An *agency* is a legal relationship in which one party (the agent) represents the other (the principal) in business dealings. The agent may deal for and legally obligate the principal.

What Types of Agents Are There?

The principal types of agents are:

1. *General agents.* Such a person or organization has a general power to enter into contractual activities for his or her principal. Managers are an example.

2. *Special agents.* These persons have more limited duties, usually exercising less discretion. Frequently, they have the duty to sell only a single item. Many are referred to as manufacturer's representatives.

3. *Other agents.* There are several types of agencies that operate on a very limited, if not sporadic, basis. These include stockbrokers, attorneys, and others who provide a service on an irregular basis.

As a manager, your managerial authority makes you an agent of the organization in a legal sense. While this does not mean that you are liable for company debts, it does mean that you act in an official capacity and commit the organization by managerial decisions. What follows about agency law on the next few pages is essential basic information that can help you become a more effective agent of management and of the firm.

NOTE: Union stewards are in a similar agency role when they act officially for the union.

How Is the Agency Created?

Most agencies are created by mutual written agreements resulting from considerable advance thought. However, an agency may be established by verbal agreement, by implication, or by the appearances of the situation.

> A CASE-IN-POINT: Bingo ran a launderette. Hilton actually operated the business, as Bingo was hardly ever there. Several of the dryers needed repairs, which Hilton was unable to make himself. He contracted for repairs, but Bingo refused to pay. Bingo would be held liable for the debt since by his actions in placing Hilton in charge, he had implicitly given him the authority to make necessary business judgments.

Does a Person Always Reveal He or She Is Acting as an Agent?

It is normally permissible for a person to conceal the fact that he or she is making contracts for an undisclosed or hidden principal. When an agent does this, he or she is clearly making the contract based upon ability to carry out its terms and conditions. Should the third party become aware of the principal's identity at any time during the course of the contract, he may elect to deal directly with the principal. Should it be necessary for the third party to bring legal action on the contract, he must elect to bring the suit against either the now disclosed principal or the agent. He cannot sue both.

What Is Meant by Scope of Agent's Authority?

The scope of an agent's authority is the extent to which he or she may act to obligate his principal based upon the express, implied, and apparent authority the principal may have given the agent. Principals are liable for the agent's acts done within the scope of his authority, otherwise they are not.

> A CASE-IN-POINT: White works for Howing Home Sales, Inc. He is to sell merchandise to homeowners, collect 25 percent of

the selling price (his commission), and forward the sales agreement to his district office. On both his ID and the sales agreement are prominent statements that read "Sales representative is authorized to collect from customer, at time of sale, exactly 25 percent of the purchase price. Balance within thirty days." Lancelot paid the whole amount of the sale to White who then disappeared. Lancelot will still have to pay Howing 75 percent of the contracted amount.

More frequently today, principals are being held liable for fraudulent conduct of their agents. This liability may exist whether the principal directly participates in the fraud or not. Obviously, this places a premium on the selection process when hiring agents.

What Are the Duties of the Agent to the Principal and the Principal to the Agent?

The duties of the parties to each other are primarily determined by the contract into which they enter. The agent's duties to his principal might be to:

1. Show loyalty.
2. Return sums collected for the principal.
3. Obey instructions.
4. Not represent more than one principal without permission.
5. Have no conflicting interests.
6. Keep information of benefit to his principal confidential.
7. Exercise care and skill.
8. Communicate knowledge learned that is of value to the principal.

A CASE-IN-POINT: An agent sold his principal's products to himself but concealed this information. He then resold the products to others and made substantial profits, which should have gone to the principal. This is considered a conflict of interest. Upon discovery, the agent will be liable to the principal for damages.

How Is an Agency Terminated?

Terminations usually occur by some agreement between the parties. One party may, however, discharge the other, which may result in a breach of contract action with possible damages.

In any event, it is important for the principal to notify third parties who have dealt with the agent and advise them that the agency has been terminated. If this is not done, third parties have the right to assume the agency still exists and continue to deal with the agent. However, the former agent may be liable to the third party because of failure to give proper notice.

> A CASE-IN-POINT: Bix fired Louie as his agent after representing Bix for years. Although Bix was justified in terminating Louie, he couldn't accept Bix's action and continued making deals. Bix's only announcement of the termination of agency was a small ad in the local newspaper, and most of the third parties dealing with the agent were unaware of it. Bix will be subject to the contracts Louie makes in his behalf unless he gives direct personal notice of the termination to the specific third parties.

HOW BUSINESS ORGANIZATIONS ARE FORMED

The type of organization affects how you do business, as well as how you and your boss might be liable. The three principal forms of business in the United States are the sole proprietorship, the partnership, and the corporation. Each has its particular legal advantages and disadvantages.[2]

What Is a Sole Proprietorship?

The least complex form of business operation is the sole proprietorship. The business is operated by a single owner who has total control of the operation. He or she receives all the profits and accepts all the liability. His liability extends to the full extent of all his assets.

What Is a Partnership?

A partnership is an association of two or more persons or business organizations to conduct business as co-owners for profit. All partners' total assets are at risk in the partnership operation. Further, a partner can put the other partner's assets at risk.

---

[2] Business organizations were discussed in detail in Chapter 9. This section is concerned primarily with the legal aspects of business organizations.

How Are Partnerships Created?

Partnerships are created by contract, with no specific formalities required. To determine if a partnership is desired, the intent of the parties must be examined. The question "Did they associate to conduct business for purposes of making a profit?" must be answered yes.

What Is a Limited Partnership?

A limited partnership is a special type of partnership created by statute. The organization consists of one or more general partners who have regular partnership liability and one or more partners whose liability is limited to the amount they have pledged to invest. This type of arrangement has been used extensively for high-risk ventures and tax shelter arrangements.

Besides the limited partner's financial liability, he is also limited in his participation in the management of the venture. The general partner(s) take the risk, but they are the exclusive managers of the organization. Usually, the general partner is the promoter of the organization and deals himself a good portion of the profit, if not salary and other benefits.

What Are the Partner's Obligations to the Partnership?

Generally, the duties and investment that the partners themselves establish for each other, and to which they all agree, determines their obligations. Besides contracted obligations, there are implied obligations such as loyalty, good faith, and the duty to disclose to the other partners all information that is acquired with respect to partnership business. The parties must account for funds and property of the partnership and for the activities assigned to them. Most, if not all, of these requirements are contained in a document called a Partnership Agreement, or Articles of Partnership.

Those who put a partnership agreement together frequently adopt the Uniform Partnership Act (UPA) as a basis for the agreement. Matters normally included in a partnership agreement relate to compensation, individual investment, sharing of profits and losses, performance of tasks, and management of the organization. These are usually agreed to separately from the UPA.

When Does a Partnership Terminate?

A partnership may terminate by agreement, court decree, or death of a partner. Generally, the winding up of partnership affairs is done by agreement.

It's wise for a partner to make third parties aware of the dissolving (termination) partnership lest innocent parties who dealt with the partnership be placed at some disadvantage. The partnership could, in some way, be held responsible.

What Is an Inc., or a Co.?

Corporations are identified by several possible abbreviations. A *corporation* is a form of business organization created by statute that may be sued. Corporations provide a relatively efficient way to finance a business operation (selling shares). The corporation allows for limited liability of its owners, and it is not affected by bankruptcy of an individual connected with the corporation. Nor does death or incapacity interrupt its legal continuity.

Corporations come in all types, including public (TVA) and private (Maytag), domestic (incorporated in the state in which it is operating) and foreign (out of state), closed (with limited owners) or open (Boeing), and professional associations (made up of professionals, that is, medical and legal).

How Is a Corporation Created?

Corporations are created via formal legal procedures as prescribed by the state that will allow the incorporation.

The typical procedures, which may vary in your state, include:

Step One:	Incorporators form together.
Step Two:	File with the state Articles of Incorporation, which include the corporation's name, legal address, statement of purpose, and identification of types, kinds, and quantities of shares to be issued.
Step Three:	Stocks are then sold.

| Step Four: | Code of regulations or by-laws are agreed upon by shareholders. These self-governing rules usually specify date of annual meeting, form of stock certificates selected, number of members on Board of Directors, number and title of officers and their duties, and restrictions on sale of stock. |
| Step Five: | Meeting of Board of Directors where the appointment of officers, the authorizing of payments of bills, and setting up of other arrangements are made, including selection of a CPA, a bank, and the establishing of a dividend policy and many other necessary details. |

From that point on the shareholders will meet at least once a year at the Annual Meeting. The Board of Directors meets as required. The day-to-day operations will be in the hands of the officers of the corporation.

How Do Corporations Terminate Operations?

There are specific procedures set by the various states on formal dissolution of a corporation. The details of these procedures are too complex to go into here. It should be noted that few corporations formally dissolve. Most simply go out of business. Or they may be bought out for cash or exchanges of stock or merge with other corporations.

What Is an Ultra Vires Act?

Corporations that perform acts outside the scope of the "purpose" clause of its Articles of Incorporation are said to have committed an *ultra vires* act. Fines, loss of its charter, and suits by stockholders or the public may follow if ultra vires acts occur.

HOW TO DEAL WITH EMPLOYER LIABILITY UNDER THE LAW

Are Employers Liable for Employees' Actions?

Employers benefit from the labors of their employees. Hence, the courts hold that when an employee does something improper while working for his employer, the employer may be held liable. This includes many actions that an employer may have expressly forbidden of an employee. The doctrine proclaiming responsibility is called *respondent superior,* or "let the master answer for the acts of his servant." The doctrine applies only when the employee is on the job or during the course of the employment.

> A CASE-IN-POINT: Apple is a sole proprietor. He decides to hire an employee who will allow him some leisure time and the opportunity to expand his sales and profits. Apple hires Lemon to make deliveries, do stock inventory, and wait on customers. One day Lemon tackles a person he suspects of shoplifting. The person turns out to be innocent. Apple must pay the customer's claim since Lemon was about Apple's business.

Under certain conditions, employers are responsible for other actions of their employees. Such actions may include fraudulent conduct, misrepresentation, willful and wanton disregard of the contract rights of others, and other unconscionable activities done in the course of the employer's business. This assumes the employer knew or should have known what the employee was doing.

> A CASE-IN-POINT: Ajax Company employees are on strike. They have formed a picket line in front of the building, which is located in a densely populated area. Mannix, the manager, enters the company driveway only to be confronted by angry workers and a human chain. In order to avoid hitting them, he swerves the car and crashes into the front porch of the house next door, which belongs to Mrs. Crabtree. Crabtree sues the company for damages to her house and pain and suffering due to loss of her cat, which she claims was so scared by the crash that it ran away. Is the company liable? The union? Neither. Mannix is liable, although he might take action against the picketers.

What Are Independent Contractors and How Do They Differ from Employees?

Independent contractors are those people who accomplish tasks that frequently are performed by employees. Because they are "independent," they are not liable for their actions, either to themselves or other parties.

Examples would include those who typically operate free of direction when accomplishing some action, such as the termite removal company, the roofers, or Joe's Plumbing and Heating Co.

Any of these contractors have basic characteristics in common. After you agree upon the job to be done and the price to be paid, they do the task in the manner they consider proper, based upon the particular circumstances. Since they are on their own, the law distinguishes them from employees, over whom the employer has direct control. The result is a very limited or nominal standard of liability for their actions.

> A CASE-IN-POINT: Bingo Tree Trimmers, Inc., is hired to trim the trees in your backyard. While trimming, Bingo himself causes a huge limb to˙smack into a neighbor's garage, causing $300 in damages. Bingo will be required to assume liability and settle with the neighbor.

What Is an Employer's Liability to Employees?

An employer (and/or a manager, as agent) has several obligations to his or her employee, one of which is to pay an agreed salary as provided for by law. Another duty is to provide a safe place to work. The employer is also liable under a number of federal and state laws, to provide the employee with certain other benefits.

GUIDELINES FOR UNDERSTANDING THE LAWS GOVERNING EMPLOYMENT

This section describes the principal laws that establish employer's obligations.

Fair Labor Standards Act (FLSA). Congress passed this law in 1938. Although not the first wage and hour legislation, its original and amended coverage makes it among our most significant labor laws. The purpose is to raise wage rates, cut long working hours, and reduce child labor abuses. It does not cover fringe benefits.

The most discussed section of the law sets minimum wages. Originally established at twenty-five cents per hour in a limited number of job categories, the law now covers virtually all workers in interstate industry.

A more ambiguous section of the Act sets the age at which certain groups of children may begin working if the "labor is not oppressive." You cannot employ sixteen-to-eighteen-year-olds in hazardous occupations, nor can you employ any child under the age of sixteen. You may, however, hire children who are fourteen or fifteen with Department of Labor permission.

NOTE: More than thirty-five states have their own minimum wage laws, and there is legislation limiting child labor in a number of states.

Age Discrimination in Employment Act(s). These acts are really amendments to the FLSA. They make it illegal for firms employing more than nineteen workers to discriminate against current workers or applicants for jobs solely because they are forty years of age or older.

The Wage Rate Acts. Several laws have been enacted, beginning in 1933, that cover certain types of workers on various federal or federally financed projects. The Davis-Bacon Act requires most workers on construction projects to be paid no less than the prevailing area wage rate for their craft. The Walsh-Healy and the Service Contract Acts do likewise for production and service workers.

Overtime Acts. Portions of the FLSA and the Work Hours Act of 1962 establish criteria for the payment of overtime wages. Generally, time and one half of the regular hourly pay rate will have to be paid if the employee works more than forty hours in one week.

Equal Pay Act. As amended in 1972, this law applies to all workers covered by the FLSA and executive-level personnel. It provides that no employer may discriminate on the basis of sex in the payment of wages when the skill, effort, and responsibility required are equal for both sexes. This law is, of course, consistent with the earlier civil rights legislation.

Civil Rights and Equal Employment Opportunity Acts. As in the case of the FLSA, the original Civil Rights Act of 1964, which barred any manner of discrimination by employers based upon race, color, religion, sex, or national origin has been amended on numerous occasions. Included here are practices that pertain to hiring, firing, promotion, demotion, wages, and all other conditions and privileges of employment.

The Equal Opportunities Act of 1972 is broader than any of the other labor laws. The business need only "affect commerce" and have fifteen employees during each working day for any twenty weeks in the current year or in the next prior year. Most public and private educational institutions are subject to this law, as are state and local governments. The majority of labor unions and committees for training, including apprentice instruction, are also subject to the Act.

A variety of federal agencies exists to administer the law, both in the private and public sectors. Compliance is also monitored by federal agencies.

Affirmative Action (Executive Order 11246). Many of the previously discussed provisions are the cornerstone of Affirmative Action Programs, which prescribe a positive course of action for employees to prevent and remedy discrimination in employment and promotion opportunities. While the executive order applied originally to federal contractors, it has been generalized in practice and by court decisions to nearly every organization in all types of industries, public or private. To meet affirmative action criteria, a firm must set goals, compile data, and have a plan for positive action to provide opportunities for those subject to discrimination. Your personnel department has more information should you want to study this in more detail.

Occupational Safety & Health Act. OSHA was enacted in 1970 and requires employers to provide a safe work environment. The law is enforced by the Department of Labor. More than that, the Department has been charged by Congress with the task of setting the standards of safety that employers must meet or exceed.

Social Security Act. Enacted in 1935, this legislation has been amended countless times. Many separate categories of beneficiaries are covered by this "insurance" program. Originally intended to supplement a person's savings for retirement, the program is funded by employer and employee contributions from wages. Among many things now included are Medicare for the elderly; disability benefits; survivor's benefits, including children, spouses, ex-spouses; and medical benefits for many who never contributed to this program. The self-employed are, in most cases, obligated to contribute to the program.

Unemployment Compensation rules and regulations were established as part of the Social Security system. States have their own systems, having been motivated to do so by the federal law. Each state administers its own program under federal supervision.

Employers who have more than three employees must participate in the unemployment program. They pay a percent of wages earned per employee, up to a predetermined annual total. A minimum benefit of twenty-six weeks is available.

Employee's Retirement Income Security Act (ERISA). This law, more commonly known as the Pension Reform Act, was passed in 1974 and affects more than 35 million workers. The law sets rules for private pension systems. This is a highly detailed act, but here are a few of the more important provisions:

1. Establishes eligibility by age.
2. Establishes eligibility by years of service.
3. Assures vesting rights—accrued retirement credits that the company cannot take back.
4. Defines benefits.
5. Requires pension benefits be insured by a federal agency.
6. Requires annual accountings to be filed by employers.

Worker's Compensation Laws (Employees Liability Insurance). These laws are in force in virtually all states. Very simply, they provide for medical coverage and indemnity for permanent injuries and death sustained by workers on the job, virtually regardless of fault.

LABOR LAW: HOW TO DEAL WITH UNION VERSUS MANAGEMENT ISSUES

What Are the Particular Employer Practices Forbidden by the Wagner Act?

The Wagner Act of 1935 (National Labor Relations Act) forbids certain unfair labor practices against employees and includes provisions making it easy for workers to unionize. The National Labor Relations Board (NLRB) was created to administer the Wagner Act.

The law applies to managers at all levels and forbids certain practices, including:

1. Discrimination in hiring or retention of a person due to union activities.
2. Dominating the unions by employer contributions or cooperating union officials (company unions).
3. Interfering with unionization efforts.
4. Refusal to bargain collectively.

A CASE-IN-POINT: Blarney Builders learned of an effort by some of its workers to form a union. Blarney paid above-average wages and treated their people well. Posters in the plant and notes in the pay envelopes advised everyone that all workers who joined the union would be discharged. The organizing workers filed a complaint with the NLRB, and Blarney's actions were ruled an unfair labor practice.

What Other Acts Followed? Did They Make Things More Difficult for Management?

Today, the obvious problems brought to the employer by the Wagner Act have been slightly diluted by a combination of new laws.

The *Taft–Hartley Act of 1947* (first amendment to the Wagner Act) attempts to lessen the Wagner Act's effect by prohibiting certain actions of unions. The law:

1. Outlaws the forcing or preventing of an employee to join a union.
2. Prevents unions from forcing employers to discriminate against employees who do not join unions.
3. Prevents the union from refusing to bargain with the employer.
4. Prevents the employer from paying for work not performed.
5. Prevents charging new union members excessive initiation fees.
6. Outlaws secondary boycotts.

The law is also notable for its "cooling off" period. Any proposed strike or lockout that threatens the national security may be enjoined for an eighty-day period. During such time, the Federal Mediation and Conciliation Service attempts to work out the parties' differences.

Landrum–Griffin Act of 1959 (second amendment to the Wagner Act). This law was necessary since the Taft–Hartley Act did not go far enough to deter union corruption. Landrum–Griffin requires the following:

1. Greater detailed reporting and disclosure of financial activities by unions and affiliated groups.
2. Democratic procedures for election of union officials.
3. The creation of a more informative atmosphere within the unions themselves.

In What Other Areas Does Government Regulate Business?

This question may be answered by detailing a wide range of laws that prohibit or control certain unjust business activities.

Intellectual Property Law. The segment of law covered here pertains to products of the mind such as patents, copyrights, trade and service marks and trade names, and trade secrets. The improper use of any of these can run the user afoul of federal and state law and government regulation.

Patents are granted to those who create a new, useful, and novel device that adds to mankind's storehouse of knowledge. The U.S. Patent Office grants the inventor a seventeen-year right of exclusion that prevents others from making, selling, or using the concept without permission. Those who violate the monopoly right of the inventor are said to infringe on the patent and may be sued in civil court for damages.

Copyrights are similar to patents with respect to federal statutory protection. A copyright, obtained on a wide variety of "literary" creations, is no good for the life of the creator, plus thirty-five years. Both copyrights and patents require disclosure in order to receive protection of the law.

Trademarks, service marks, or trade name are protected in statute on both the state and federal level. It is generally believed that business utilizes these identifiers to gain large market shares of a product.

> A CASE-IN-POINT: Precision Tool Co. (PTC) operated for years in Indiana and Ohio and developed a solid reputation with its customers. Many years later Precision, Inc., started in business selling essentially the same product line as PTC in the same geographical area. PTC sought to have Precision, Inc., enjoined from using the word *precision* in its name. PTC prevailed. The court said the public would be confused since the word *precision* meant PTC to the public. Also, PTC had developed in the minds of the public a secondary meaning—that is, when they thought "precision," they were thinking Precision Tool Co.

Trade secrets are defined as anything that gives you a competitive advantage. They are protected by common law and by contract (usually with employees). Although many trade secrets are made worthless by today's reverse engineering techniques, they are still protected closely by industry for the competitive advantage they may provide, even if only for a short period of time.

Interstate Commerce. Besides the power to regulate trade with foreign countries, the federal government has the power to regulate commerce "among the several states." The principal field of commerce that most frequently gains our attention involves transportation that crosses state lines, including various rail, motor, water, and air carriers. Interstate communications are regulated by the Federal Communications Commission (FCC).

Anti-Trust. In the past ninety-plus years, the federal government has utilized its power over interstate activities to control, prohibit, and, in some cases, encourage certain business practices. Primary enforcement responsibility rests with the United States Department of Justice.

The Sherman Anti-Trust Act (1890) is the grandfather of all laws passed by Congress to promote competition in interstate commerce. It has two main provisions:

Section 1 declares "that every contract, combination in the form of a trust, or conspiracy in restraint of trade or commerce among the several states, or with foreign nations is illegal."

Section 2 provides "every person who shall monopolize or attempt to monopolize or combine, or conspire with any other person(s), to monopolize any part of the trade or commerce among the several states or with foreign nations . . . " is guilty of a crime.

A violation of the Sherman Act has come to be interpreted to require the following:

1. A coming together of two or more parties.

2. An unlawful agreement.

3. Suppression of trade.

Fundamentally, the Act must be interpreted with the so-called "Rule of Reason." Simply put, common sense must prevail when the Act is applied.

> A CASE-IN-POINT: The Standard Oil Company of New Jersey case is the standard reference when it comes to illustrating the application of the Act. Standard entered into price-fixing deals. They also limited production of petroleum products and their distribution and were also guilty of controlling other concerns via holding companies, all designed to monopolize trade. Standard, as it then existed, was broken up and prohibited from ever engaging in such activities again.

The Clayton Act (1914) followed fast on the heels of the Sherman Act. Its more significant provisions are as follows:

Section 2 makes it "Unlawful for any person engaged in commerce . . . to discriminate in price between different purchasers of commodities of like grade (in the U.S.)" . . . where the effect substantially lessens competition.

Section 3 prevents tie-in sales or tie-in leases and price fixing that would prevent or lessen competition.

Section 7 prevents a corporation from buying stock or assets of a company, where such action might allow for the lessening of competition or tend to create a monopoly.

The Clayton Act is obviously more specific than the Sherman Act. It prohibits particular transactions and sets more standards to determine noncompliance.

> A CASE-IN-POINT: RCA Corp., through improper use of its properly obtained United States patents, restricted its customers to purchase certain of its products. It was held as an unfair trade practice since it restricted trade and prevented the free flow of commerce. It was an "illegal use of a legal monopoly."

The Federal Trade Commission Act (1914) is a companion to the Clayton Act. It provides, via its Section 5, that unfair methods of competition and unfair or deceptive acts or practices are unlawful in commerce. It also establishes the Federal Trade Commission (FTC) to pursue the objectives of anti-trust legislation. Today, the FTC is an administrative force to be dealt with carefully by business. It should be respected, if not feared.

What Is the Privacy Act of 1975?

This recent legislation establishes detailed guidelines for federal government agencies with respect to the disclosure of personal records information. The collection and retaining of personal information by government agencies is limited to the agencies' specific needs.

OTHER AREAS OF PROTECTION THROUGH REGULATION

Are There Other Federal Regulations to Be Aware of?

All the federal regulations that might apply to you or your employer cannot possibly be covered here. Some of them, however, are described as follows:

The *Clean Air Act* and *Air Quality Control Act* became effective in the late 1960s. They are administered by the Environmental Protection Agency, which also administers the *Federal Water Pollution Control Act*, the *Noise Control Act*, and *Solid Waste Disposal Act*, and various acts dealing with pesticide controls.

The *Consumer Product Safety Act* was enacted during the surge of consumerism of the 1970s. It protects the public from unreasonable risk of injury associated with consumer products.

The *Fair Credit Reporting Act* requires that consumer reporting agencies use equitable means when reporting on the credit worthiness of consumers. Obsolete and inaccurate information must not be disseminated. The FTC administers the Act.

For close to fifty years, the *Federal Securities Act* has affected those who issue securities to the public. It requires certain disclosures and certification by the Securities and Exchange Commission (SEC) prior to the issuance of the security. Criminal penalties exist for failure to comply with the law.

One of the principal accomplishments of the *Food, Drug, and Cosmetic Act* is the establishment of the Food and Drug Administration. Many times amended, this law is effective over a wide area of consumable products to prevent foods and drugs that are not fit for consumption from being made available to the public.

These are the main laws that regulate business and individuals. Information about specific laws concerning your business may be obtained from most industry trade associations, congressmen and congresswomen, government agencies, or through other sources inside and outside your company.

In summary, you have looked at the major governmental laws and regulations that affect your organization. Some have greater impact on higher management than on lower level management; however, *all* have relevance for you because they shape the situation and the options you face. There are also laws not covered here that pertain to certain industries, such as health care, agribusiness, aerospace, mining, and communications. Many govern the product end, but some also have to do with processes as well. You are encouraged to learn more about the particular legal constraints that are important to your organization.

Developing Your Professional Dimension

Throughout these pages, we have stressed your role as part of the management team—and of the management profession. The managerial job today requires professionalism, and tomorrow calls for even more. It's only a matter of time when managers at all levels will be required to meet professional accreditation standards, just as accountants, purchasing agents, and engineers already are.

Personnel managers and specialists have a formal accreditation process through the American Society for Personnel Administration (ASPA), which is rapidly gaining recognition in industry. For managers, the best-known formal accreditation is the Certified Manager (CM), granted by the Institute for Certified Professional Managers (ICPM).

The following pages contain the ICPM Statement of Purpose and Code of Ethics. Further information on the Institute and Certified Manager accreditation is available from the Institute.

In addition to the ICPM, there are other professional affiliations you might find beneficial. For example, most metropolitan areas have foremen's clubs, and if you are an NMA member, you no doubt are part of a management club. There are also many community service organizations that have a professional orientation, such as Kiwanis, Rotary, and the Jaycees.

Institute of Certified Professional Managers

What Is the Institute of Certified Professional Managers?

The Institute of Certified Professional Managers received its initial grant from The Brown Foundation, The International Management Council, and The National Management Association.

Members of Professional Management organizations had espoused feelings that there were too many people who had stumbled into management positions by virtue of the fact that they happened to be the best technician, or accountant, or engineer. People needed direction in training and study in order to become professionals in their new field. In 1974, in order to meet the needs of these people, a joint task force consisting of IMC and NMA members met with management educators to create the Institute of Certified Professional Managers.

The task force was assisted by a consultant, Dr. Robert Fulmer. Dr. Fulmer, a George R. Brown professor of management at Trinity University in San Antonio, Texas, aided the task force in the early development of the Institute. He also assisted in developing the purpose, organizational structure, and membership criteria.

The purposes of the Institute are four-fold, and current Institute strategies are designed to uphold and fulfill these goals. The purposes are

1. To recognize management as a profession.
2. To provide direction for study in the supervisory and managerial field.
3. To provide a critical, third-party evaluation of managerial competence.
4. To recognize demonstrated competence in the managerial field.

Structurally, the Institute is headed by a Board of Regents and the Executive Director of the Institute. The Regents meet twice a year and are the policy-making body. The Executive Director carries out the policies and handles the administrative activities of the Institute.

Institute of
Certified Professional Managers

ICPM

Code of Ethics

I will recognize that management is a call to service with responsibilities to my subordinates, associates, supervisors, employer, community, nation, and world.

I will be guided in all my activities by truth, accuracy, fair dealings, and good taste.

I will earn and carefully guard my reputation for good moral character and citizenship.

I will recognize that, as a leader, my own pattern of work and life will exert more influence on my subordinates than what I say or write.

I will give the same consideration to the rights and interests of others that I ask for myself.

I will maintain a broad and balanced outlook and will look for value in the ideas and opinions of others.

I will regard my role as a manager as an obligation to help subordinates and associates achieve personal and professional fulfillment.

I will keep informed on the latest developments in the techniques, equipment, and processes associated with the practice of management and the industry in which I am employed.

I will search for, recommend, and initiate methods to increase productivity and efficiency.

I will respect the professional competence of my colleagues in the ICPM and will work with them to support and promote the goals and programs of the Institute.

I will support efforts to strengthen professional management through example, education, training, and a lifelong pursuit of excellence.

Index

A

Absolute standard method of measuring performance, 163-164
Acceptable quality levels (AQL), 331
Accounting:
  cost, 321, 323-328
  department, role of, 311
  reports, 320
Active feedback (listening), 95-96, 239-240
Administrative agencies, 338-340, 342, 369
Advice, principle of compulsory staff, 310
Affirmative action, 370
Age discrimination in employment laws, 369
Agency:
  creation of, 361
  definition of, 360
  termination of, 362-363
Agents:
  disclosure and, 361
  duties of and to, 362
  scope of authority of, 361-362
  types of, 360-361
Aggressiveness, assertiveness versus, 86, 89-90
Air Quality Control Act, 376
American Society for Personnel Administration (ASPA), 377
Analysis:
  breakeven, 324-326
  controlling and, 57
  decision making and, 61-63, 65-66
  external, 39, 41
  force-field, 28-29
  internal, 40-41
  planning and, 39-41
  psycho-, 233-234
  ratio, 326-328
  risk, 65-66
  situation, 39-41
  Transactional Analysis (TA), 70-71, 73-74, 76-86, 93, 98, 234

Analysis *(cont'd)*
  variance, 323-324
Anti-trust laws, 374-375
Assertiveness:
  aggressiveness versus, 86, 89-90
  definition of, 86
  guidelines for an assertive manager, 89
  how to achieve, 86, 89-90, 93-94
  with your boss, 141
Assigning of work, how to handle, 52-53
Attitudes:
  balance and, 30
  checklist for building good, 189
Audio-visual aids, 110
Awareness, 96
  conscious, 97, 98
  nonverbal, 98, 100
  subconscious, 97, 98
  superconscious, 97, 98

B

Bahke, E. Wright, 212
Balance, how to achieve, 29-31
Behavior:
  balance and, 30
  modification, 234
Behaviorally anchored scale for measuring performance, 172-173
Berne, Eric, 70-71, 76, 97, 234
Body language, 98, 100
Bonoma, Thomas V., 129-130
Boss, your:
  assertiveness with your, 141
  conflicts and, 140-141
  how to make him/her look good, 141-142
  how to work with the leadership style of, 286-287
Brainstorming, description of, 278-279
Breakeven analysis, 324-326
Brown Foundation, 379
Budgeting, 320-321

Notes

Notes